FINDING *Love*
in the
MIDST *of* WAR

FINDING *Love*
in the
MIDST *of* WAR

The Untold Story of the Abandoned Soldier

Teresa V. La Greca

Redwood Publishing, LLC
Orange County, California

Printed in the United States of America
First Printing, 2020

Published by Redwood Publishing, LLC
Ladera Ranch, California
www.redwooddigitalpublishing.com
info@redwooddigitalpublishing.com

Book Design by Redwood Publishing, LLC
Cover Design: Michelle Manley
Interior Design: Ghislain Viau

ISBN: 978-1-952106-03-3 (paperback)
ISBN: 978-1-952106-04-0 (ebook)

Library of Congress Cataloguing Number: 2020900511

Disclaimer: The author has recreated events, locales, and conversations from her and her family's memories of them. It's almost impossible to recall a conversation word for word. You might forget minor details. So, dear reader, please be cautioned that names, dates, places, events, and details may be slightly different from your own memory of such a time and/or event, however this book is a memoir of the author's events, and they will be told as such.

10 9 8 7 6 5 4 3 2 1

To those soldiers abandoned on the battlefield.

TABLE OF CONTENTS

PROLOGUE

*M*y father seldom spoke about the war. Like many soldiers, he managed to leave those days behind and go on with the business of living, toiling as a farmhand and policeman in Sicily and a busboy, waiter, and restaurateur in America. I've always known my father served in the Italian army and that he was stationed in Greece because that's where he met my mother. I never thought about much else. It wasn't until 1956 that I first learned my father had fought on the wrong side. The realization hit me hard and filled me with shame. I was eleven, and yet I remember as if it were only yesterday, cowering in my seat as my history teacher told the class that Germany and Italy declared war on the United States on December 11, 1941.

Prior to that day, the only thing about World War II that had interested me was that my parents had met and fallen in love during it. I thought it remarkable that they were able to get together at all considering that their countries were on opposite sides. Falling in love with the enemy had to be dark and forbidding, and at the same time, impossibly romantic. It also made me ponder the power of fate, destiny, and roads taken. After all, if it hadn't been for the war, in all likelihood, my parents would never have met. I also found it intriguing that my parents' marriage took my Italian father back to his roots. I once asked him how we got our name, even suggesting that our ancestors were most likely Greek.

I remember his response well: "Me, Greek? *Che stupidaggine!*"

"It's not foolish, Dad; just think." I could see I was irritating him but I continued nonetheless, "It has to be that one of our ancestors emigrated from Greece to Italy and had a Greek name that Italians couldn't pronounce, so they called her 'La Greca.' Do you ever wonder what her real name was?"

Dismissing me with a wave of his hand, he replied, "No! I don't waste time with *fantasia.*"

"Remember El Greco, the Greek painter? His real name was *Domenikos Theotokopoulos*. Spaniards couldn't pronounce that, so they called him 'El Greco.'"

"I don't know about El Greco, but I can tell you for sure, we are not Greek!"

"Now you can't really say that, Dad. After all, Mom *is* Greek, so that makes your children at least half Greek."

The only times our father said anything remotely relating to the war was usually in response to our whining about being cold or hungry.

Coming home from school, I'd run into the kitchen and cry out, "Is there anything to eat? I'm starving!"

Thrusting a handful of potato peels at me so forcefully I nearly fell backward, my father would bellow, "Here, eat!"

"Yuck! Who eats potato peels?"

"You, if you are starving!"

Running in from the cold, I would make a mad dash for the radiator and purr, "Oh, it's so nice and warm! It's freezing outside. I nearly froze to death!"

That's when I'd encounter his wrath: "What? Froze to death?! You have warm clothes! You have hat; you have coat; you have boots! You don't know what freeze is!"

Then he'd go on to describe in excruciating detail the frigid Albanian weather, how he had to bury himself in the snow to keep warm, so food deprived that he'd eat raw onion shoots he'd dug out of the frozen ground.

Starving and *freezing.* Those two words never failed to set him off.

He'd pace about, arms flailing, eyes practically popping out of his head, and roar, "You don't know how lucky you are . . . lucky you don't know what it is to starve or freeze."

Of course, I always thought he was exaggerating, or as Italians say, *fare di una mosca un elefante.* When I think about it now, there were so many opportunities, so many times when I could have asked, "Dad, why did you have to sleep in the snow? Didn't the army have cots and blankets for you? Why didn't you have food? What were you doing in Albania?" But no, all I cared about was dodging his lectures.

A few years ago, a good friend gave my mom the novel *Corelli's Mandolin* by Louis de Bernières, thinking she'd find the parallels interesting. Like my dad, an Italian soldier, Captain Corelli, is stationed in Greece and falls in love with Pelagia, a Greek girl. Mom shared the book with me, and while we both enjoyed the novel, we agreed that Corelli and Pelagia's story was a sad tale of unrequited love, whereas my parents' love story went on to flourish.

In the novel, a soldier constantly grumbles about the treacherous Albanian terrain, the miserable mind-numbing cold, and soldiers not having appropriate clothing and boots for the bone-chilling weather. He speaks of soldiers fearing losing their limbs to the "white death" more than being shot. Reading those passages gave me a new understanding of the horrific experiences my dad must have endured. I learned that in addition to having to cope with the Albanian winter, Italian soldiers had to deal with dwindling food supplies. England had air and naval bases in Crete that allowed for British planes to routinely intercept the caravan of mules transporting supplies. Because of food shortages, soldiers resorted to stealing from the scythe-wielding Albanians who'd lob your head off if they found you in their cornfields.

I would have loved to have heard my father's story. I heard bits and pieces here and there, but there were many gaps. I wish I'd had the opportunity to sit with him as he recounted his war adventures and what he endured in the service of his country. After battling cancer, my father passed away on February 9, 1992, at the age of seventy-one. Now I'm left with regret for all the things I never asked. However, I'm fortunate that my mom possesses a remarkable memory and has filled in some of those gaps. She has told me of my father's harrowing war experiences, how she and my father met and fell in love, and what everyday life was like before the war and how it changed when Italy declared war on her country.

THE FAMILY TREE

*D*ear Reader,

Before you get too deep into this story, I think it might prove very helpful for you to have access to my family tree. With this, I hope who's who becomes clear, or, if you find yourself thinking *Wait, who is this...?* as I introduce new people along the way, you have something which you can reference.

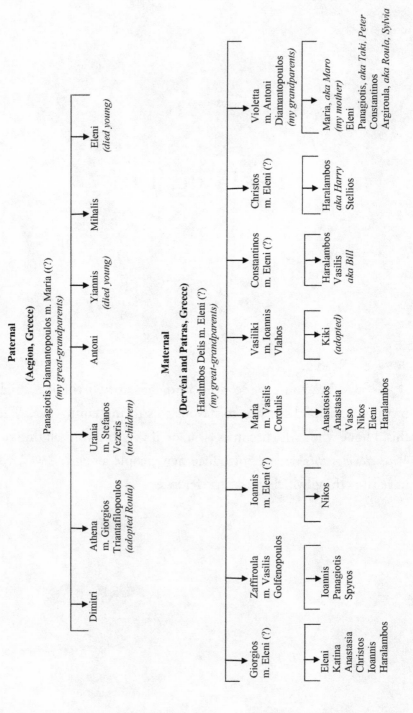

My Mother's Family

Paternal

(Aegion, Greece)

Panagiotis Diamantopoulos m. Maria ((?))
(my great-grandparents)

Dimitri

Athena
m. Giorgios
Triantafilopoulos
(adopted Roula)

Urania
m. Stefanos
Vezeris
(no children)

Antoni

Yiannis
(died young)

Mihalis

Eleni
(died young)

Maternal

(Dervéni and Patras, Greece)

Haralmbos Delis m. Eleni (?)
(my great-grandparents)

Giorgios
m. Eleni (?)

Eleni
Katina
Anastasia
Christos
Ioannis
Haralambos

Zaffiroula
m. Vasilis
Golfenopoulos

Ioannis
Panagiotis
Spyros

Ioannis
m. Eleni (?)

Nikos

Maria
m. Vasilis
Cordulis

Anastosios
Anastasia
Vaso
Nikos
Eleni
Haralambos

Vasiliki
m. Ioannis
Vlahos

Kiki
(adopted)

Constantinos
m. Eleni (?)

Haralambos
Vasilis
aka Bill

Christos
m. Eleni (?)

Haralambos
aka Harry
Stelios

Violetta
m. Antoni
Diamantopoulos
(my grandparents)

Maria, *aka Maro*
(my mother)
Eleni
Panagiotis, *aka Taki, Peter*
Constantinos
Argiroula, *aka Roula, Sylvia*

xiv

THE FAMILY TREE

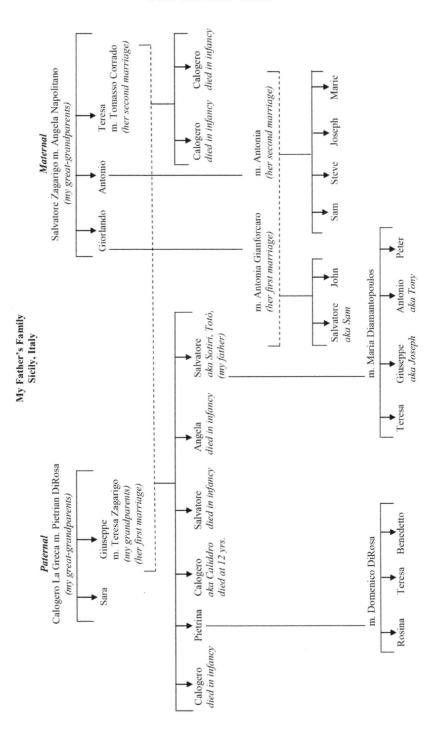

My Father's Family
Sicily, Italy

Paternal
Calogero La Greca m. Pietrian DiRosa
(my great-grandparents)

Sara   Giuseppe
m. Teresa Zagarigo
(my grandparents)
(her first marriage)

Calogero
died in infancy

Pietrina

Calogero
aka Caliidro
died at 12 yrs.

Salvatore
died in infancy

Angela
died in infancy

Salvatore
aka Sotiri, Totò,
(my father)

m. Domenico DiRosa

Rosina   Teresa   Benedetto

m. Antonia Gianforcaro
(her first marriage)

Salvatore
aka Sam

John

m. Maria Diamantopoulos

Teresa   Giuseppe
aka Joseph

Antonio
aka Tony

Peter

Maternal
Salvatore Zagarigo m. Angela Napolitano
(my great-grandparents)

Giorlando   Antonio   Teresa
m. Tomasso Corrado
(her second marriage)

Calogero
died in infancy

Calogero
died in infancy

m. Antonia
(her second marriage)

Sam   Steve   Joseph   Marie

xv

PART ONE
GREECE

1

Italy Declares War on Greece

THE FIRST RAYS OF SUNLIGHT streamed through the window panes, the sky was blue, the air crisp and thick with anticipation. Yet, my mother was somewhat apprehensive this morning. She would be going to a new school. The week prior the students learned that due to their large class size, some students would be assigned to another all-girls school. The school Mom had been attending was just a couple of blocks from home whereas the one she was assigned to was across town, about a mile away. Her mother gave her bus fare but she decided to walk and use the money to buy pastries at the Italian bakery.

On her way to school, Mom met up with her friend Koula. Koula at times seemed to be reticent and had an air of solemnity about her. Mom would later understand why when she visited her friend at home and saw the framed photo of a little boy dressed in a sailor's suit. Koula told Mom that the boy was her older brother, that she had never met him and that he lived in England with his father. Years later, Mom learned that Koula's mother had been married to an Englishman whose work required him to frequently travel abroad. Disenchanted with her husband's long absences, she had an affair. When her husband found out, he divorced her on the grounds of adultery and was granted full custody of their six-year-old son. The only connection she had to her son was his photo.

As the girls walked, they heard music playing.

Mom turned to Koula and said, "Why is that music playing today? It isn't Independence Day."

"Didn't you hear? It was on the radio this morning. Italy declared war on Greece."

My mother thought it was a joke.

"That can't be true, Koula! Our parents wouldn't let us go to school if there was war."

Koula shrugged, and they continued on their way. They passed by the Italian private school, and it was closed.

* * *

It was 9:30 a.m., the latest Pappou (my grandfather) had lazed in bed. He was not looking forward to the crutches. As he sat upright, a sharp pain shot up his leg. He took a moment to steady himself, picked up the crutch, and placed it under his armpit. With the first crutch securely in place, he picked up the other one and—finally standing—made his way into the dining room.

Yiayia (my grandmother), seeing him hobbling in, screamed, "What are you doing?! You shouldn't get up by yourself! Why didn't you call me? You could have fallen!"

"Well, I didn't fall. Here, take these," Pappou said as he handed her the crutches and lowered himself onto a chair. "How about some breakfast? I'm hungry."

"You must be. You haven't eaten a thing since yesterday morning. I have your favorite, *koulouri* (a ring of bread sprinkled with sesame seeds) with yogurt and honey," Yiayia said, handing him the newspaper before dashing off into the kitchen.

"That sounds good," Pappou said. He unfolded the newspaper and the huge headline jumped off the page, jolted him, and he cried out, "Where are the children?"

"It's Monday. They're in school. Why? What's wrong?"

"Did you see this?"

"What? Oh my God, when?"

"Five o'clock this morning. If there's war, why weren't the schools closed? Why weren't we warned? What a time for me to fall and . . . and why did I sleep late? The children would be home!"

"Taki and Eleni are just across the street. But Maro . . . Maro started that new school. It's so far! I must go and get her."

"No! Don't do that! She may be on her way home, and you'll miss each other," Pappou said.

*   *   *

When Mom's first class ended, the girls went out to the schoolyard for recess. As soon as Mom stepped outside, the rumble of a low-flying airplane made her look up. She was not the only one. There were people out on balconies looking up and cheering. Heads filled every window of the school. Then four more airplanes appeared. As the airplanes flew past, black shapes fell from their underbelly, followed by booming explosions and clouds of smoke. It was then

5

that she realized the falling objects were bombs! The professors tried to maintain order by blocking the school gate, but the hordes of rushing girls were too much as they pushed their way past the gate and onto the street. Mom ran out too, and as she was running, she could see a building in the distance crumbling onto the pavement. There was chaos, smoke, and debris everywhere. The deafening roar of the low-flying bomber planes frightened her, and she sought shelter in a store on the way home. It was a pottery shop, and when a bomb exploded nearby, pots and vases fell from the shelves and shattered at her feet. She once again ran out onto the street. As she struggled to get home, it seemed as if everyone were moving in slow motion, dreamlike. At an intersection, policemen blew their whistles, telling people to lie on the ground.

As Mom lay on the ground her hands covering her head, she remembered Aunt Vasiliki's dire warning, "You'll cry tomorrow!" It was just last night that her aunt had uttered those words. Earlier that day Pappou had fallen, injuring his ankle. Yiayia called for the doctor. Mom was leery of the doctor because his treatment regimen utilized leeches, which were thought to prevent blood clots. She found the leeches not only frightening, but also disgusting. That evening, as the doctor was tending to Pappou, Aunt Vasiliki, Yiayia's older sister, who often came over to give Yiayia a hand, led the children out to the veranda. Mom suddenly broke into a fit of laughter for reasons she still isn't sure of. Seeing her laughing hysterically, her siblings began laughing as well. Their appalled aunt scolded them, telling them they should be ashamed of themselves for behaving like a bunch of hooligans while their father was in pain. But her scolding only made them laugh all the more, their laughter quickly growing to a rousing crescendo.

Their exasperated aunt waved a finger at them and said, "If you don't stop that insolent laughter, you'll cry tomorrow!" To this day, Mom shudders at how prophetic her aunt's words turned out to be.

After those around her got up off the ground, Mom, too, got up and ran. As she was running, frightening thoughts ran through her mind: a bomb falling on her; her parents hurt, or worse; her home bombed, demolished like the building she saw collapsing into a heap. Through clouds of smoke, she saw faces etched with fear, images seared in her brain that would fill her dreams with nightmares for a very long time to come. It was only after the planes had left that the air-raid siren sounded. When Mom finally made it home, she was relieved and ever thankful to discover that her parents, her siblings, and her home were safe.

The bombing had begun at ten o'clock in the morning and had lasted no more than one hour. Mom's family later learned that the Italian schools had previously closed, so the Italian children would be safe at home when the bombing started. There was a large Italian community in Patras, many having immigrated to the harbor city just across the Ionian Sea. They'd brought with them their political and social ideals, established residency in the vicinity of the Catholic Church, developed an independent press, and established private schools.

The war began on Monday, October 28, 1940, a month after Mom's eleventh birthday. On the way to school, patriotic music played across the town. The sounds reserved for special holidays were confusing on this autumn day. Prior to the bombing, there had been no warning, no air-raid sirens. But by the day's end, over one thousand people had been killed.

The bombing lasted seven months, and the schools remained closed the entire time. Mom loved school and missed going. She loved all of her classes and received high grades in History, Latin, French, Greek, and Ancient Greek. She wasn't particularly good at math but fortunately her teacher was engaged to her cousin Eleni and tutored her. As far back as Mom can remember, students had greeted their teachers by extending their arm in a Fascist salute. It was widely known that Ioannis Metaxas, the prime minister of Greece, was a Fascist and a Germanophile. His foreign policy directed that Greece maintain a neutral stance between England and Germany, as Germany had become Greece's largest trading partner. His death on January 29, 1941, only three months after Italy had declared war, is shrouded in mystery to this day.

The winter of 1940 to 1941 was one of the coldest on record. The frigid weather and food shortages caused massive suffering, especially for the elderly and the very young. The shortages were the result of farmers and wholesale grocers stockpiling goods. The hoarding led to the emergence of the black market, where speculators didn't trade in currency; they opted for gold or other valuable commodities. The black market and rationing were the only means of food supply in urban areas. Inflation was rampant, resulting in the drachma losing much of its value.

Mom witnessed the war-fueled greed when she accompanied her mother in search of oil. Yiayia reluctantly tucked under her arm her treasured Persian tablecloth that had been given to her as dowry, and set off.

"How much oil will you give me for this?" Yiayia asked.

The man unfurled the tablecloth, and after careful examination, scratched his bearded chin and said, "For this, I can give you one liter."

Indignant, Yiayia folded the tablecloth, put it under her arm, and started off—but not before telling the greedy man, "We'll do without the oil. This war won't last forever!"

The International Committee of the Red Cross distributed canned vegetables, sardines, Spam, and corned beef. Unfortunately, the organized efforts by the Orthodox Church and the Red Cross were unable to meet the needs of the population, and the situation remained grim. It is estimated that Greece suffered approximately three hundred thousand deaths during the Axis occupation as a result of the famine. Those fortunate enough to have land to grow food fared better. My grandparents eventually made good use of their land.

Before the war, Pappou's vineyards had produced an assortment of table grapes and wine grapes. His vineyard had boasted the sweet, seedless sultana grape. Once ripe, the clusters were cut from the vine, hung up, and dried, producing large sultana raisins. He also grew the hardy winter grape, which grew sweeter once exposed to frost, the vines soaring as high as forty feet, turning the shriveling grapes into raisins. With the help of hired field hands, Pappou grew olives, fruit trees, and vegetables. Plants were watered through a series of irrigation ditches, and the harvested fruits and vegetables were taken to market. The income generated from the farm and Pappou's grocery store had provided for the family.

But now, with the war on, Pappou could no longer afford to keep his workers, so the family had to pitch in. They pulled up the flower beds, cleared some of the vineyards, and primed the land for planting wheat, potatoes, tomatoes, cabbage, peas, string beans, zucchini, and pumpkins. Yiayia canned and bottled the harvested vegetables and made preserves from cherries, blackberries, and citrus fruit peels.

9

Yiayia, too, was forced to cut back, discharging her maid, Andreana, who had been with her since the birth of her first child. Not only did Yiayia have to contend with the housework and gardening, she also had to make clothes for her growing children. With the drachma losing much of its value, Yiayia couldn't afford to buy fabric, and so she utilized the drapes, just as Maria had done in *The Sound of Music*. She used the bed linens and curtain linings for dresses and shirts, and the blue cotton upholstery for durable smocks.

Yiayia worried about the food shortages and began pilfering flour, sugar, and other staples from Pappou's grocery store. Pappou caught her on more than one occasion and reminded her that the rationing rules applied to them also. This didn't deter Yiayia, and with the aid of her children, she continued to take what they needed in small quantities.

Many fled the city for the countryside, where they would be safer. Some who remained saw this as an opportunity to profit, resulting in widespread looting of abandoned homes. When the war ended, those who had fled returned to discover their homes ransacked. It had to be disheartening to learn that a compatriot, a neighbor, or possibly a friend would add to the misery war brings.

The police had the monumental task of trying to keep order. Prisons were becoming crowded not only with looters and other criminals apprehended, but also with Italian men. The police began rounding up men of Italian descent and jailing them as political prisoners. It didn't matter that many had lived in Greece for generations and were Greek citizens. To deal with the glut of wartime prisoners, schools were converted into prisons.

At the start of the war, a young soldier was executed in the schoolyard across from my grandparents' home. A newlywed, he had been conscripted into the army and then deserted. He was tried and found guilty—the penalty: death by firing squad. His wife stayed in our underground shelter. Huddled in the basement, they heard the gunshots, and the young widow wailed. There was nothing anyone could do to ease her anguish.

Mrs. Tofalos, a relative of Aunt Vasiliki's husband, Ioannis, wanted to take her children to the countryside, where they'd be safer. A widow, she lived with her son and daughter, who were in their teens and were always smartly dressed in the American clothes their older brother sent. On the day they were to leave, the air-raid siren sounded quickly followed by the roar of a plane. The plane dropped its bomb, filling the air with smoke and shrapnel, and instantly killing both children. Their devastated mother kept them at her home for three days until she was finally persuaded to have their bodies taken for burial. Mom was given a couple of the daughter's dresses, and while she was grateful, those dresses would be a sad reminder of that unfortunate young lady.

During the seven months that Greece was bombed, the family moved up the street into a room in the rear of their grocery store. Yiayia's brother Ioannis owned the building and lived on the second floor with his wife, Eleni, and their son, Niko. There were two stores on the street level. One was Pappou's grocery store and the other a coffee shop. In the rear of each store was a large room with two beds, a small kitchen and bathroom. The floor below had two apartments that were rented out, and the land sloped so that the rear of the apartments was on the street level and the front was underground. Beneath both apartments was yet another room that spanned the entire building and served as a bomb shelter that held about fifty people. Whenever the air-raid siren blared, the tenants went down to the shelter, carrying kerosene lamps, and sat silently on benches, chairs, and the floor. When the all-clear sounded, they went back upstairs. The bombings came in spates, sometimes every night for a week, then nothing for days. Before going to bed, they placed their clothing where they could easily find it. However, in their panic and the dark of night, they often grabbed the wrong clothes, so most nights they slept fully dressed.

* * *

It was on a warm April day, the sky a crystal blue, that Mom and three of her girlfriends ventured out to the horticultural school, where her friend's father was a custodian. Spring was Mom's favorite season. It was the time of year when lemon, orange, and cherry trees sprouted their blossoms, filling the air with their wondrous aroma. Mom had been looking forward to this day, as it would be a peaceful refuge from the bleating goats, cackling chickens, and chores. The girls marveled at all the different flowers and colors, taking in their fragrance, when suddenly the serenity of the day was shattered by the all-too-familiar roar of the air-raid siren, followed by the high-pitch wail of the Stuka dive bombers. The girls looked up at the sky, now plastered with Stukas, and made a run for the school's shelter.

"Maro, your dress!" her friends screamed. "Take off your dress!"

"What?"

"Your dress! Take it off! The planes will see your red dress, and we'll be targets!"

"Don't be silly," Mom said. "The planes are flying so low, they can see the color of our eyes."

The girls huddled together in the shelter. When the all-clear sounded, they exited. There was no sign of the Stukas; they had flown past, once again revealing the blue sky. Fearing the planes might return, the girls rushed home.

"You missed the planes," Eleni said. "There were so many!"

"We saw them too. They flew by the school," Mom said. "We stayed in the shelter."

"The mama goat got hurt," Eleni told her.

"How?"

"She got hit with shrapnel," Taki said. "Babá went to get the doctor."

"Where is she now?" Mom asked.

"She's in the garden. Let's go see her," Eleni said as she led the way. The goat was lying on her side, her daughter, Tomboy, standing over her.

"Do you think Tomboy knows her mother is hurt?" Taki asked.

"She knows," Mom said. "Animals know a lot, even crazy Tomboy."

The poor mama goat lost her eye after being hit with shrapnel, but she lived.

That day, the planes also bombed the port.

* * *

On March 7, 1941, Prime Minister Winston Churchill deployed fifty-eight thousand British and Australian troops to Greece. In April, German forces invaded on the ground and from the air, forcing the British and Australian troops to retreat. Thousands were captured. Italian, German, and Bulgarian invaders made their way into Greece. Germany occupied and administered Athens and Thessaloniki.

Bulgaria controlled the eastern portion of the country. And Italy occupied the Peloponnese peninsula, including the Ionian Islands. The school across the street from my grandparents' house, which had been converted to a prison, was taken over by the Italians and used as their barracks.

The British began bombing areas occupied by the invaders. In Patras, they bombed the hotel housing Italian army personnel. Mom saw the funeral procession for the officers and soldiers killed as it traveled past our house on its way to the nearby Italian cemetery. The British, in an attempt to bomb the barracks on a hilltop, missed their target and hit a house instead. In what had to be a miracle, a woman who moments before had given birth, made it out alive clutching her newborn.

As the German troops advanced into Greece, King George and his government fled to Crete, and on April 18, Alexandros Koryzis, who had only assumed the role of Greek prime minister on January 29, took his own life. The bombing finally stopped when Greece surrendered on April 23. After the capitulation, white sheets unfurled from homes, shops, and church steeples. The Germans bombed Piraeus Harbor in Athens, destroying the port, so the Allied troops began their evacuation through the port in Patras. Through her window, Mom watched the parade of British trucks and tanks rumble past, heading for the port, leaving Greece to fend for itself.

2

My Mother's Family

M Y MOTHER, THE FIRST OF FIVE children born to Violetta and Antoni Diamantopoulos, was born in Patras in 1929. My yiayia, believing she could improve the texture of her daughter's hair, which she thought a bit too fine, shaved it all off. To her dismay, when it grew back, the curly blonde locks were replaced by thick, straight, black hair. When Mom was about a year old, Pappou purchased from Yiayia's brother Constantinos a house that was adjacent to the large parcel of land Yiayia received as dowry. The house, located on the outskirts of Patras, was built in the 1840s as the summer residence of the governor of Achaia state in Peloponnesus. The stately three-story house was quite imposing when compared to the typical single-story dwellings in the area, and it had all the modern conveniences of the day: electricity, indoor plumbing, wood-burning stoves, and two full bathrooms.

A second daughter, Eleni, was born in 1931, followed by a son, Panagiotis—nicknamed "Taki"—in 1934, and a second son, Constantinos in 1936. Yiayia was fortunate to have a maid to help with the children and chores because the laundry alone was a major undertaking. The intricate, backbreaking chore was carried out in the outdoor shed. It began with the soaking of the whites—sheets, pillowcases, and towels—in an enormous tub. After scrubbing it all on the washboard, the laundry was heaped into a basket with holes at the bottom so that the water funneled into a second basket underneath. A small cloth bag filled with ash, a whitening agent that worked much like bleach, was placed on top of the whites. Buckets of boiling water heated on the outdoor hearth were slowly poured over the load; the water drained into the second bucket and was used to wash the darks. Nothing was wasted. I find it incredible that black ash can make anything white, but it worked, according to Mom. It managed to turn everything a sparkling white and was eco-friendly to boot. The laundry was line-dried and smoothed with irons filled with hot coals. Because the process involved so much time and labor, laundry was done only every two or three weeks. After learning what Yiayia and the women of her day had to go through, I will never again complain about the clang of my tumble dryer. After all, what is it that I have to do: sort, load, add detergent and softener, and push a button or two?

According to Yiayia, a housewife's best friends were dusk and dawn, the times of day when she'd tend to her chores unimpeded. It was a principle she passed on to her daughters. Growing up, I never saw Mom sitting idly. After tucking us in, she'd iron or mend clothes or do whatever other work was needed. Even while watching television,

Mom's hands were kept busy sewing, knitting, or snapping string beans. At times she'd enlist our help, having us hold the skeins of wool that she wound into balls.

I'd complain, "Mom, can't we just sit and watch television?"

"It's a waste of good time, just sitting doing nothing," Mom would reply.

I'd protest, "We're not doing *nothing*! We're watching television!"

Yiayia, like most mothers of the day, was a stay-at-home mom. She was a passionate cook and spent hours in her kitchen. Everything was made from scratch, including the *phyllo* that she used to make *spanakopita* and *tiropita*, spinach and cheese pies. There were no gadgets, no electric mixers or blenders. Cream and eggs were whisked into perfect peaks by hand. Yiayia made tempting desserts, such as *baklava* filled with ground walnuts and doused in honey that melted in your mouth, and the mouthwatering *galaktoboureko*, sweet custard encased in flaky, buttery phyllo topped with citrus-flavored syrup. *Diples* (Mom's favorite), thin sheets of dough folded and fried into crispy packages drizzled with honey and dusted with cinnamon and ground walnuts, were so irresistible to the children that Yiayia had to keep them hidden. Mom, who had an insatiable sweet tooth, would scour the house in search of them, once dropping the ceramic container, shattering it and all the *diples*, landing her in a heap of trouble.

When Constantinos was six months old, one of his eyes began to protrude. My grandparents sought the help of physicians in Patras, and not getting answers, moved on to Athens. The specialist in Athens said that Constantinos had an aggressive form of eye cancer and little could be done. The little boy constantly pressed his temples with his hands, as if he were trying to squeeze out the pain. Yiayia prayed to Saint Paraskevi, patron saint of eye ailments, even dressing her son in a miniature monk's robe, promising him to the Orthodox Church if only he would be spared.

It was a little after midnight when Mom and her siblings were awakened by their father, who told them Constantinos was asking for them. Mom was nine and sensed by her father's somber tone that something was terribly wrong. The children climbed out of bed and filed into their parents' bedroom, where Constantinos was sitting up in his crib. He greeted them with a sweet smile, calling out to each by name and waving his little hand as if saying goodbye. It was more than Mom could bear. She rushed out of the room so that her little brother wouldn't see her cry. Constantinos died quietly in his sleep that night, just weeks after his second birthday.

Mom and Eleni crept into bed holding on to each other.

Eleni, just seven, asked, "Why did Constantinos have to die?"

"He was very sick," Mom replied.

"Will Mamá and Babá die?"

"Everyone dies," Mom said.

"What happens when we die?"

"We go to Heaven."

"Is Constantinos in Heaven now?"

"Yes, he is in Heaven with God."

"Will we ever see Constantinos again?"

"Yes, we will see him in Heaven."

Mom has no memory of her brother's funeral other than the little white casket being carried out of the house. It was the first time she had seen her parents cry. Sadness permeated their home, and for many nights Mom cried herself to sleep.

The medical bills were staggering, and my grandparents had to sell a parcel of land to cover them. A young couple purchased the land and built a house on it. While they were neighbors and good friends, Mom doesn't remember their names, but she does recall that everyone called the young woman "Kefalonitisa," as she hailed from the island of Cephalonia. It was common practice in Greece for people to be called by their place of origin. A woman from Patras was called "Patrinia"; one from Aegion, "Aegiotisa"; and one from Italy, "Italida." It was also considered courteous to address women by their husband's first name. Yiayia, for example, was called "Kyria (Mrs.) Antonya." I don't think this practice to be courteous at all. Talk about losing one's identity!

The stress and heartache in caring for a terminally ill child took a toll on Yiayia. Her doctor advised rest and warned against having more children because a pregnancy could strain her already weak heart—not only in carrying the child, but also nursing and caring for the infant. However, about a year after Constantinos' death, Yiayia was once again pregnant. She worried that her children might be left without a mother, but terminating the pregnancy was out of the question.

Pappou had two sisters, Athena and Urania, who lived in Aegion. Both were married, and both were childless. Athena, the older of the two, would constantly plead with my grandparents to let her have one of their daughters, arguing that she and her husband were in a better position to provide sufficient dowries. As much as she pressed, my grandparents would not give up their children. When Athena first learned of Yiayia's pregnancy, she wasted no time making her case, saying she would hire a wet nurse and care for the child. Yiayia finally relented, telling her sister-in-law that she would agree on the condition that Athena would take the child at birth.

In September 1939, their fifth child—a daughter—was born. Athena lamented that she hadn't been able to find a wet nurse and asked Yiayia to nurse the baby until she was able to find one. Yiayia who'd never wanted to give up her baby in the first place was having second thoughts. The baby turned out to be exactly what the family needed, for it eased the pain and dispelled the sadness that had seeped into their home after Constantinos' death. My grandparents named their baby girl Argyroula and called her "Roula." Mom was a devoted big sister and a great help to her mother. She fed her baby sister, changed her diapers, cuddled with her, and read her nursery rhymes. Roula slept in a crib near Mom's bed, and as she grew bigger, would jump onto the bed, wanting more play. As a toddler, Roula often ran after her twelve-year-old sister, holding on to her smock and crying when she left for school.

While Mom loved going to school, she also loved summer breaks because it meant more days at the seashore. Mom and her siblings walked to the beach, met up with friends, and dove into the blue sea under the watchful eye of their mothers who sat on the white sand under their wide-brim hats. Mom doesn't recall seeing anyone in bathing suits. Instead, women wore dresses, girls wore slips, and boys wore undershirts and shorts. Sunbathing was not stylish, as a tan implied that one toiled in the fields.

At midday, the children changed out of their wet clothes into dry ones and traipsed home, where they used the garden hose to wash the sand off their feet. For their lunch, Yiayia usually made the children's favorite, an omelet filled with chopped meat that was sautéed with onions and tomatoes, served with slices of crusty bread. Afterward, everyone, including Pappou, took their afternoon nap.

The family was by no means rich, but Mom doesn't remember wanting for anything. They had nice clothes but not many. Like most girls her age, she had a couple of dresses, a tunic for school, a couple of smocks for home, and two pairs of shoes—one for Sunday and one for everyday wear. They didn't have dolls, so they played games such as spin the top, jump rope, hopscotch, and soccer.

The children pitched in with the household chores; helped in the garden; tended the chickens, rabbits, and ducks; and milked the goat. The family had two goats: a mama goat, who was gentle, and her daughter, who was quite unruly and mischievous. She had to be watched when not tethered because she trampled and ate the plants. The times Mom took the young goat to the stud farm, she fought any buck that attempted to mount her and bucked so hard that Mom was dragged to the ground. Because of her wild nature and refusal to be bred, they called her "Tomboy." She remained of little use to the family until the day she was served on a platter.

Taki and Eleni worked alongside my grandparents in the garden, venturing out early in the morning to avoid the midday sun. Mom stayed behind to tend to Roula, tidy up, make the beds, and prepare breakfast. When my grandparents and the little field hands returned, they were treated to a bowl of hearty porridge, warm bread served with butter, and Yiayia's homemade preserves, as well as a pot of brewed green tea. Eleni and Taki constantly teased their big sister, telling her how easy she had it, loafing around while they were out doing real work. They often entertained her with this little ditty:

> "*Oh, Maruchos has no care,*
> *Always resting in her chair!*
> *While we're toiling in the sun,*
> *Maruchos is at home having fun!*"

Eleni and Taki played hard and fought hard. They were fierce rivals and constantly played pranks on each other. Yet, though they needled each other and got into mischief, they couldn't stand being apart. One day, as both were climbing up a tree, Eleni lost sight of her little brother. Frightened that he had been taken by phantoms, she ran into the house, crying. When she spotted him sitting at the kitchen table, grinning from ear to ear, she was furious that he had once again tricked her. At meal times, they drove Yiayia to frenzy by refusing to eat until they were certain their plates contained equal amounts, even going as far as to weigh their plates on the kitchen scale. They didn't care what or how much was on their big sister's plate, but *their* plates had to pass muster.

No one had telephones then, so family and friends just dropped in. Yiayia, who took pride in making her home warm and elegant, was always ready to receive company. Their spacious, well-appointed living room accommodated a sofa, twelve armchairs, a delicately carved armoire, and a bevy of occasional tables. The sofa and armchairs were upholstered in luxurious wine-red velvet, and the floor-to-ceiling windows were adorned with drapes of the same fabric. The Chinese porcelain vases were filled with freshly cut flowers from the garden, their fragrance permeating throughout the house. Visitors were treated to *tourkiko* (Turkish coffee) or a cool drink with pastries or some other *glyko*. *Mastiha*, a white licorice-flavored paste heaped on a teaspoon and dipped in a tall glass of ice-cold water was the children's favorite. Evenings, the family ventured to the *plateia* to enjoy the local music. There, the children danced and had ice cream and cake.

It was only after the bombing had stopped that Aunt Athena and her husband, Georgios, began visiting again, showering little Roula with lots of gifts and attention. Athena would place Roula on her lap, regaling her with stories of their home in Aegion, telling her she would have her very own bedroom, lots of pretty dresses, and lots of dolls and toys to play with. Yiayia tried putting a stop to her sister-in-law's antics, reminding her that since she had reneged on her promise to take the child at birth, she no longer felt compelled to keep her end of the bargain. Athena argued that she had done her best to find a wet nurse, but with the war on and all, it was difficult. She pleaded with Yiayia, telling her to think of Roula's future, once again insisting that she and her husband would provide a substantial dowry.

Mom feared that it was only a matter of time before her aunt would lure her little sister away. Whenever their parents reprimanded her, Roula put on her coat and hat, gathered up her gifts from Aunt Athena, and threatened to leave for Aegion, where she said she would be loved. Mom turned out to be right. In 1942, when Roula was three, my grandparents reluctantly agreed to let Athena take Roula. Sadness once again filled the house. Yiayia would always regret her decision and hated herself for giving into the pressure. It was as if she had lost yet another child. She slid into depression and came close to having a nervous breakdown. Mom pleaded with her parents to let her visit Roula in Aegion; if anyone could bring her little sister back, it was she. But with the war on, her parents wouldn't allow her to make the one-hour bus trip to Aegion.

Pappou and Yiayia

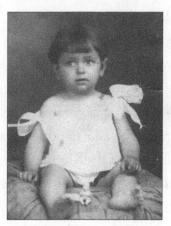

*Mom with her straight
black hair*

Mom, Taki, and Eleni

*Pappou, Eleni,
and Mom*

Mom in the costume worn on
Greek Independence Day

Mom in the garden in photo
taken by Dad

Yiayia with Eleni, Mom, and
maid, Andreana

Aunt Urania
and Yiayia

3

My Parents Meet

TO THIS DAY, AS CLOSE AS I like to think we are, there are certain things my mom is not comfortable talking about. When I ask about her meeting and falling in love with my father, she's reluctant to speak of it, asking, "Why do you need to know that?"

"You have to admit, Mom, it's not like falling for the boy next door."

"What can I say? We saw each other. He liked me, and I liked him."

"But how did he first approach you? What did he say?"

"The first time I saw him, he didn't say anything. I mean, we didn't really meet."

"What do you mean you 'didn't really meet'?"

"I remember it was on a Sunday in January of 1943. My mother and I were on our way to visit a family friend. We were walking along the avenue. Your father was walking with two matronly women, and as they approached, our eyes met."

"Who were the women?"

"They were Italian-Greeks. There were many Italian-Greeks in Patras. They fraternized with the soldiers, inviting them into their homes. Your father said many would help the soldiers with the Greek language."

"So what happened next?"

"When our eyes met . . . I don't know how to describe it; I don't really understand it myself. I remember being drawn to him. It was his eyes. His eyes were brilliant and mesmerizing and had a certain magnetism . . . hypnotic-like . . . that drew me in. I felt an electric spark run through me. It was only for an instant, and then all three walked ahead. But your father turned to look at me."

"Maybe he, too, felt the spark."

"Perhaps . . . maybe that's why he kept turning to look at me."

"You had to be looking at him too."

"I was not."

"Then how would you know he was looking at you?"

"Well, maybe I did look up once or twice. What can I say? Your father was very handsome. He had lots of shiny black hair, broad shoulders, slim hips . . ."

"You noticed a lot for someone who wasn't looking!" I teased. "It sounds like love at first sight!"

"Oh, I don't know about that. But it was then that I realized that he was an Italian soldier."

"That had to be a letdown!"

"Not only an Italian soldier, but the dreaded occupier," Mom said, nodding.

"What did you do?"

"I told myself to forget him; he's the enemy. But I couldn't stop thinking about him. I had never felt anything like that before. I remember thinking, *What kind of power does that soldier possess for him to have such an effect on me?* And, of course, I was flattered that such a handsome man would even notice me."

I can understand why Mom was captivated. When I look at photos of Dad as a young man with his perfectly trimmed moustache, they bring to mind the dashing cinema stars of the day: the swashbuckler Douglas Fairbanks Jr., the daredevil Errol Flynn, the sensuous Ronald Colman, and the devilish glint in his eyes gave him the essence of the rogue Rhett Butler. Dad, too, must have been captivated, as he later told Mom that he often returned to the street where he'd first seen her, hoping to run into her. He said he could have died when he discovered that all he had to do was to cross the street. He couldn't believe that she lived right across from the barracks where he'd been stationed for well over a year!

Dad in photos taken before and after the war

It was the most my mother had divulged, and I didn't want the conversation to end, so I dashed into the kitchen and got some brie, crackers, wine glasses, and a chilled bottle of Pinot Grigio.

Driving the corkscrew into the bottle, I asked, "So when did you see Dad again?"

"About a month later. I was out on the balcony and saw your father in the schoolyard. At first, I wasn't sure it was him. He was standing there with his hands on his hips looking up at me as if he, too, wasn't sure I was the girl he had seen that day."

"Did he say anything to you then?"

"No, but now that he knew where I lived, he'd come by the house, stand below the balcony, and sing."

"Did your parents notice?"

"I don't think so, because on evenings, the soldiers came out to the schoolyard, played music, and sang."

"What songs did Dad sing?"

"Italian songs. I didn't understand Italian then, but I liked the songs and his melodic voice. One was 'Dormi, Dormi,' a song that was also popular in Greece."

"Did you go out on the balcony when he sang?"

"At times I stepped out to look."

"How romantic! You must have felt like Juliet being serenaded by Romeo. Did he say anything to you then?"

"He spoke a little Greek but not much. He told me his name and asked me for mine."

"Did you tell him?"

"No! I didn't say anything. Then he started following Eleni and me on our way to school."

"I thought schools were closed during the war."

"They were closed during the bombing. After Greece surrendered, schools held half-day classes."

"Did he say anything when he followed you?"

"Not at first. He just walked behind us at a respectable distance. He later told me he'd followed us so that no one would bother us.

Eleni was not happy about it. She screamed and even cursed at him saying, 'Why are you following us? What do you want? Go away!' But he just ignored her."

"I can see Eleni doing just that. She was always feisty and fearless."

Mom had often told us about the dandelion-picking episode. They had gone picking dandelions on their Aunt Zaffiroulas' property by the cemetery when Eleni and Taki strayed onto a neighbor's property, knowing perfectly well they were trespassing. When the neighbor spotted them, he came after them, screaming, "Thieves! Come back here, you little thieves!" Eleni and Taki took off like bats out of hell, but Mom froze, unable to move. Eleni screamed at her, "Don't just stand there, dummy, run!" Furious, the man threatened them, saying, "Wait till I get my hands on you!" And even though Eleni was only eight, she fearlessly yelled back, "Oh yeah? You'll have to catch us first!" Unable to catch the two, the man settled on Mom. He grabbed her hand, causing her to drop her basket, and said, "We'll see what your mother has to say about your thieving!" When they reached the house, Yiayia was already at the door. Huffing and puffing, the man complained of her children's thievery, making special mention of her disrespectful and defiant daughter. Knowing full well that Mom was too timid to talk back, let alone be disrespectful and defiant, she told the man, "You've got the wrong one. It's the other one you want!"

Eleni would also entertain us with stories, telling us, "When we were little, your mother was the shy, quiet one. Not me! I wasn't quiet, and I wasn't shy. She liked staying home. I liked going out to play. I climbed trees. I got scratches and bruises, but I didn't care; it was fun. I liked to race. I was so fast! I ran faster than *everybody*, even the boys. I was a real tomboy!"

31

I was seven years old when I first met my Aunt Eleni in New York in 1952. There was no trace of that tomboy. She was a glamorous twenty-one-year-old who had traded her scrappy look for the sophisticated fashions of the 1950s.

Mom went on to tell me about the day she and her little sister had their first big fight.

"On our way to school one day, your father handed me a rose. I didn't dare take the rose, and it fell to the ground. As he bent to pick it up, Eleni yelled at him, 'Get lost you dirty dog!' Your father didn't understand what she'd said, so he smiled and winked at her. That really got her going. 'Got something in your eye?' Your father said nothing, and she screamed, 'What's the matter—can't talk? You'd better beat it, or I'll get my father after you!' I told her to stop, that he wasn't doing anything wrong. Then she turned on me: 'Maybe you like him following you, but I don't! I don't like it one bit! I'll tell Mamá and Babá that you talk to soldiers.'"

"Eleni was protecting her big sister from the bad guys," I said.

"She made me so mad, I started yelling at her. 'I'm not talking to anybody!' I screamed. 'It's you who's doing all the talking. Maybe if you didn't say anything, he'd go away.' Although your father didn't understand what we were saying, he could see we were arguing."

In spite of Eleni's outbursts, Dad continued to follow them, at times snapping photos of them, their house, and the garden. He loved taking photos and was always at the ready, with a camera strapped around his neck. He took photos of the soldiers during drills as well as during their free time, had the film developed, and gave the prints to his buddies. Among his papers, we found a document signed by

Colonel Commander Alberto Osti, authorizing Dad to use his camera in the "operation zone." Dad often spoke of his prized camera that went missing sometime during the war.

"How was it that Dad had so much time?" I asked. "Didn't he have duties?"

"The Italian soldiers were occupiers then. They went on patrol and on maneuvers. They didn't raid or burn villages like the Germans later did.

Dad was resourceful in his attempts to befriend Mom's family. He first approached Yiayia, and in his fractured Greek, offered her a loaf of bread that the Italian soldiers called *pagnotta*. The delicious freshly baked bread was hard to refuse, especially when compared to Yiayia's homemade bread. Since flour was scarce, she had to enhance it with ground acorns, potatoes, or whatever ingredients were available. Pappou suffered from ulcers, and her bread was hard on his digestion. For that reason alone, she agreed to take the bread that Dad offered her. A proud woman, she didn't want to be indebted to the soldier, and so she only took it in exchange for something else. She thought a cup of goat's milk made for a fair trade. Dad took the cup of milk and after walking until he was out of sight, tossed the milk onto the ground. He later told Mom he didn't drink milk and had only taken it so as not to offend her mother. Once, Dad gathered up the courage to ask Yiayia if he could come inside, and she responded by chasing him away with her broom.

Mom came down with a bad cold and stayed home from school. Dad, concerned he hadn't seen her approached Eleni, who, of course, wouldn't give him the time of day. Then he decided to call on Yiayia, who was furious that he'd asked for her daughter. As she attempted to slam the door on him, Dad stopped it with his foot. Mom, who was up in her bedroom, heard her mother and sister shouting, got out of bed, and tiptoed down the stairs.

She heard Dad speaking in Greek, pleading with her mother, saying, "*Thélo na do ti Maria! Thélo na do ti Maria! Den tha páo méhri na do ti Maria!*" (I want to see Maria! I want to see Maria! I won't go until I see Maria!)

Mom, standing on the stairway, called out to Dad, "I'm OK. I'm here."

Yiayia, now furious with her daughter, ran after her. Dad looked in and saw her give him a little wave before rushing up the stairs with her mother close behind. Pleased to have seen her, Dad left happy.

Yiayia followed Mom up to her room, and screamed, "Shame on you, coming out in your nightclothes! And since when do you talk to Italian soldiers?"

"I came down because I heard the shouting. Now he's gone, and it's nice and quiet."

"Nice and quiet! When your father hears about this, it won't be nice and quiet!"

"All he wanted was to see that I was OK and . . ."

"Why should he care if you're OK? What is he to you? And where have you seen him?"

"Eleni and I see him on our way to school."

"He goes to school with you?"

"He doesn't go to school; he just follows us to make sure no one bothers us and . . ."

"Well, I don't want him following you and your sister. What would people think, seeing you with the Italian?"

Not having much luck with Yiayia, Dad began frequenting Pappou's grocery store. The store had a few tables and chairs outdoors where during the early evening, men would sit to enjoy a glass of wine. Dad would go in, order a glass of wine, and make small talk, speaking in Greek interlaced with Italian. Dad found Pappou charming and likable, and he was pleasantly surprised to learn that he spoke Italian.

Pappou had traveled extensively before settling down. He was a solo adventurer, who at seventeen years of age, had left his parents, siblings, and the security of his home to sail on a merchant ship and see the world. After a couple of years, he grew weary of life at sea and jumped ship in New York harbor. He traveled throughout the United States, working in restaurants before settling in Galveston, Texas. He, along with a fellow Greek, purchased a restaurant near the busy port of Galveston. The location guaranteed a steady flow of patrons and longshoremen who came not only for the gyros, hamburgers, freshly caught seafood, and Greek salad, but also a game of pool. It was in Texas that Pappou was granted US citizenship.

Pappou was in America during the Spanish flu pandemic of 1918 that killed more than half a million Americans. He told us he survived the deadly flu because he not only chewed on raw garlic, but also wrapped it in cloth and hung it around his neck. Pappou never stopped extolling the powers of garlic! We believe he survived because the pungent garlic smell kept everyone at bay.

In 1928, twenty-two years after leaving his homeland, the solitary life in America became tiresome, and he returned to Greece. His experience as an immigrant in turn-of-the-century America must have been a bad one because Mom often heard him say, "If you're seeking to exact revenge, give him a one-way ticket to America!"

Back in Greece, a matchmaker introduced him to Violetta Delis. The youngest of eight children, she was strong-willed and had a reputation for being difficult, having refused more than a few marriage proposals and at twenty-four, was considered an old maid. He was immediately drawn to the dark-haired beauty. She, too, was drawn to Antoni, who at thirty-nine, possessed not only a calm steady nature, but also wit, charm, and a dry sense of humor. Never before had she known a man who was so knowledgeable, who had crossed the Atlantic, dabbled in foreign languages, and made her feel so at ease. He proposed, and she readily accepted.

In America, Pappou lived among Greek and Italian immigrants and learned Italian. Dad was much more comfortable with Pappou than Yiayia, not only because he spoke Italian, but also because, unlike Yiayia, Pappou had an easygoing nature.

After a few visits, Dad grew more confident and took the conversation further, telling Pappou, "I met your daughter, a lovely girl. I would like your permission to call on her."

"Son, you must be in the wrong place. My eldest daughter is only thirteen and much too young to have callers."

"Thirteen? Did you say thirteen?"

"Yes. She is thirteen!"

Understandably Dad was taken aback. He believed he'd been courting a young lady of seventeen, not a thirteen-year-old. Mom's maturity is an attribute I inherited. Both Mom and I were tasked with the responsibility of looking after our younger siblings, which undoubtedly contributed to our being mature beyond our years. When I was twelve and a bridesmaid at my Aunt Roula's wedding, I wore a gown and pumps, and even got to wear lipstick, which Dad wasn't too thrilled about. As I was being introduced to the groom's family, a woman practically screamed, "That's not possible. She can't be twelve; she looks at least twenty-five!" Horrified, I ran into the bathroom with my mother in tow. Through my tears I said to my twenty-seven-year-old mother, "Mom, they think I'm old like you!"

That September, I started the seventh grade. I was four inches taller due to a summer growth spurt, and I was miserable! I spent that whole school year hunched over in an effort to conceal my height and full bosom. There's a family photo that to this day still makes me cringe. Looking at it, one sees three adults and three little boys, when really, there's only a two-year difference between my eldest brother and me. So I can certainly understand why Dad thought he was courting a young woman, and not a little girl.

After Pappou regained his composure, he said, "Look here, Salvatore, when the war is over, you will return to Italy. If you feel the same way about my daughter, you will come back to Greece."

I'm sure he thought that once the soldier returned to Italy, he would forget Greece and his daughter.

"I did not know Maria was so young," Dad said. "I understand. But can I see her sometime so we can get to know each other and—"

"No, you cannot. I already told you! She's too young!"

Dad would not give up. He continued following Mom to school and observed her from the school rooftop as she picked vegetables and tended to the chickens and goats. He'd call out to her, and when she looked up, he'd snap her picture, once getting a great shot of barefoot Mom (children walked barefoot around the house and the grounds so as not to wear out their shoes) chasing a chicken that was trying to escape.

He befriended their neighbor Chrysoula, a close family friend who would later become my godmother. She lived with her parents in a house they rented from my grandparents. In her early twenties, Chrysoula—unlike my mother—was an extrovert and a bit of a flirt. Dad asked her to intercede on his behalf. Mom doesn't know why her friend agreed to help, but she always suspected that she had a crush on him. Dad gave her a photo and asked her to give it to Mom. But instead of handing it to her, Chrysoula placed it in Mom's textbook. While in the classroom, a classmate borrowed the book, and when she saw Dad's photo, squealed with delight. The girls passed the photo around, laughing hysterically and teasing Mom about her dashing Italian soldier.

As Mom tried to retrieve the photo, their professor walked in and shouted, "What's going on here?"

The girls froze, including the girl holding up the photo.

"Let's have a look," the professor said as he took the photo out of the girl's hand. "Well, well, what have we here?"

He turned the photo over and read aloud the Italian words Dad had written, "'*Ti voglio bene.*' How very nice! Now to whom are these words dedicated?"

All eyes turned to Mom, whose face burned with a deep blush.

The professor called her up to the front and asked, "What is the meaning of this?"

"I don't know," Mom said. "Someone must have put it in my book."

"So this isn't yours?"

Mom, still red-faced, looked down at the floor and said nothing.

The professor said, "Very well then—if you can't say, I'll have to speak to your parents!"

He then called the class to order, and everyone took their seats. When the class ended, Mom approached her professor and coyly said,

"Professor, I think the photo belongs to my neighbor. She borrowed my book yesterday, and she may have put it in my book by mistake. Can I have the photo so that I can return it to her?"

Her professor, somewhat leery, handed the photo to Mom but not before saying, "Tell your friend to be more careful next time. Also tell her to be especially careful of the company she keeps!"

Clutching the photo, Mom went on her way. She told herself it wasn't a total lie. After all, it was Chrysoula who must have put the photo in her book. She gazed at Dad's handsome face and read the words he had written her over and over again.

She'd liked him from the start. When Dad learned Mom's name, he began calling her Mariella. She loved the musical sound of it and the way it rolled off the tongue. She was flattered not only by his attention, but also his persistence. The fact that he'd tried to endear himself to both her parents meant that his intentions had to be honorable. She was also impressed that he was learning her language. Both my parents had a flair for languages and would go on to speak each other's language with ease, their accents so indiscernible, some thought Mom was Italian, and Dad, Greek.

After learning of their daughter's suitor, my grandparents kept a close watch on her. It was the summer of 1943. School was out, and she was not permitted to venture out alone, not even on the balcony. Dad decided to once again enlist the help of Chrysoula, who asked Mom to come up to her apartment. When Mom showed up, the shock of finding Dad there frightened her so greatly that she ran out. The failed attempt spurred Chrysoula to try again. This time, she asked Mom to accompany her to the garden to pick some tomatoes. At the garden gate, Mom turned and saw that her friend was no longer there—but Dad was. He opened the garden gate for her, but instead of going in, Mom ran back into her house. Dad wrote love notes to her in Italian, stuffing them into her pocket. He wrote of *amore* and his wanting her to be his *sposa*. She was able to decipher the words he wrote using her French and Latin textbooks. At times, she had trouble reading his handwriting and wished he would print instead of writing in cursive.

One evening as Mom was washing the dishes, she heard a tapping on the window. She looked out and saw it was him. Afraid her parents would hear, she held a finger to her lips and motioned that she'd come out later. When she finished with the dishes, she managed to sneak out. They were together for only a couple of minutes when they heard Yiayia calling. Dad gave Mom a quick kiss and ran off. Afterward, all she could think about was the garlic she had eaten. Dad took pleasure in teasing her, saying he'd never forget that their first kiss tasted of garlic.

Mom started meeting him in the garden, where they would sit under the stars. She helped him with Greek, and in the process, she learned Italian. He'd speak to her in Greek interlaced with Italian, saying, "When your parents see how much we love each other, they will give us permission to marry. We will live in Italy. You will love Italy."

How romantic it all sounded to her, but at the same time, how improbable. She knew her parents would never agree. They'd say they knew nothing about this man, nothing except that he was an enemy occupying their country. She tried to remind herself he was a man whose country was at war with hers. But she couldn't help herself. She couldn't understand these new feelings welling in her. Perhaps it was the war. In wartime, we never know what's going to happen, so we grab any happiness we can while there's still time. She was Juliet and her Romeo was an Italian soldier. This was what true love was all about: insurmountable joy and sorrow.

It was late at night in early August, three weeks after their first kiss. Everyone had gone to bed when Mom heard tapping on her bedroom window. Afraid the others might hear, she agreed to join Dad in the garden. She crept down the stairs and went out to him. There was a full moon, and countless stars lit the sky. They held each other and kissed. He spoke tenderly.

"I can't wait for the day when we are married and together always."

I asked Mom how was it that she had her own bedroom. She explained saying that when they were little, she, Eleni, and Taki slept in one room and that when Roula was born she went on to share a room with Roula who slept in a crib. When Roula went to live with their aunt and uncle in Aegion, Mom had the room to herself. Eleni and Taki didn't mind as they preferred each other's company over their big sister's.

Later that month, Uncle Georgios visited from Aegion and decided to stay the night. To Mom's horror, he was given her room. She had no way of getting word to Dad and could only hope he wouldn't come to her that night. But he did, and while in her room, he stumbled in the dark, waking Uncle Georgios. Realizing his blunder, Dad practically jumped out the window. Uncle Georgios' shrieks were heard throughout the house, and everyone rushed in. She tried to remain calm, but when Uncle Georgios recounted the episode, all eyes were on Mom who was beet red, looking as guilty as the goat that tore up the vegetable patch. Her father walked over to her and slapped her face, the first time he had ever done so. Her mother sobbed, saying the family was ruined. Mom somehow found the courage to speak.

"We love each other," she said. "We want to marry."

"You love each other? You want to marry?!" Pappou screamed. "You don't know what you are saying! What do you know about love? You're just a child! You don't know anything about this man!"

Yiayia shook uncontrollably, silently weeping and constantly crossing herself.

"How could this happen?" Pappou demanded. "Our smart, responsible daughter . . . what could have possessed her?"

Seeing the grief and anguish she had caused her parents, Mom dropped her head in shame. She had disappointed and hurt them. She had no idea what they would do.

The next day, Dad headed for Pappou's store. He must have thought this out carefully. He knew Yiayia held nothing but disdain for him and that he would never win her over. He began by professing his love for Mom, telling Pappou that she, too, loved him and that he hoped he would give them his blessing. Pappou must have wanted to do more than slap him, this man who had seduced his daughter had the audacity, the nerve, to ask for his consent. Yet, at the same time, he must have thought the man to have courage to come and face him as he did. He was furious but also measured.

He spoke calmly, repeating what he'd told Dad the first time, "When the war is over you'll return to your country. If you feel the same, you will come back for Maria."

I've often wondered why my grandparents didn't report Dad to the authorities. I can only surmise that they wanted to avoid a scandal.

Dad at right on violin

Dad second from right on sax

Italian troops during maneuvers in Greece

Italian plane

Port in Patras

Italian troops in Aegion

*Slim pickings at the
outdoor market*

*Col. Commandant
Alberto Osti
inspecting his troops*

Soldiers on maneuvers

Officer at headquarters

Alberto Osti, Col. Commandant

Document granting Dad permission to take photos

4

THE ARMISTICE

THE LOUD STOMPING OF BOOTS startled Mom awake. She leaped out of bed and ran into the living room, where her parents stood by the window; a light breeze stirred the curtains. She felt the ground shake as the cannon thundered down the narrow street and a contingent of German soldiers marched toward the barracks. They came to a halt at the gate and a German soldier raised a megaphone to his mouth and shouted in Italian.

"The Italians are being ordered to come out with their hands up," Pappou whispered. "I hope they do, because if they fire that cannon, the whole block will be blown up."

The Italians, in no position to challenge, began filing out with their hands up.

The previous night, the barracks were deathly quiet. There was no music playing, no singing, no merrymaking, just an eerie stillness. The troops had heard the reports over the radio that Italy had surrendered to the Allies. After trying to make sense of the ambiguous news, some left the barracks.

Dad decided to go to my grandparents' house.

"Italy surrendered," Dad said. "We heard it over the radio. We're at a loss. We don't know what to do. There were no orders. I think we've been deserted."

"You had no warning?" Pappou asked.

"It was a shock. Nobody knew. We're sure the barracks will be taken over by Germans. Some of the men left. I decided to come—"

"Where did they go?" Pappou interrupted.

"Some went to the mountains, others—"

"Will you be going to the mountains?"

"I was hoping if—until we find out what's going on—you will allow me to stay. I know it's a lot to ask, but . . ."

"It's more than a lot! Do you know what the Germans will do to my family, to Maria, if they find you here?"

"It will only be a day or two. If I can stay in the shed—"

"What difference will that make? We will be accused of harboring you. The answer is no! I can't risk the Germans finding you here."

"Just a day or two, that's all I ask," Dad pleaded. "We should know something by then. We heard there will be ships taking us to Italy."

Mom reached for her father's hand and pleaded, "Babá, it will only be a little while, just until he can get back to Italy."

"Antoni, he said the ships will be arriving," Yiayia said. "He can't go back to the barracks if it's not safe."

Dad, touched and more than surprised by Yiayia's words, said, "Thank you."

"Has everyone gone mad? Did all of you forget that the barracks are a stone's throw away? When the Germans take over—and they will—he could be picked up at any time! And heaven help us if they find him here!"

"Antoni, there's the attic and—"

"So you've decided, then!"

"He said it will be a day or two," Yiayia said.

"It appears I've been overruled by the women in the house," Pappou said. "You can stay, but only for a day. Two at most! I hope your army doesn't take too long getting you and all those miserable wretches out of Greece!"

That night Dad spent a sleepless night in the attic. After hearing of Italy's surrender, there were reports that Italian ships would transport the soldiers to Italy. *Are the ships really coming?* he wondered. *And if so, when will they get here? Should I return to the barracks? Should I head for the port? Or should I head for the mountains?* He paced up and down, thinking long and hard well into the night, wondering what he should do.

Early the next morning, Dad, too, heard the stomping of boots. The shock of seeing German troops already at the barracks with their cannon jolted him as did the sight of his buddies coming out with their hands up.

At that moment, Mom went up to the attic and asked Dad, "What will the Germans do to them?"

"I don't know . . . take them prisoner or . . . Your father is right. I can't stay here. It's dangerous with Germans across the street. My staying will endanger everybody. The ship may be at the port. I should make a run for it. I have to get on that ship."

"What if the ship isn't there?"

"I don't know. I'm not sure about anything anymore. All I know is that it's dangerous to remain here."

"The mountains would be safe," Mom said. "My father has friends in the mountains."

Dad didn't want any harm to come to my mother's family and thought it would be best if he left. At the same time, he had an uneasy feeling, a premonition that the ships would not be at the port and that he'd be walking into a trap. Orders and instructions surely would come! Their government wouldn't leave their soldiers at the mercy of the Germans. Or would they?

No orders came. There were no instructions. One thing was certain, the armistice would endanger these soldiers more than actual combat, for it put them at the mercy of the Germans, experts at exacting revenge. Abandoned by their army and their country, the soldiers were left with three options: join the Germans, surrender to them, or attempt to blend in with the population while trying to find their way back to Italy. Some were lucky and found work on farms. A fortunate, well-connected few found refuge and did their utmost to stay out of sight, which was not an easy feat, as the Germans were relentless in their pursuit, taking out their hatred and frustration on them.

Dad decided not to go to the port, opting to go to the mountains instead. He would later learn that the ship transporting soldiers to Italy had been bombed, and all on board had perished. All those men happy to be going home sitting at the bottom of the sea.

Once Dad was ensconced in the attic, it was difficult for my grandparents to put him out. Mom was heartened to hear her mother tell her father, "We cannot in good conscience turn him away. Somewhere a mother waits for a son's return." There were two rooms in the attic. The larger room had two windows, which provided light and ventilation. The smaller room was used for storage. Yiayia's idea of the attic turned out to be a good one. Just above the attic was a crawl space, a safe and secure place for Dad to hide in the event the house was searched. Pappou had the carpenter install paneling on the ceiling to conceal the opening leading to the space.

Pappou rambled almost daily about the risk they were taking.

"You'd better do your part," he warned. "You have to stay out of sight. You can't confide in anyone. Collaborators and informants are everywhere. No one can be trusted. And you're to speak Greek only. No Italian here!"

"I'll do my best."

"You have to do more than your best! And, from now on, your name is Sotiri."

"Why Sotiri?"

"It's Greek for Salvatore."

When Mom and I returned in 1970, Greece was ruled by the military junta, the Regime of the Colonels (1967–1974), where, once again, informants terrorized the population. We were stunned by the hostility we encountered. Waiting at the bus stop, Mom asked the driver in Greek if the bus went to a certain beach. It wasn't only the gruff bus driver, but also the entire busload of men who hollered, "*Kyria mou, ti lei apano?*" ("Madam, what does it say above?") On a public beach, when Mom asked our cousins what they thought about the junta, she was met with silence. Thinking they hadn't heard, she asked again and was again met with silence.

It was only after Mom's stepmother had closed the windows and drawn the shades back at home did she whisper, "People are afraid to talk in public. There are informants everywhere, and one has to be on guard and not speak, especially against the government."

"Is it really as bad as that?" Mom asked.

"It's worse! There are people who have disappeared. No trace!"

Coming from America, we couldn't understand the new lack of freedom in Greece, the cradle of democracy. After all, it was the ancient Athenian leader Cleisthenes who had introduced a system of political reforms that he called *demokratia*, or "rule by the people." Now with the junta in power, not only did the Greek people not rule, they also couldn't speak. I found the situation intolerable, and at times I couldn't suppress my frustration.

While riding on a bus with my mom's stepmother whom I called aunt, I asked in my flawed Greek, "*Theia*, where is King Constantinos?"

My aunt, knowing full well that because of my fractured Greek the other passengers would surmise I was a foreigner, simply smiled and said, "I don't know, dear. Maybe he's on vacation."

When we returned home, she let me have it: "Didn't I tell you we don't speak of such things!"

It was on September 10, two days after the armistice, which also happens to be Dad's birthday that Dad, dressed in shorts and an undershirt, snuck into the barracks. He needed civilian clothes and thought the army uniforms and blankets could be useful. He reasoned that he had more right to the Italian-issued supplies than the Germans did. Mom and Yiayia ripped open the seams of the uniforms and submerged them into a tub filled with boiling water and a chemical to remove the color. The fabric was then dyed and used to make trousers, jackets, and coats.

While in the barracks, Dad was spotted by Gianni, his good friend, who, having no other option, had joined the Germans.

"You'd better get out," he warned. "I heard DiBenedetto tell the Germans you were in here."

"Why would he do that? We're friends. We played in the band together."

"You know how it is these days. He probably wants to score points. Don't think about that now. Just go. You haven't much time."

"Thanks, Gianni, I—"

"Get going! You can thank me later . . . if you make it!"

Dad ran out the rear and threw the uniforms and blankets over the gate into Aunt Eleni's backyard. Aunt Eleni was married to Mom's Uncle Constantinos, who died when he was only thirty-eight. A widow with two young sons and in financial need, she had sold a section of the property to the government for the school to be built.

Dad headed toward the back of our house and, not wanting the Germans to find him there, slipped on a pair of trousers and a shirt and went out the back again. He placed a ladder against the eight-foot garden wall, and as he climbed up, was spotted by the soldiers on the school rooftop.

Mom happened to be in the attic and could see three soldiers mounting a machine gun on a tripod and aiming it in the direction of the garden. The German began firing as an Italian held the belt that fed the bullets into the machine gun. Amid the thunderstorm of gunfire, Mom heard Chrysoula screaming, "They're shooting at Salvatore!" Then suddenly, the shooting stopped. The German shouted as all three men grappled with the machine gun that had apparently jammed. They cleared the jam and began firing again, but Dad was already over the garden wall. Dad continued running through the tall vineyards and brush, periodically flopping onto his belly. The shooter, thinking he'd gotten his mark, stopped firing. That's when Dad got up and began running again.

Mom said the stop and start of the gunfire went on for what seemed like an eternity. Every time the shooting stopped, her heart stopped, fearing Dad had been killed. She heard the people who'd come out onto the street shouting, "What's happening? Who's doing all that shooting? Who are they shooting at?" She also heard Chrysoula once again cry out, "They're shooting at Salvatore!"

The soldiers, having lost sight of Dad, stopped firing. Mom ran downstairs and saw Pappou at the door, as the soldier who had held the ammunition belt forced his way in the house. He must have seen Dad making his escape through our garden. He grilled Pappou, who simply shrugged and, speaking in Greek, told the soldier he hadn't seen anyone or anything. Frustrated, the soldier turned to leave, but not before warning Pappou of the consequences for harboring a fugitive. A few minutes later, Mom saw the German soldier running with his ferocious dogs through their vineyards, most likely in search of Dad's body.

Dad ran the three-quarters-of-a-mile stretch, crisscrossing the vast field of dense brush, tall vineyards, and farms. When he reached the end of the strip directly across from the cemetery, he spotted Ioannis, Aunt Zaffiroula's son.

Panting, he blurted out, "Germans … dogs … are after me!"

"Follow me!" Ioannis said as he led Dad to a spot where, by luck, earlier that day, he had dug a ditch. "Jump in! I'll cover you with stuff that won't smell so good. Cover your nose and mouth!"

Ioannis covered Dad with bundles of cane and hay, and shrewdly topped everything off with manure so that the dogs would be thrown off the trail. Sometime later, Ioannis, who was tending to the cows and goats, saw the German with the dogs searching the grounds and not finding Dad, continued on his way.

Mom was overcome with grief, thinking Dad was lying somewhere wounded or dead. She breathed a big sigh of relief when Ioannis arrived and let them know that Dad was alive and well and in their shelter. Dad returned a couple of days later, visibly shaken. Afraid the Germans would come looking for him again, Pappou said they had to find another hiding place and that Dad could no longer stay in the house.

He called on his friend Vouchinas, who was harboring four Italians on his farm. The men tilled the soil and tended the animals, doing whatever was needed in return for food and shelter. Pappou asked if he could take in Dad, and Vouchinas readily agreed.

At times, Dad grew restless and returned to Mom's house. My grandparents weren't pleased by this, fearing he'd be seen not only by the Germans, but also by informants lurking about.

Considering the consequences for harboring Italians, I wondered aloud to my mother why Greeks were willing to help Dad and other Italians.

"The Italians were stationed in Greece for over two years," Mom told me. "Your father, like many of the soldiers, frequented cafés and restaurants and mingled with the population. Two of his friends married girls in our neighborhood."

"Did you know them?"

"Yes, I knew them both," Mom said. There was Maria, our dressmaker, who married Paolo, and Efthehia married Ettore."

"How did their parents feel about their marrying Italians?"

"Maria's parents weren't happy. There were rumors Paolo had a wife in Italy."

"How would Maria's parents know that?"

"Paolo's cousin told them Paolo was married and had two children back home. Paolo denied it, and Maria chose to believe him."

"Did they ever find out if he was married?" I asked.

"I heard that after the war, he never returned to Greece."

"He could have died."

"He could have."

I learned that there was no deep-seated enmity between Italians and Greeks; their histories and cultures had been intertwined for thousands of years. Some soldiers were given refuge in Greek homes, and many joined the partisans to fight the Germans. My grandparents would go on to help other stranded soldiers as well as my dad. One was Carlo. Pappou found him in our garden. He had escaped from Cephalonia, was picked up by fishermen, and then was dropped off at the beach near our home. By the time he reached our garden, he didn't have the strength to go on. He begged Pappou for help.

"Where can I hide you?" Pappou asked.

"Please . . . I beg you—"

"I can't take that chance. There are Germans all over the place."

"Just for a little while?"

Seeing the bedraggled man in his thorn-ripped uniform with scratches to his arms and face, Pappou replied, "It's not that I don't want to help . . ."

"If you can spare a little food, old clothes, anything—"

"What's your name?" Pappou asked.

"Carlo."

Pappou couldn't turn the man away. There were three sheds in the garden. One housed the chickens. The second was a storage room for wine and canned and bottled fruit and vegetables. And the third was used for laundry.

Pappou led the man into the third shed and said, "Wait in here, Carlo. I'll be right back."

He then went into the house and retrieved some antiseptic, a pair of trousers, a shirt, and a blanket.

"Where are you going with those?" Yiayia asked.

"They're for someone in the shed."

"Who's in the shed? Not another Italian!"

"Who else is hiding these days? Can you get him some food?"

"Go to him. I'll bring the food," Yiayia said.

Pappou cleaned the man's scratches, applied the antiseptic, and handed him the clothes and blanket. Yiayia brought in a tray containing bread, some meat, a piece of feta cheese, and a glass of red wine—and quickly left.

Dad would visit Carlo, who told him of the carnage he'd witnessed in Cephalonia, saying the *Tedeschi* (the Italian word for "Germans") had executed thousands of unarmed Italians. Dad couldn't fathom their former allies killing in such a cold-blooded way. This wasn't warfare; it was murder, and it was beyond barbaric!

I can only imagine the anguish these two men felt. I'm certain they had many questions, such as, "How could our country abandon us, her soldiers, leaving us stranded? What are we supposed to do now? How do we get back home? Is anyone in charge? Does anyone care? What kind of war is this when we are ordered not to fight the Germans and left at their mercy? And why are the Germans taking it out on us? Don't they know we had nothing to do with that armistice, that we were just as ignorant?"

The Cephalonia Massacre was the brutal mass execution of the men of the Italian Thirty-Third Acqui Infantry Division by the Germans on the island of *Cephalonia* in September 1943. Following the *Italian armistice,* the Germans tried to disarm the Italians. The Italians resisted, and in a battle that lasted nine days, 1,315 Italians were killed. It was only after running out of ammunition that the Italian resistance surrendered. Over five thousand unarmed men were executed, and three thousand drowned when the German ships taking them to concentration camps were sunk by the Allies. It was one of the largest *prisoner-of-war* massacres of the war.

Ten days after arriving in our garden, Carlo, the shed-dwelling refugee, was well enough to travel. Pappou had him taken to Vouchinas' farm, where Dad sometimes stayed. My grandparents were relieved that Carlo was finally gone and that they no longer had to worry about him being found on their property.

On October 13, 1943, one month after surrendering to the Allied forces, Italy declared war on Nazi Germany, making this already dire situation for those stranded soldiers even more so. How were they to fight Germany? They had no leader, no battle plan. Many joined the Greek partisans in the mountains to fight against their former ally.

The Greek rebels hiding out in the mountains were a major problem for the Germans. In order to discourage the population from harboring and supporting rebels, the Germans killed those they suspected of being rebels, looted their villages, and set fire to them—burning them to the ground. By June of 1944, 879 villages were totally wiped out, leaving more than one million Greeks homeless.

The German occupation brought darkness and despair to the Greek people. They had not felt the same level of fear and oppression during the Italian occupation. For the most part, the Italians tried to befriend the people, whereas the Germans made no attempt to do so, and, in fact, went out of their way to frighten the Greeks into submission. They threatened them with reprisals, warning that for every German killed, nine Greeks would be executed, their bodies exhibited in the town square. And they kept their word. Nine men were hanged in Olga Square and were kept there for two days for all to see. Hostages were taken at random, and if a German soldier was killed that day, the hostages were hanged. If there were no incidents, they were released that night. The Germans repeated this exercise daily.

The Nazis, in their form-fitting uniforms and shiny leather boots, appeared to be invincible and defiant, when in reality most were filled with fear bordering on paranoia, and as a result, they terrified the population with impulsive threats. Nazis were never at ease. They never walked; they marched robotically. When you encountered a Nazi on the street, you avoided eye contact. When the Italians had occupied the barracks, children would wait outside for the cook, who'd come out to fill their little bowls. Children who had not been afraid to approach an Italian would never approach a Nazi. Whereas the Italian-imposed curfew was in effect from midnight until 7:00 a.m., the German curfew was in effect from 7:00 p.m. to 7:00 a.m. In addition, the Germans ordered shutters closed during curfew, making it oppressively hot, especially in summer.

The Italian occupation was relatively mild in that there were a small number of executions and atrocities committed compared to those committed in the German- and Bulgarian-occupied zones. Despite Italy's alliance with Germany, the Italian military occupation officials generally protected the Jews in their zone and ignored German demands to implement the mass murder of Jews. Thousands of Jews in the German-occupied zone fled to the relative safety of the Italian occupation zone, and the highest Jewish survival rate in Nazi-occupied Europe was in Italy. The Germans were more than displeased that the Italians protected Jews not only in their territory, but also in parts of occupied France, Greece, the Balkans, and elsewhere. Joseph Goebbels, Hitler's minister of propaganda, wrote the following in his diary on December 13, 1942:

> The Italians are extremely lax in the treatment of the Jews. They protect the Italian Jews both in Tunis and in occupied France and will not permit their being drafted for work or compelled to wear the Star of David. This shows once again that Fascism does not really dare to get down to fundamentals but is very superficial regarding problems of vital importance.

It was in November that my grandparents consented to my parents marrying. That same month, my grandparents were faced with yet another unforeseen and unwelcome event. Mom was the first to hear the German's heavy footsteps. She looked down from the upstairs window and saw the soldier standing at the front door.

She immediately ran to the back window and called out to Dad, "There's a German at the door! Take Eleni and Taki to the shed, and stay there until I tell you it's safe!"

She then ran downstairs to join her parents. She saw Pappou standing at the door, reading from a piece of paper. Yiayia motioned her into the kitchen.

"I have a requisition for your house," said the soldier, who spoke in English with a smattering of Greek. "Five soldiers will be billeted here. I will need to inspect the house."

Pappou, still reading, frowned and in English said, "I have a wife and three children. I don't think my house can accommodate so many."

"I am required to inspect the premises!" the soldier snarled.

"Yes, of course," Pappou said as he motioned for the man to enter.

There were two small apartments on the first floor, each with a separate entrance. The apartment on the left had been rented before the war and was presently vacant. It contained one large room, an eat-in kitchen, a bathroom, and a small room that housed Yiayia's loom. Pappou told the man that the apartment on the right was currently occupied by a couple and their two young children.

At that point, the tenant appeared, looking somewhat dazed. Seeing the German in the hall, she retreated to her apartment. The woman, who often appeared to be intoxicated, had confided to Mom that she'd never had so much as a drop of liquor before her husband introduced her to wine. Unfortunately, she went on to develop a thirst for the "drink of the Gods" that at times seemed unquenchable. She'd often plead with Mom, cajoling her for just another little glass. Sometimes Mom obliged her.

Pappou led the man through the vacant apartment. They walked through the main room and into the kitchen, where Yiayia and Mom stood. The soldier nodded and walked past them into the small room and bathroom.

After completing his inspection, he said, "And upstairs?"

"There's a kitchen, living room, dining room, three bedrooms, and a bathroom."

"We go up."

"Of course," Pappou said.

After walking through the rooms, the German returned to the living room and stood in the center of it, his legs apart and arms akimbo. Shifting his gaze from the veranda to the balcony, as if taking in the view from each, he finally announced, "This will do."

Pappou argued, "But there is not much room downstairs for my family!"

"These are my orders," the soldier replied.

Defeated, Pappou asked, "When will you be arriving?"

"We will come in two days. This will give you time to prepare."

"What do we do to prepare?"

"Remove things you require."

"How long will you stay?"

"That, I cannot say."

The soldier headed back down the stairs, with Pappou in tow.

Pappou closed the door behind the German and said, "Looks like we'll be having company for a while."

Fear flashed through Yiayia from the tips of her toes to the top of her head. "What are we going to do now? And what about Sotiri? He can't stay here anymore!"

"*Kyria mou*, take it easy. You will make yourself sick. We have two days to think about what we have to do. The first thing is to get the upstairs ready. We have to take what we need down and move what we can up to the attic. I will think about what we do with Sotiri."

As Mom listened, she wasn't thinking about the things that had to be moved. She was thinking about where they could safely hide the man she loved. With the Germans occupying their home, it would be impossible for him to stay in the attic; the opening to the crawl space that the carpenter had so artfully concealed could not be used. That November day's devastating unforeseen blow threw their plans out the window.

"Maro, where are Sotiri and the children?"

"Oh, I forgot about them. They're in the shed. I'll get them," Mom said as she headed out.

Yiayia turned to Pappou and asked, "Who can we trust to take Sotiri?"

"I've been thinking about that. You know, I've been impressed with the way he's picked up the language over the three months he's been here. He's become quite fluent. What if we say he's our son?"

"You can't be serious! He speaks Greek, but he speaks with that accent of his."

"Oh, I don't think the Germans will be able to tell the difference."

"Are you willing to take that chance? They will never believe he's our son! First of all, he doesn't look like us, and second, he's much older than the others. How will you explain that?"

"Well, I can say he's a son from a previous marriage . . . that I was married to an Italian who taught him the Italian language . . . and that will explain the slightly different accent."

"*Slightly* different? His accent is more than slightly different. He sounds like an Italian speaking poor Greek."

"Now you're just being critical. I don't think his Greek is so poor."

"Those Germans will see it right away. That idea is crazy! The best thing is to send him to a farm somewhere in the mountains. That way, he will be out of the way and out of our lives."

"Do you forget that you and your daughter, against my wishes—"

"I thought it would only be for a day or—"

"Well, he's here now, and we have to deal with it. Here you are!" Pappou said as Dad and the children filed in. "I'm sure your sister told you we will be having company."

"Babá, you're not going to let those lousy Germans stay here?" Eleni asked.

"We don't have a choice, Eleni."

"Tell them we don't want them here!"

"Where are they going to sleep?" Taki wanted to know.

Pappou rubbed his palms together briskly and said, "We'll talk about all that later. First, we eat! Girls, help your mother in the kitchen."

Mom set the table as Yiayia brought out the steaming bowl of *fasolada* (bean soup) and Eleni brought out the bread, feta cheese, and olives.

As Mom filled the water glasses, Pappou said, "Maro, get the bottle of *retsina* and the wine glasses."

When they finished their meal, Pappou said, "The Germans will occupy the rooms upstairs. You are never to go up there. I want you to stay away from them. You are not to talk to them. You must always be polite. We must not make them angry. Our lives depend on it."

Pappou could see by their somber faces that his words had frightened the children.

"There's no need to be afraid. Just do as I say, and everything will be all right."

Mom's house wasn't the only one that the occupiers billeted. Her aunts and uncles—Vasiliki and Ioannis next door and Eleni and Ioannis up the street—also suffered the intrusion. Billeting with the locals kept the Germans in close proximity, and more importantly allowed them to avoid bases where they could be attacked, not only by the Allies, but also by the growing number of resistance fighters.

There was much to be done before the intruders arrived, and the relatives helped one another prepare. Beds, bureaus, clothing, and other items they required were brought downstairs. Most of the living room furniture, as well as the velvet drapes and area rugs, were carried up to the attic. Because of their size, the sofa and the armoire could not be moved.

Two days later, the five Germans arrived, loaded down with their gear and sleeping bags. Yiayia and the children scurried into the kitchen, and Dad stayed out of sight, leaving Pappou to greet them. Pappou decided that if the need arose, he would go with his plan of passing off Dad as his son.

The soldier leading the group was the same one who had come to inspect the house. He greeted Pappou, and all five men went up to their quarters. For the most part, they kept to themselves and were seldom seen. Most mornings, they barreled down the stairs in their heavy boots, waking up the entire household. Mom looked out the window and saw them leaving with all their gear, and while she hoped they wouldn't return, they always did. Sometimes they were out for hours, and other times, for days. Life with the Germans was unpredictable and nerve-racking.

A month into the German home invasion, the cabbage patch was plundered, the entire crop gone. The cabbage heads were there one day and gone the next. Pappou was sure the Germans, world-renowned for their sauerkraut, were the culprits. The cabbage had not been in any danger when the Italians had occupied the barracks—the zucchini perhaps, but not the cabbage. My yiayia would have loved to have taken a broom to those brazen thieves and Eleni would have joined in with a big stick.

*　*　*

On December 1, 1943, my parents were married in Saint Andrew's Catholic Church in Patras. The only people who attended the service were my grandparents and two witnesses. They left for the church at different intervals so as not to arouse suspicion. With more German troops patrolling the city, the Italians who were trying to blend in with the locals were having more and more of a difficult time. Adding to the peril were the Greeks and Italians who had become informants. Mom and Dad would spend their first night as man and wife in the small room that contained Yiayia's loom.

The morning after the wedding, Vouchinas, one of the witnesses, called on Pappou and said, "Sotiri can't come to my farm anymore. The Germans raided my place yesterday and took the men. My mother told them they were migrant workers, but they didn't believe her. It's lucky they didn't harm her."

"Did they take Carlo?" Pappou asked.

"They took everybody."

"Poor fellow . . . escapes from Cephalonia only to be caught again!"

A few days before the wedding, a neighbor asked Dad if he would be staying with his in-laws. Trusting him, Dad confided that he'd be hiding out at Vouchinas' farm. Dad wasn't sure if the man was an informant, but the possibility that he was, sickened him. He learned a very important lesson: trust no one.

My grandparents were running out of options for hiding Dad from the Germans. They knew it was dangerous for him to remain in the city and that the mountains would be safer. Pappou approached his friend Dimitri, who had a farm in Balla, a village high in the mountains, accessible only on foot and by horse. Mom was godmother to Dimitri's daughter Maria and had visited the family a few times before the war. Afraid of traveling on horseback, she'd always walked there.

My parents told Pappou they wanted to flee together.

"A wife should be with her husband," Dad said.

"Are you out of your mind?!" Pappou barked.

"When *you* married, *your* wife went with you," Dad said.

"Yes, she went with me all right, but then I didn't have to worry about Germans, did I?"

Secluded on Dimitri's farm, Dad grew lonely at times and periodically made his way back to Mom's, traveling by moonlight and sneaking into the house before dawn. Pappou always chastised him, saying that he was putting the family at risk. Whenever Mom heard gunshots, she was terrified, thinking he'd been spotted. As time went on, Dad's visits grew longer, and eventually, he did not return to the mountains.

John, one of the Germans, asked Pappou, "What is his relationship to your family?"

"Why, he's my son."

"Is that so? He does not look like the others. He is much older, no? And I believe he speaks Greek with some accent."

Being the calm and collected man he was, Pappou didn't let this deter him.

"Yes, he is older than the other children. He is my son from my first marriage. My first wife was Italian, you know. She spoke Italian to our son so he would learn her language."

Pappou hoped the explanation would satisfy the man, and it apparently did because the subject never again arose. My parents believed that John, the friendliest of the lot, knew all along that Dad was an Italian soldier who, because of his relationship with Mom, was being sheltered by the family. Fortunately, the Germans didn't seem to care. As a hopeless romantic, I would like to think that in those bleakest of times, they wanted love to prevail.

That December, the Germans presented Pappou with another requisition order—this time, for his store. Because of the store's strategically attractive location, a corner building on the main road, they ordered him to close up shop. Pappou protested, saying that they were now taking away his livelihood—but it was to no avail.

He reluctantly packed up his stock and moved it into the house. Because of food shortages and infrequent deliveries, there wasn't very much to pack. As if life weren't difficult enough, it became even more chaotic. German soldiers were living upstairs. Customers were coming in to buy canned goods that were stacked, along with sacks of flour, on top of the bureau. And, in the middle of it all, the family was passing off an Italian soldier as a family member. Yiayia was being pushed closer and closer to the edge.

And, as if all this weren't enough, Mom added to the chaos.

One morning, she woke up nauseous so she approached her mother who was in the living room with Aunt Vasiliki.

"I'm nauseous," Mom said. "Could it be something we ate last night? Does anybody else feel nauseous?"

"No, I don't think so," Yiayia said. "Just drink some *gazzosa* (fizzy lemonade). It will make you feel better."

The next morning Mom woke up nauseous again. She took Yiayia's advice and drank the *gazzosa*, which made her feel better. However, when the nausea returned the next morning, Mom was concerned and once again approached her mother.

"Nauseous again?" Aunt Vasiliki shouted.

"Maro, when did you start feeling sick?" asked Yiayia.

"About three days ago . . ."

Her aunt chimed in, "Oh, I don't think it has anything to do with what you ate, *koritsi mou.*"

"What do you mean?" Mom asked.

"Oh, nothing . . . just . . ."

"Vasiliki! That's enough!" Yiayia squealed. "Maro, pour yourself a tall glass of *gazzosa*. It will make you feel better."

Mom plodded off to the kitchen wondering why her mother and aunt were acting so strange about a little nausea.

When Mom was out of earshot, Aunt Vasilki groaned, "She's pregnant I tell you! What are you going to do now?"

"We'll deal with it like we deal with everything else," Yiayia sighed.

Yiayia got a hold of Pappou and Dad and directing her glare at Dad said, "Did you know Maro has been having morning sickness for three mornings now?"

"Morning sickness? She didn't say anything to me? What's wrong with . . ."

"She's pregnant, that's what's wrong!"

"Are you sure? How do you know?" Dad said.

Now it was Pappou's turn to glare at Dad. "Didn't I tell you to be careful? Didn't I tell you that this is not the time to bring a child into the world!"

"And Maro is just a child herself!" Yiayia lamented. "There's only one thing to do. We have to terminate the pregnancy. It's early and there's time . . ."

"That could be dangerous. More dangerous than having the baby . . . and a sin!" Dad said. "And it's something Maro and I have to decide for ourselves!"

Dad stormed out of the room and went into their bedroom where Mom was waiting. Speaking tenderly he said, "Maro, why didn't you tell me you weren't feeling well?"

"I told you I don't like it when you call me Maro," Mom said. The first time Dad called her Maro she complained, "Not you, too! I hate the name Maro! I like it when you call me Mariella."

"We're in your father's house. While I'm under his roof, I have to call you what your family calls you. Why didn't you tell me you weren't feeling well?"

"It's just a little nausea. I'm not really sick. The *gazzosa* helped. I feel better now," Mom said. "I don't know why everyone is acting so weird over a little nausea, especially Aunt Vasiliki."

"You're right, you're not sick. We're going to have a baby and . . ."

"We're going to have a baby? How do you know?"

"You get nauseous in the beginning," Dad said.

"We're going to have a baby! How wonderful! I want to have a little girl . . . a little girl that looks like you . . . a little girl with your beautiful eyes and your black hair and . . ."

"So you want us to keep the . . ."

"Why of course! Why would you even ask such a thing? Don't you want our baby?"

"Of course," Dad said. "Of course I do. More than anything!"

It was only recently that Mom confided that I could have been aborted. She had kept this from me all these years, thinking it would cause me to resent my grandparents. I have told her that I can't resent my grandparents because I can understand their concerns for her. What is most important to me and what heartens me most is that my parents chose to give me life.

*　*　*

Although there was a kitchen upstairs, John often came down to use the stove downstairs and chat with Dad and Pappou. One day, Mom and Dad walked in on John as he was cooking cabbage. The pungent odor drove Mom out of the room.

John ladled a couple of spoonfuls onto a plate and slyly told Dad, "Here, this is for your little sister."

Dad managed a weak smile and took the plate.

He found Mom out on the veranda and said, "John said this is for you."

Mom eyed the pilfered cabbage and said, "Why for me?"

"I think he guessed we're not brother and sister."

"What do you mean?"

"Well, he wants you to have this. He must know you're pregnant."

"How could he know? I'm not even showing!"

"He just knows."

"Do you think he'll make trouble?"

"I don't think so. He's enjoying himself too much."

My parents didn't believe that John had ever bought Pappou's story about Dad being his son. The reason John offered Mom the cabbage was because he most likely believed in the myth that if a pregnant woman smells food, she has to have a taste to ensure a healthy baby. A few days later, John gave Mom a pair of blue suede pumps. She was uncomfortable taking the looted items, but she didn't want to offend him. He had always been civil to the family and she didn't want to say or do anything to change that. She took off her shoes, which she had stuffed with newspaper to cover the hole on the sole, and eased into the pumps. They were a perfect fit. John smiled and walked away before she could thank him.

John, sensing Pappou to be a kind man and a good listener, often confided in him. The two conversed in English because Pappou didn't speak German. John told him that his mother had written him, saying that his wife had run off with a man, abandoning their two young children. He said his mother was presently caring for them. He hoped the war would end soon so he could return home, where he hoped to find a good woman to be a mother to his children.

Dad grew to be at ease with the Germans, often visiting them in their upstairs quarters. They, too, often visited with Dad and Pappou at the kitchen table or walked the grounds. Despite the language barrier, they managed to communicate, often utilizing their hands. However, Yiayia and the children always made themselves scarce whenever the Germans were around.

Mom worried that Dad was getting too comfortable for his own good. As time went on, his complacency charged her concern. He'd complain of being cooped up, saying he felt closed in and needed to get out. He ventured out more and more, and the times he was late returning, Mom was filled with anxiety. One day as Mom was walking to her doctor's office, she was shocked to see him walking a few steps behind her, flashing a big smile.

"What are you doing? You're not supposed to be out!" she exclaimed.

Dad took her hand in his and said, "I thought I'd tag along to make sure nobody bothers my wife."

"It's dangerous for you to be out here!"

"What's there to be afraid of?"

Just then, a group of German soldiers approached. Mom froze in her tracks.

Dad draped his arm around her and said, "No need to be afraid. Just keep walking and talking, and don't forget to smile."

The group walked past, Mom still shaking. She had not forgotten the day he was almost killed in dodging gunfire.

"Weren't you the least bit afraid? If that machine gun hadn't jammed, you could've been killed."

"Not the way that idiot was shooting. He couldn't hit a thing."

"I don't understand you!" Mom said.

"Just remember, these *Tedeschi* smell fear, so when you see them, stay calm. And also remember, no sad eyes. They look for that. The last thing you want to do is look scared or run. That only makes them suspicious. That's what gets you in trouble!"

Dad was brimming with confidence, most likely believing that *acting* confident was as good as *being* confident.

My parents had their very first quarrel on March 6, 1944. Mom remembers the date not because of the quarrel but because of what happened later that day. The family had dinner at midday, and on this day, with the food already on the table, Dad had yet to return from one of his outings. Mom stepped out and was relieved to see him.

"Sotiri's coming," she announced to her family members.

A couple of minutes passed and Pappou, more than annoyed, said, "I thought you said he was coming. Where *is* he?"

Mom stepped out again. No Dad! Aunt Vasiliki's and Chrysoula's houses were the only two he could have gone into.

She saw Chrysoula sitting on her doorstep, shucking peas, and asked, "Have you seen Sotiri?"

"No."

"He was out here a moment ago. Where could he have gone?"

"I just came out and haven't seen anybody."

Mom went up to her aunt's, and not finding him there, ran back home.

"What happened?" Pappou asked. "He couldn't have just disappeared unless the earth opened up and swallowed him."

"He's nowhere! Nowhere!"

Mom looked out again and saw him ambling toward the house.

"Where have you been?" she demanded.

"Why? Were you looking for me?" he asked.

"Where *were* you?"

"I was at Chrysoula's."

"What on earth for?"

"I just wanted to see what you'd do if I disappeared."

It was the first time she was truly disappointed in him.

"You think that's funny? It's not! It's cruel. You are a cruel child. Grow up!"

Dad enjoyed playing practical jokes. April Fools' Day was a favorite of his. The trouble was that his jokes, at times, went a bit too far. He earned the ire of my aunts once when he beckoned them to come to our home on some pretext. When they arrived, he greeted them with, "April Fools!" My aunts didn't find it funny, telling him he nearly gave them a heart attack. That didn't stop Dad though. He'd always come up with a prank to top the previous year's. But the day wasn't a total bomb because he later compensated for his bad behavior with a delicious meal for his victims. Dad loved to cook and share his labor just as much as he loved to jest.

Mom stormed into the house, refusing to talk to him.

Dad followed after her, pleading, "I'm really sorry. You're right. That was dumb. I don't know what I was thinking. I didn't mean to scare you. Really, I didn't."

"Never do that again."

"I never will. I promise."

That evening, Dad would disappear for real.

From left: Pappou, Dad, Yiayia, Aunt Vasiliki, and Eleni hauling wheat

Mom, Taki, and Eleni at the well

John and Pappou strolling through the grounds

Mom in our garden, where Dad made his harrowing escape dodging machine gunfire

Mom and Dad in the garden

Dad, at right, in civilian clothes with a family friend

5

My Father Is Captured

PAPPOU AND UNCLE IOANNIS WERE sitting at the kitchen table. Dad had gone up to visit his German friends, and trim one another's hair. (My dad and the Germans were either frugal or didn't trust Greek barbers.) Yiayia was in the living room, mending socks and keeping a watchful eye on Eleni and Taki, who were sprawled on the floor, playing with marbles.

Mom entered the living room and plopped into a chair. After that day's quarrel with Dad, she was looking forward to an uneventful evening. She was enjoying the serenity when suddenly it was shattered by thundering footsteps on the stairs. The door was partly open, and she could see Dad and two of the Germans enter the kitchen, sporting crew cuts. Mom wished the Germans would stay in their quarters and not invade their space. She also wished Dad wouldn't encourage them. She warned him time and again that if he ever slipped and was found out, it wouldn't only be he who'd suffer the consequences. Dad argued that it was better to befriend the Germans than not. What would they do, Mom wondered, if they discovered that he was an Italian soldier hiding under their noses?

As dangerous as the situation was for the family, I can't help but laugh, thinking of *Hogan's Heroes*, the TV sitcom depicting the Germans—especially Sgt. Schultz and Col. Klink—as incompetent, bungling fools.

One of the men reached into a huge sack, pulling out items and placing them on the table. Mom looked over to her father and uncle, and she could see by their downcast eyes that they, too, were envisioning the carnage that must have taken place that day. The men were speaking a mixture of Greek and English when suddenly the talking stopped. Mom looked up and saw that her father, uncle, and Dad were now standing. It was then that she noticed three other men in the room. She hadn't heard them come in. At the time, the front door was kept unlocked to accommodate the Germans' erratic schedule.

Mom strained to look closer. There was a Gestapo agent, an Italian soldier, and a Greek civilian. She recognized the civilian and was horrified. His name was Anagnostopoulos, and he lived nearby with his two unmarried sisters. In his early thirties, he was tall, attractive, well educated, and fluent in several languages, German being one. He'd landed a position as a translator and was despised, not because he worked for the Germans, but because he was a Nazi collaborator who had proved himself invaluable to their war effort. At the end of the war, when the Germans fled Greece, he went with them in order to avoid punishment—leaving with no thought of his sisters. (This man piqued my interest because not only did he share the name of Spiro Agnew, who had shortened it from Anagnosto-poulos, he also shared his fate. Spiro Agnew, President Nixon's vice president, was forced to leave his office in disgrace.)

Dad was standing at attention with arms outstretched as the collaborator patted him down searching for weapons.

Pappou walked into the living room and as he went past Mom whispered, "I knew it was a matter of time before he got caught. He doesn't listen. He doesn't stay put. Now some informant has turned him in."

Yiayia drew the children to her. Mom could barely move out of the way as the three men stormed into the living room. Although terribly frightened, she couldn't help being struck by the incongruity of the two soldiers. The German, in his perfectly tailored uniform with brass buttons and polished black leather boots, made an impressive figure, whereas the Italian, in his ill-fitting uniform and scruffy boots, looked rather inept.

The collaborator, with an air of authority, sauntered around the room and, speaking in Greek, asked, "Who is the wife of the Italian?"

Mom, terrified, her reply barely audible, said, "I am."

Ogling her, he said, "Get your coat. You are to accompany your husband."

Pappou stepped forward and said, "My daughter is a minor. I want to go with her."

"By all means," replied the collaborator.

Mom, now terrified, needed to use the bathroom and had only taken two steps when the collaborator walked past her and into the bathroom, making sure there was no means of escape. Satisfied, he waved her in.

When she came out, she saw him holding Dad's coronet, which had been hanging on the wall.

"Do you know any other Italian soldiers?" he mockingly asked Mom.

Glaring at the lout, she replied, "No."

My parents and Pappou were escorted out and into the waiting van, where three other Italian soldiers were huddled. Mom recognized Paolo and Ettore. She was startled to see them and even more so that their wives were not with them. She couldn't understand why she alone had been ordered to accompany her husband. Mom saw the smug look on the collaborator's face. She had not been truthful when she'd told him she didn't know any other Italians, but she didn't concern herself with him. There was much else to worry about. Their house might be burned down; her family, imprisoned, or—God forbid—executed, and there was the possibility that her unborn child would never know its father. And then there was the guilt, the overwhelming guilt, that she'd brought this on her family.

The van stopped outside the prison, and they were ordered out. Mom was taken to a cell containing women who appeared to be ladies of the night. The women teased her, wanting to know what an innocent like herself was doing there. It was torture for her, sitting in that cold cell and not knowing what lay ahead. She was anxious about Yiayia, who was most likely enduring a sleepless night.

The next morning, Mom and Pappou were taken to an office where two Gestapo agents and a Greek civilian, who was serving as an interpreter, were waiting. Mom didn't know the civilian personally, but she knew *of* him. It was common knowledge that his daughters, all four of them, were involved with Italian and German officers and that they were well compensated for their services. His perfectly coiffed and smartly dressed daughters strutted on the *plateia*, indifferent to the suffering of those who didn't have the means to buy food, let alone clothes and shoes. There were many Greeks who spoke German and worked as translators, but not all were collaborators. Mom's cousin Haralambos was scorned for working for the Germans. He argued that he wasn't helping the Germans; he was helping the Greeks deal with them.

During the questioning, Pappou volunteered that my parents were married.

It was at this point that the obnoxious Greek turned to Mom and asked, "Why did you marry the Italian? Was it because you didn't have food to eat?"

What a ridiculous question, she thought. *How could a soldier in hiding, desperately dodging Nazis and overzealous informants, possibly provide for anyone?* She glared at the despicable man, a man who, for profit, had turned against his own people. She wanted to tell him this, to humiliate him as he tried to humiliate her. But she didn't. There was safety in silence. She may have been young and naïve, but she was wise enough to know that he was in a position of power and could make their already dire situation worse than it was.

Mom could only wonder what would happen to this arrogant man and his four daughters when the Germans were forced to flee. Would he be arrested for collaborating with the enemy? Would his wanton daughters be made to suffer the fate of women accused of sleeping with the enemy, *collaboration horizontale*? Would their heads be shaved as a mark of retribution and humiliation?

As they were about to leave, Mom remembered that Dad had asked her to try to retrieve his coronet. When she asked the Greek if she could have it back, the repulsive man replied that she could on the condition that she report to his office every morning at seven o'clock. Mom scowled at the jerk, then turned, took Pappou's hand, and walked out of the prison. To her relief, when they returned, the Germans said nothing about Dad's arrest. They had to be mortified and more than embarrassed when he was picked up by the Gestapo.

Some days later, John told Pappou, "We never believed Sotiri was your son. I have to admit, we were amused by your story."

"Well, what could I do?" Pappou said. "He's my daughter's husband."

"Given the circumstances, I would have done the same. We like Sotiri very much, a charming fellow. We enjoyed his company and are sorry he was caught. I want you to know that we wish him safety, both for his sake and Maria's."

*　*　*

Years later, I asked my mom, "Didn't the Germans shoot people for harboring Italians? How was it that we were spared?"

"We were lucky, I guess."

"It could be that since Germans were in the house, the powers that be decided not to make an issue of it. It had to be humiliating for them that an Italian soldier was hiding in plain sight."

Dad was transferred to a prison in the old part of the city, which was a distance away from our home. Mom made several trips to the prison but was turned away each time. The last time she attempted to see him, the prison guard told her that Dad was on the truck that had just left. She asked where the truck was headed, and the guard said he didn't know.

Two weeks had passed when a woman called on the family, saying she'd met Dad at the Athens prison. Dad asked her to let the family know where he was and that he was well.

Pappou said he'd take the bus to Athens. Mom recalls fondly that even Yiayia had come to care for Dad. She had unruly Tomboy the goat killed so that Pappou could take a hearty meal to him. Pappou found Dad to be in fairly good spirits, but when he returned a month later, he learned that Dad was no longer there. This was a crushing blow. Just having known he was in that Athens prison was a comfort to Mom. Now that she no longer knew where he was, she despaired, assailed with frightening thoughts: she might never see him again; he could be dead, and she, a widow at fifteen. She felt helpless, and all she could do was pray for his safe return. So pray she did.

* * *

During the war, the Red Cross provided pregnant women with supplies needed for their babies' delivery. Mom was eight months pregnant when she and her friend Kefalonitisa, who was pregnant with her third child, went in for their supplies. They walked a little over a mile, and when they arrived, they were discouraged to see the queue that encircled the building. Standing in line in the blistering heat that July day, with the sun's rays beating down on them, made some of the women swoon. One woman fainted and was carried inside.

When Mom finally reached the glass window, the young man asked, "Your name?"

"Maria La Greca."

The man looked up at her quizzically.

"What kind of name is that? It isn't Greek!"

"It's Italian," Mom said.

"You have to report upstairs."

"Upstairs? Why upstairs?"

Pointing to the double staircase, he said, "Up those stairs."

Mom, alarmed and confused, walked toward the staircase. She hesitated a moment to see if anyone else was directed to go upstairs. No, she was the only one. She wondered if it was because of the Italian name she had given. She then saw that the man had left his post at the window and was walking toward the other side of the double staircase. Not comfortable with the prospect of being alone with him, she returned to the line. When a woman screamed at Mom, accusing her of jumping the line, Kefalonitisa told the woman that Mom had been in the line and had stepped aside. Mom, relieved that her friend had come to her defense, walked up to the window, where she was once again asked for her name. This time, she gave her maiden name and was given the items without delay.

"What was that all about?" Kefalonitisa asked.

Not wanting to get into it, Mom said, "Oh, I don't know. The fool most likely wanted to show how important he is."

* * *

A month later, as it was approaching curfew, Mom went into labor. The midwife had two other women scheduled to deliver that day and could not make a house call. Mom, accompanied by Yiayia, made the twenty-minute trek to the midwife's house, in a neighborhood that was heavily populated by Italian-Greeks. After walking almost a mile in the oppressive August heat, they finally reached their destination. Later that night, they heard gunshots and people screaming.

"What's happening?" Mom asked.

"Those lousy krauts," the midwife said. "They're going house to house, snatching Italian teenage boys and girls for their labor camps."

That night, the Germans abducted a schoolmate of Mom's, an Italian-Greek girl named Epiphania. Before the war, Epiphania had traveled to Italy along with other young Italian-Greeks at the invitation of Mussolini's government. When Epiphania returned from Italy, she flaunted her fashionable Italian shoes. Mom thought the pointy-toed shoes odd. The two ten-year-old girls would taunt each other, Mom mocking Epiphania's shoes, and Epiphania Mom's hat. She'd point at Mom's beret, giggle, and call her *Gallida* (Frenchie). During the Italian occupation, Epiphania's family socialized with the Italian soldiers, inviting them into their home. Mom learned that Epiphania's family, like other Italian-Greeks, was deported to Italy after the war, but doesn't know if Epiphania ever returned from the German labor camp she'd been sent to.

* * *

Between 1943 and 1944, the Germans were becoming more and more desperate and began drafting Greeks to fight against the Resistance. Some were taken to the Eastern Front and used as cannon fodder. Many who feared German conscription, joined the Resistance, choosing to die fighting against—and not *for*—the Germans.

Mom recalls that in Aunt Vasiliki's house, there lived a woman whose husband was an electrician, and he had a permit to stay out after curfew. While he was known by most of the Italian guards, one night a new guard was on duty, and upon seeing the man out after curfew, he shouted, "Halt!" When the man reached into his pocket to retrieve his permit, he was shot dead. The widow's teenage son joined the Resistance, and sometime later, her younger son was drafted by the Germans to fight the Resistance. If the Greek boys did not obey the order to shoot against their countrymen, they themselves were viciously shot in the back by the Germans shadowing them. A sad song encapsulated this tragic time:

> *Fathers against sons;*
> *Brothers beating brothers;*
> *Friends stabbing friends;*
> *How long before it ends?*

* * *

The gunshots and screams went on well into the night. Mom was filled with terror, thinking some stray bullet would find its way into the midwife's house. In the throes of labor, she stifled her cries, sinking her teeth into her palm. At four o'clock the next morning, I made my entrance. Mom was thrilled. She got the little girl she had wished for: a girl with a full head of shiny black hair and big dark brown eyes like her father's.

Probably due to the unsanitary conditions at the midwife's, Mom contracted an infection that plagued her for weeks, causing her to lose not only her strength, but also her hair. Because of the infection, Mom wasn't allowed to nurse me, and I was fed goat's milk. My yiayia took care of all my needs. She fed me, changed and bathed me, and sat up with me on the nights I couldn't or wouldn't sleep.

In October, two months after I was born, the five men who'd been billeted with us for almost a year left without saying goodbye. The Germans headed for the port to the waiting ships, with the Greek partisans in hot pursuit. The partisans fired at the ships, and the Germans fired back, one bomb striking a nursing home. There were many casualties that day.

When my grandparents went to inspect the rooms upstairs, Yiayia was outraged at seeing the nails the Germans had hammered into the armoire to hang their belongings.

Shaking her head she asked, "How could anyone be so cruel, so heartless, as to drive nails into a work of art?"

After the Germans left, Roula and her adoptive parents came to visit. Two years had passed since she'd left for Aegion. Roula was now five, and seemed to have no memory of her parents or siblings. It was apparent that she was quite spoiled, enjoying the attention she received as an only child. It was at this time that my grandparents reluctantly agreed to sign the adoption papers, making Aunt Athena and Uncle Georgios Roula's legal guardians.

With the Germans gone and the curfew lifted, life was slowly returning to normal. But there was still no news of my father.

6

THE ITALIAN ARMY DISINTEGRATES

I SAT IN MY SIXTH-GRADE HISTORY CLASS as my teacher lectured the class on World War II. When it came to Italy, aside from the fact that she fought on the Axis side, the only other major fact covered was Italy's surrender to the Allies. The war continued with the Allies fighting Germany and Japan. It was as if the Italian army ceased fighting, packed their gear, and went home. I would later learn that there was much more to the story. Italy's surrender was by no means the end for her or her soldiers. The armistice put those men who were abandoned on the battlefield in more peril than actual combat did. The fighting in Italy was so savage and so horrendous that Italian soldiers and civilians who lived through it don't talk about it.

Eager to learn how my dad and those stranded Italian soldiers who were left at the mercy of their former ally dealt with their plight,

I came across a scattering of books, which revealed that little had been published. I learned that the Italian theater was one of the most neglected in World War II, and the contribution of Italian soldiers who fought on the Allied side was even less known.[1] The histories of World War II published in Italy rarely mention the events involving the abandoned Italian soldiers after September 8, 1943.[2]

In 1943, after recurrent military defeats, King Victor Emmanuel III ordered Mussolini to resign. Mussolini refused, and on July 25, he was arrested, and Italy set up a new government headed by Pietro Badoglio, who arranged for an armistice with the Allies. After weeks of negotiations, the armistice was finally signed in Sicily on September 3. It was agreed by all parties that the armistice be kept secret until Italy's armies could withdraw and the Allied invasion of Italy was well underway. However, the Germans learned of their ally's surrender the same way Italy's armed forces did when on the evening of September 8, before the necessary plans were put in place, Badoglio pressured by General Eisenhower announced it to the whole world. Sometime after midnight, a broadcast to all military units went out with a directive that summed up instructions for reacting against German violence and concluded: "*In no case are you to take the initiative in hostilities against German troops.*" These instructions put the army in the worst possible position for facing inevitable German aggression, aggravating its uncertainty and disorientation.[3]

Among the conditions included in the armistice was an Allied commitment to return the Italian troops from the Balkans back to Italy. Only twenty-four Italian divisions found themselves on Italian territory, while thirty-five divisions were occupying parts of the Balkans and the Aegean Islands. There was no assistance from

Italy or from the Allied Middle East command. It was every man for himself. The men raced to the ports but were blocked by the Germans as well as Greek partisans. There was a total lack of coordination with the Allies, and only a small part of the Italian army saved itself. In many cases, once the Italian troops had reached the coast after long, exhausting marches, they waited for the arrival of ships that never came. My father, like many stationed in Albania, Yugoslavia, and Greece, preferred to take refuge in the mountains and join the Greek partisans rather than surrender to the Germans. However, these soldiers didn't always get a favorable reception. With no assistance from Italy or from the Allied Middle East command, an army of more than a million men disintegrated within days with seven hundred thousand deported and interned in Germany.[4]

* * *

After Italy's capitulation, the Germans pushed through with their speedy occupation of Italy while the Italian military and political establishment disintegrated. The Allied commitment to unconditional surrender made a separate peace with Italy impossible and required the invasion of Italy instead. The Allied preparations for the Normandy invasion meant that only limited forces could be used for landings in Southern Italy. The Germans quickly deployed their forces and occupied Northern Italy, which the Axis still held, and reinstated Mussolini in the North. Invading Italy from the south, the German troops in Italy quickly became an occupation force and subjected their former ally to the brutal treatment they had exacted on conquered people. Some Italians would remain loyal to fascism, but most aligned themselves with the Allies and rejoined the Italian army, fighting on the side of the king. For the remainder of the war, they fought alongside the Allies against the Germans as they sought to reestablish themselves as Italian soldiers. [5]

I came across an account of a soldier's experience that was similar to my father's. He was stationed in Patras, and, like my father, he fell in love with a girl who sheltered him after the armistice. He fought alongside Greek partisans and, like many stranded soldiers, tried blending in with the population. He was eventually captured by the Nazis and transported to a labor camp in Yugoslavia that contained what he described as subhuman conditions. There, he and 253 POWs were systematically starved. A sport Germans took delight in was throwing bits of meat onto the floor, and then, as the starving prisoners attempted to pick up the dirty morsels, the Germans would unleash their vicious dogs, who would win the competition every time. [6]

At the end of hostilities, Italy was besieged by violence when Communist-controlled partisans carried out the mass murder of thousands of Italians, with little or no restraint by Allied forces of the occupation. [7]

*   *   *

I often heard my nonna—my father's mother—say, "Before the war, we could leave our doors open because Mussolini put all the mafiosi in jail. But when the Americans and the English came, they emptied the jails, thinking they were freeing political prisoners, but most were criminals and Communists."

I thought this to be nostalgia, a way of glorifying the pre-war Mussolini, but I found elements of truth in those sentiments. I learned that the Mafia had been stamped out under Mussolini, the leaders either imprisoned or escaped abroad, mostly to the US. They returned to Sicily with the US forces, posing as political refugees, and secured the release of those who were imprisoned in Italy. "Lucky" Luciano, one of the leading racketeers in New York City, was freed from prison because of aid he supposedly gave the US during the war. He was deported to Italy, where it is alleged he operated as the link between the Italian and American racketeers who were active in labor, violence, transportation, narcotics, bootlegging, and prostitution. The aid, direct and indirect, that the Allies gave to the revival of the Mafia backfired on the Allied countries, most notably the US.[8]

What surprised and shocked me most was that the pre-WWII Mussolini was lauded far and wide by an eclectic group that included Mahatma Gandhi, who called Mussolini "one of the great statesmen of our time"; Pope Pius the XI, who said Mussolini was "sent by providence" to save Italy; the American ambassador in Rome, Richard Washburn Child, who wrote that Mussolini was "the greatest figure of his sphere and time"; and Winston Churchill, who called Mussolini "the Roman genius." In a June 1933 letter to an American envoy, President Franklin Roosevelt praised Mussolini: "I am much interested and deeply impressed by what he has accomplished and by his evidenced honest purpose of restoring Italy and seeking to prevent general European trouble."

In November 1923, *The New York Times* wrote, "Mussolini's conception of power and authority has many points in common with that of the men who inspired our own constitution: John Adams, Hamilton, and Washington."[9]

The Saturday Evening Post published numerous articles praising Mussolini and his regime. Fortune magazine (May 1932) reported, "In the world depression, marked by governmental wandering and uncertainty, Mussolini remains direct . . . . He presents, too, the virtue of force and centralized government acting without conflict for the whole nation at once."[10] Two months later, *Fortune* compared Fascist Italy's social policies with those of the Democratic Party in the United States: "The Corporate State Is to Mussolini What the New Deal Is to Roosevelt."[11]

Mussolini started out as a journalist with socialist leanings who endeavored to initiate change through his writings. He attempted to preserve the peace in Europe with countless proposals to the League of Nations requesting that the harsh terms inflicted on the German people under the Treaty of Versailles be revised. It is generally agreed that the main cause of WWII was the refusal to revise the mistakes of the Treaty of Versailles. Even before Mussolini took charge of Italy as the Fascist leader, and throughout the period after 1922, he constantly urged a peaceful revision of these treaties and predicted a second European war if this was not done. No other European leader did this until Hitler arose and proceeded to revise Versailles Diktat by violent means.[12]

While a popular saying in America is that Mussolini made the trains run on time, he actually accomplished much more than that. A former schoolteacher, Mussolini raised the compulsory age of education to fourteen and increased public sector spending on schools and universities. He instituted a program of infrastructure unrivalled in modern Europe. Bridges, canals, and roads were built, along with hospitals and schools, railway stations and orphanages. By 1925, the Fascist government provided food supplementary assistance, infant care, maternity assistance, general health care, wage supplements, paid vacations, unemployment benefits, illness insurance, occupational disease insurance, general family assistance, public housing, and old age and disability insurance.

A crowning achievement was draining the *Agro Pontino* (Pontine Marshes), a low-lying area in central Italy between the Tyrrhenian Sea and the Apennine foothills, southeast of Rome. Once a very fertile farming area, the land was abandoned after the Roman Empire because it became infested with malaria. Since then, numerous drainage projects had been attempted, but none were realized until 1932 through 1934, when Mussolini drained the marshlands, rid the area of malaria, and built the town of Littoria—now Latina. He distributed the land to the peasants and settlers, giving them houses in exchange for their labor. Now the town of Latina farms wheat and livestock. His spending on social welfare programs compared favorably with the more advanced European nations, and in some respects, it was more progressive. When asked by a New York City politician about the meaning behind Italian Fascism in 1939, Mussolini replied, "It is like your New Deal!"

The world turned against Mussolini when he began his quest of acquiring colonies like many other Europeans had done. What I find ironic is the audacity and hypocrisy of the European empire builders, most notably England, France, and Belgium, in their criticism of Italy's colonial aspirations. Italy only became a nation in 1861, and therefore came late into the colonization game, long after these nations had gobbled up most of Africa, Asia, Australia, and the Americas. By 1922, the British Empire held sway over 458 million people, one-fifth of the world's population at the time, and covered more than thirteen million square miles, almost a quarter of Earth's total land area. At the peak of its power, the phrase "the empire on which the sun never sets" was often used to describe the British Empire.

However Italy's policy in conquering Ethiopia is judged, it is notable that in the few years of Italy's rule, Ethiopia reached a higher level of civilization and prosperity than it had ever enjoyed before. Slavery was abolished; roads, bridges, schools, hospitals, churches, public buildings, and hotels rapidly arose; the old towns were transformed and new ones were built; law and order were established; many forms of welfare work were instituted; diseases formerly prevalent, such as leprosy, were attacked with success; agriculture improved; and new industries were set up. Scores of thousands of Italian farmers and industrial workers settled in the country without interfering with the rights of the natives, whose own conditions were improved.[13]

It is telling that while King Victor Emmanuel III and all the male members of the House of Savoy were exiled from Italy never to return, Mussolini's family was not. Italians held the king, not Mussolini, responsible for the armistice that left over thirty-five divisions stranded and at the mercy of the Germans.

It was William Pitt the Elder, the British prime minister, who said in a speech in the House of Lords in 1770, "Unlimited power is apt to corrupt the minds of those who possess it." A quote attributed to the nineteenth-century British politician and historian Lord Acton is, "Absolute power corrupts absolutely." While Mussolini wanted to turn a unified Italy into a world power and dreamed of one day reigning over a Neo-Roman Empire, his quest would lead to his destruction and the disfiguration of Italy.

The task of historians is to record historical events as accurately as possible, based on facts and not political ideology. Unfortunately, this is not always the case. And while I don't pretend to be an expert in history or politics, I know that historians don't always see facts the same way and that biased interpretations are at times woven into facts and even falsehoods appear in their recording.

CHAPTER REFERENCES

1. Eugenio Corti, *Few Returned* (Missouri: University of Missouri Press, 1997).

2. Elena Agarossi, *A Nation Collapses: The Italian Surrender of September 1943* (Cambridge: Cambridge University Press, 2006).

3. Ibid.

4. Ibid.

5. Eugenio Corti, *The Last Soldiers of the King* (Missouri: University of Missouri Press, 2003).

6. Dr. Maria Lombardo, *A Camp Without Walls* (Rome: Italy Italy Enterprises, SpA, 2001).

7. Luigi Villari, *The Liberation of Italy, 1943–1947*, (Appleton: C. C. Nelson Publishing, 1959).

8. Luigi Villari, *Italian Foreign Policy Under Mussolini*, (New York: Devin-Adair Co., 1956).

9. *New York Times.* November 29, 1923.

10. *Fortune Magazine.* May 1932.

11. *Fortune Magazine.* July 1932.

12. Luigi Villari, *Italian Foreign Policy Under Mussolini*, (New York: Devin-Adair Co., 1956).

13. Ibid.

7

My Father Returns

MY BROTHERS AND I WERE WATCHING TV with our mom and our Aunt Eleni in our Manhattan apartment when an annoying commercial interrupted our program. In the ad, a young man runs in slow motion across a field of wildflowers toward a young woman. The woman runs toward the man, her long blonde hair bouncing with every leap.

Our aunt practically jumped off the couch and screamed, "That's how it was when Sotiri came back!"

"Came back from where?" I asked.

"From prison."

"My father was in prison?"

"The Germans took him."

"Why did the Germans take him?"

"It was during the war. The Germans grabbed Italians and took them away. Your father was gone a long time. We thought we'd never see him again."

"I never knew that," I said.

"I was so excited! I called your mother and told her to come out and to bring the baby. The baby was you."

At the time, I didn't understand much of what my aunt was talking about, and when the program came back on, I must have put it out of mind because I never asked more about it. Years later, I asked my mom to tell me about the day Dad returned.

"It's just like Eleni said. She saw your father running home, and she told me to come out. I ran out and saw a man lifting her up in the air, and when he put her down, I saw it was your father. I couldn't move. I couldn't speak. Eleni took you from me, your father pulled me to him, and we held onto each other for the longest time. I couldn't believe he was back; it was the happiness of my dreams! Even though I'd never given up hope, deep down, I couldn't help thinking I might never see him again, not knowing if he was alive or dead."

"When Eleni told me that Dad was in prison, I didn't really understand," I told my mom. "I was only ten then. I didn't know about the war. I wish Dad had told us about it; I would've loved to have heard his story."

"People who live through war want to forget it—especially the soldiers," Mom replied softly.

* * *

Dad's return in November of 1944 was a day of celebration. It had been eight months since he was taken prisoner. Mom couldn't wait for everyone to see him by her side. There had been the not-so-subtle whispers that he would not return—that he would go back to his country, where he most likely had a wife waiting for him. Mom was excited for them to see him holding me in one arm and Mom in the other.

Mom continued, "This is what your father told us."

The day we were taken from Athens, I had a feeling something was up because there were many more Germans in the prison that day. The guards unlocked the cell doors and ordered us out. There were about a hundred of us in there. We were led into the yard and ordered into a truck that took us to the railway station. At the station, we boarded a train. The car was crowded, and the German guards used their rifle butts to push us in. Some men sat or lay on the floor, and others stood. When the doors slammed shut, it was dark except for glimmers of light that shined through the cracks in the wooden slats. I started thinking that those cracks could be a way out of there. It was stifling hot, and the stench of urine and feces made it hard to breathe. I knew I had to get out of there.

"Your father hated being confined. I think he had claustrophobia," Mom noted. "He always complained about being cooped up when hiding in our attic and on the farms. That's why he'd always sneak out."

I had to escape; I knew it was my only chance. I kept hearing Carlo's words about Nazis shooting unarmed Italian soldiers. I had to make my move; it had to be now or never. I knew jumping off the train could be dangerous, as you could break bones or die from the fall, and if you were seen, you'd be shot. But the thought of staying in that stinking cattle car heading for a German prison gave me the strength to leap. There were others on the train who talked about jumping, and some said they'd risk it. We told ourselves there would never be a better time . . . that it would be impossible to escape from a prison with barbed wire fences, tower guards, searchlights, and dogs. We used our hands to pry open the wooden boards.

At night, when the train was traveling at a slower speed, we decided the time was right. I prayed for God's help and then jumped. I tumbled down a hill and came to a stop at the bottom of a gully. I sat up and looked for the others. It was dark, and I couldn't see a thing. I heard footsteps and crouched as they came closer. I looked up to see the faces of six men who promptly aimed their rifles at my head and ordered me up. They spoke Greek, and I let out a sigh of relief, thinking I'd have a better chance with Greeks than Germans. I got up slowly. I didn't know who they were or what they wanted. One indicated the way forward with his rifle. I tried to engage them in conversation, but they ignored me and told me to skáse (shut up) and keep walking.

We walked for a long time. I was exhausted. My body ached, and my mouth was dry. Climbing up hills was treacherous, and I had a hard time keeping up. When I stopped to catch my breath, I was hit with the butt of a rifle. It was still dark when we reached camp. I fell to my knees, and one of the men gave me water, which I gratefully gulped down. I looked around and saw men sitting around the fire. There were six of them, all speaking Italian. I walked over and discovered they were not restrained.

"What is this place?" I asked. "And who are these guys?"

"A partisan hangout. They're rebels. They're snipers shooting at Germans."

"Why are you here? What do they want with you?"

"No idea. We were trying to get to Italy when they got us."

"When was that?"

"About a month ago. They're brutes. They beat us for sport."

I knew I had to get out of there. I told them I was going to try to escape, and asked if they'd go with me. They said they didn't want to chance it because they'd never make it; they were too weak, and if we were caught, we'd be shot. Three days later, when the rebels were asleep, I crept out. At daybreak, I ran into another group—this time, Germans. I was sure I had been seen, so there was no point in running. I pretended to be happy to see them and told them I had escaped from partisans who were holed up in the mountains and that there were Italians there. They believed me and took me with them. I couldn't understand what they said to one another, but I could see by their gloomy faces that they were concerned. They had to know the war wasn't going well for them. Snipers were becoming more of a problem. I was with them for about a month, and one day during a skirmish with some partisans, I broke away. I was trying to find my way back to Patras when I ran into another band of partisans. Luckily, these partisans were civil and treated me well.

There were so many resistance organizations in Greece that one needed a road map. The most powerful were the Communist-leaning EAM-ELAS (National Liberation Front-National Popular Liberation Army) and EDES, the nationalist right-leaning guerilla force bolstered by the British.

On November 12, 1944, Dad was in Thessalonica, approximately a seven-hour train ride from Patras. It was in Thessalonica that he applied for and received safe passage to Patras. Mom found his application for certification, which stated that he had been a comrade in arms serving in the IX Division from May 4 to July 11, 1944, under the command of Chief Kikitsas. It also stated that on July 11, he'd been captured by the Germans during a battle near Samarina. He was taken to Ioannina, and from there to Thessalonica. After refusing to register as a Fascist, he was consigned to work as a laborer. Sometime in late September, he once again escaped from the Germans, taking refuge in the B Sector of the East Department of the National Liberation-Front of the city, where he handed over a Luger and eighty cartridges. Dad's safe-passage certificate states, among other things, that he had joined the fight against the Germans.

I asked my mom, "Did Dad say if he ran into any of the men who also jumped that night?"

"At the time your father didn't say very much, and I don't remember asking him too many questions. Remember, I was young—only fifteen."

"What about Paolo and Ettore, the two guys who were picked up the same night Dad was? Were they with him on that train?"

"He didn't say. Sometime later we heard that it was the father of our dressmaker, Maria, who had informed on all three."

"Why would he do that?"

"He wasn't happy about Maria marrying an Italian, so he informed on Paolo. And to avoid drawing attention to himself, he also informed on your father and Ettore."

"But his daughter was already married to Paolo."

"She was also expecting his baby," Mom said. "We heard that Paolo never returned to Greece, leaving Maria and their son behind."

"Maybe he died," I said. "What about Efthehia? Did Ettore make it back?"

"After the war, Efthehia went to Torino with her young son and stayed with her in-laws. When Ettore returned to Italy from the German labor camp, he was extremely thin and weak but otherwise OK. Efthehia's younger sister later went to visit her. She met a Torinese and married him. The last I heard is that the sisters settled in Torino with their husbands."

"Did Dad say what he did while he was with the Germans and partisans?" I asked.

"He didn't say much. I'm sure he didn't want to relive what he'd been through, and I certainly didn't want him to. The only thing that mattered to me was that he was back. Later, there were other things in our lives to think about, so the war faded. It was only when your father was ill that he began reminiscing about it. In his last days, while in fits of pain, he asked God why He was making him suffer now. I heard him say once, 'God, did you spare me then to have me go through this now?' It was then that he began talking more and more about the war—at times, hallucinating. Once, he sat up in bed and reached out with his hand, saying the olives were ready for picking. He didn't talk about the fighting. He talked about the hunger, the cold, the fear, and the struggle to stay alive."

I was four months old when Dad returned. My parents were thrilled that they were finally free to go out as a couple, free to visit relatives and friends, free to go on walks, and free to enjoy the simple things in life that one takes for granted.

8

My Parents' Greek Orthodox Wedding

YIAYIA HAD WORKED DILIGENTLY at building trousseaux of embroidered bed linens, tablecloths, and napkins. She strived to have ample dowries so that her daughters would be well positioned to find ideal husbands.

But the war changed all that. It brought not only misery and deprivation, but also an interloper to seduce her young daughter, an impressionable girl who came to abandon all for what she believed to be love. *What does a fourteen-year-old know about life and love? Infatuation—that's what it is!* Yiayia thought to herself.

Yiayia knew nothing of the foreigner who came uninvited into their home and into their lives other than he was a soldier at war with her country, a foreigner who spoke a language different from hers—and if he practiced a religion, it was most likely also different from hers. To say her daughter's choice for a husband was a disappointment is an understatement. But Yiayia had no strength, no fire with which to go up against a fourteen-year-old's infatuation.

She dreamed of those tranquil days before the war when her only concerns were her children's health and their grades in school. She knew there was nothing she could do to undo my parents love for each other, but she was determined to have at least one of her dreams realized: to see her daughter married in the Greek Orthodox tradition. She was not at all happy with their rushed Catholic ceremony. Only four people witnessed my parents' pledge in front of God to love, honor, and obey one another, and because of the German occupation, they couldn't even leave for the church together. Since the service was held in a Catholic Church, Yiayia felt that in the eyes of *her* church—the Greek Orthodox Church—her daughter was not married. So she set a plan in motion, inviting relatives and close friends, and arranged for the priests to conduct the service in their home on January 27, 1945.

"Tell me again, why are we doing this?" Dad asked.

"I already told you. Mamá doesn't believe we're really married unless we have a Greek service," Mom explained as she cradled me in her arms to breastfeed me so that I'd be quiet during the service.

"And the priests come to the house?" Dad asked.

"Yes."

"At least our wedding was in a church."

"People get married at home."

"Catholics marry in church."

Mom ignored him, saying, "Mamá invited all the relatives. I hope they come."

"I'm sure they will," Dad sneered. "They'll want a good look at the enemy."

"Stop that! Our wedding was so rushed. There was no celebration, nothing. This will be just a little celebration to remember our wedding."

"Does this mean I'll have to remember two wedding anniversaries?" Dad teased.

"There you go again! You promised to behave."

"OK, I'll be good."

"The service will be simple. Mamá has been cooking for days. I hope that for her sake, everyone shows up."

"Oh, they'll come all right, if only just for the food."

It is customary in Greece, as in most countries, for guests to bestow wedding gifts upon the couple; however, in this case, the relatives banded together and decided not to do so. Even though Dad had returned and not dishonored the family, these relatives felt the need to hurt Mom, letting her know in no uncertain terms that they were not at all pleased with her choice for a husband, that by choosing to marry the enemy, she had brought shame on the family. She understood why they might feel that way, but it hurt nonetheless. She was happy for her mother though that they came at all.

Uncle Christos, who was also Mom's godfather, served as her *koumbaro* (similar to a best man but the role is a bit more involved in the Orthodox marriage tradition). When the war started in Greece, Uncle Christos was forced to close both his shoe factory and his store because the government mandated that employers pay salaries to the families of those employees who had been conscripted into the military. He couldn't afford to do so, so he closed down both businesses.

On one of our trips to Greece, I met Uncle Christos' sons, Haralambos and Stellios. It was remarkable how much Stellios, who
is tall and lanky with blond hair and hazel eyes, resembles Mom's
brother Taki, not only in looks, but also in demeanor. His brother,
Haralambos, on the other hand, is shorter and stockier with blue eyes
and brown hair. Everyone calls Haralambos "Lambis," but I call him
"Harry" because he is anything but a lamb. I especially like Harry
because when I met him, I found him to be not only charming, but
also attentive to both Mom and me. He took us to the Achaia Clauss
Winery, where I first tasted Mavrodaphne, a sweet dessert wine made
from the red grapes grown in the vineyards overlooking the Gulf of
Patras. On that tour, we learned that its founder Gustav Clauss hailed
from Bavaria and named the wine Mavrodaphne in memory of his
fiancée, Daphne, a lovely black-haired Greek girl who unfortunately
died before they could be married.

* * *

The two priests arrived and took their places. The guests gathered
in the living room, and while they were not exactly overjoyed to
meet the groom, they were at least civil. Dad looked somewhat ill at
ease in Uncle Ioannis' black suit, periodically tugging at the sleeves,
which were way too short. He hoped no one would notice his ankles
sticking out of the pant legs. He was standing by the *koumbaro* when
the door suddenly opened, and his bride, on her loving father's
arm, walked toward them. She looked absolutely resplendent in
her cousin Katina's wedding dress, which fit her perfectly, the lace
veil framing her radiant face. Gazing at his beautiful bride who was
holding a large bouquet of white calla lilies, Dad forgot about his
short shirtsleeves and pant legs.

The priests blessed Mom and Dad and placed the *stefana*, Greek wedding crowns, on their heads. The *koumbaro* interchanged the crowns three times as witness to the sealing of the union. The crowning was followed by a reading of the Gospel and brief prayers. A cup of wine was given to Mom and Dad, and they each drank three times from the common cup. This ritual serves as a reminder that the couple shall share everything in life, joy as well as sorrow, and that they will bear one another's burdens, the token of a life of harmony. One of the priests took Dad's arm and Mom's and led them around the table three times as an expression of joy. He held the cross and the holy gospel, and on each circle, Mom and Dad kissed the cross. At the conclusion of the ceremonial walk, Mom and Dad returned to their places. The priest then blessed the wedding couple, removed the crowns from their heads, and implored God to grant them a long, happy, and fruitful life together. At the end of the service Mom, Dad, Uncle Christos, and the priests signed the act of marriage.

When the service ended, Eleni, my thirteen-year-old aunt, carried me into the room.

"What a sweet child!" both priests exclaimed as they reached out to take my little hand—at which point I let out an ear-splitting howl followed by a flood of tears.

"Eleni, take the baby upstairs," Yiayia said. Then, turning to the priests in way of apology, she said, "The black robes and beards frightened the child."

"Yes, of course, of course. Whose child is she? I don't remember baptizing her," said one of the priests.

"She's our daughter," Dad replied, "and she's already been baptized."

The priest frowned and said, "You have a child?"

111

"Yes, Papás," Yiayia said. "If you remember, I told you they were married last year in the Catholic Church."

"Yes, yes . . . but the child . . . the child has to be baptized Greek Orthodox."

Dad, now more than annoyed, said, "She was baptized in the Catholic Church! One baptism was enough for Christ; one should be enough for our daughter!"

"Well, if we knew there was a child, we wouldn't have come!" the priest said as the two headed out the door, choosing not to partake in the wedding toast.

The relatives congregated at one end of the room, eyes downcast and not uttering a word. Yiayia forced a smile as Pappou took her arm and in a booming voice, said, "Let's eat!"

With that, everyone filed into the dining room.

Mom pulled Dad aside and asked him, "Would it have been a big deal if our daughter were to be baptized again?"

"It is a big deal to me! Why, the *nerve* of those pompous priests, acting as if Catholic weddings and Catholic baptisms don't count! It's insulting. I agreed to do this for you, but I expected you to show respect for me and my religion."

"Of course I respect you. And I respect your religion. December 1 is the day we were married and the day we will always celebrate our wedding. Today's ceremony was for my mother. It meant so much to her to see us married Orthodox."

"You said the service was going to be simple. What a production! I thought it would never end. I was beginning to lose it. And what about those crowns?! Your uncle put them on, then took them off, put them on, and took them off again! It's like he couldn't make up his mind. And how many times did we kiss the cross and sip that lousy wine? The least they could have done is to have some decent wine. And all those trips around the table? I thought we were on a merry-go-round."

"In the Greek Church, everything is done in threes, even the sign of the cross," Mom explained. "It's for the Father, the Son, and the Holy Ghost."

"I know, I know, but I think they're overdoing it just a little bit, don't you? But I'll apologize to your mother and father about the priests."

"It wasn't only the priests that upset Mamá," Mom said. "Did you notice that no one brought gifts? I really don't care, but my mother is very upset about it."

"Tell her to forget it! Who needs their lousy gifts anyway? *Cara*, you know, with all the nonsense, I didn't tell you how beautiful you look. You really are beautiful!"

Mom, smiling, wrapped her arms around her husband's neck and kissed his lips.

Mom in Cousin Katina's wedding dress
and Dad in Uncle Ioannis' suit

Poor Yiayia! The wedding that she had so much looked forward to had turned out to be a total fiasco. She was disappointed that the relatives felt it necessary to openly hurt her daughter. Mom, too, was hurt. She couldn't understand why the priests were so disagreeable. But when she stopped to think about it, in the grand scheme of things and after all they had been through, these problems were small and didn't amount to much.

A month later, Mom's cousin Eleni, who was engaged to the teacher who had tutored Mom in math, had her wedding. The same relatives went out of their way to pick the finest crystal, china, silverware, bed linens, and other essentials for the bride. Some even took the two-and-a-half-hour bus ride to Athens to find the perfect gift. Mom believes the reason they went over the top was to make certain that if she hadn't gotten the message the first time, she would most definitely get it this time around. Mom was especially hurt that her favorite aunt and uncle, Vasiliki and Ioannis, had also slighted her. Both had always been kind to her, especially Uncle Ioannis, who was always patient and willingly gave of his time.

Dad took this occasion to casually tell Mom, "Your Uncle Ioannis is a homosexual."

Furious, Mom replied, "What a terrible thing to say! Besides, you're wrong. He's married to my aunt!"

"I'm only telling you what I know."

"Well, you're wrong!"

Years later, Mom learned that Dad had been right. When the family first became aware of Ioannis' homosexuality, they advised Vasiliki to divorce him—that according to the law, she had every right to. But Vasiliki refused, saying that Ioannis was a sweet, caring man; that she loved him; and that the rest was unimportant. I believe the "rest," as Aunt Vasiliki delicately referred to sex, is important in a marriage. It's said that "Marriage has many pains, but celibacy has no pleasures." In my opinion, marriage without romance and sexual intimacy is not a marriage at all. Sweetness and caring without the rest wouldn't be enough for most. But then, Vasiliki lived at a time when refined women didn't speak of such things.

PART TWO
SICILY

9

THE LONG AND WINDING ROAD TO SICILY

THE UNRELENTING RAIN MADE FOR a perfect backdrop to the day that my grandparents would be made to suffer yet another humiliating blow. The first when their daughter was stripped of her citizenship for marrying an Italian soldier. The second was today, when she was being forced to leave her country. They had hoped that Mom and I would depart for Italy when the war ended, fearing that with the war still on, travel was unsafe.

It was in the spring of 1945 that the Allies began repatriating stranded Italian soldiers to Italy. The Greek government, retaliating against Italy, deported all Italians. It didn't matter if they had been born in Greece and had lived in Greece for generations.

At the time, most of Europe followed *jus sanguinis* (right of blood). *Jus sanguinis* is still the most common means of passing on citizenship in many European countries. America follows *jus sanguinis*. Pappou was an American citizen living in Greece and passed on his American citizenship to his children even though they were born in Greece. America also follows *jus soli* (right of soil). This gives unconditional citizenship to anyone born on US soil, whether the mother is a tourist passing through or a person entering the country illegally. Many feel that *jus soli* is being abused, encouraging women to give birth in the US, knowing that the child will automatically become an American citizen.

Dad was to leave first, and Mom and I were to follow. However, on the day before his scheduled departure, two government officials came to our home and notified Mom that she and her child had to leave with her husband, and if she didn't comply, she would face prison. The fact that I was born in Greece didn't automatically grant me citizenship, as a child's nationality was determined by the father, and not the mother or country of birth. I'm certain the government wasn't concerned about breaking up our family. On the contrary, they wanted to prevent children fathered by foreign soldiers from becoming wards of the state.

Mom remembers the frenzy well. Because of the dampness and humidity, the wash was hung indoors. Relatives and friends came to help, bringing their irons to speed up the drying process. Mom was given extra diapers and other essentials for the journey.

To add to her humiliation, Mom would embark on the journey with a black eye. A couple of days prior, Mom in one of her more playful moods, had snuck up on my ticklish father as he slept, and tickled his side, causing him to spring up, landing an elbow to her eye. A superstitious woman told Mom the black eye was an omen that she would never return to Greece. Mom wasn't superstitious and didn't believe in silly omens, and, as it turned out, would return several times.

It was at the port that it all sank in. For Mom, leaving was bittersweet. While she was looking forward to her new life, parting with her family and not knowing when she'd return was more difficult than she had imagined. Tears flowed all around. She embraced her parents, brother, and sister, telling them she would be back, but not really believing it herself. Mom cradled me in her arms, and with Dad at her side, boarded the French liner.

The first leg of the trip, an overnight sail, gave my parents an inkling of how arduous the trip would be. Those passengers who didn't have sleeping compartments had to make do with deck chairs. The wooden chairs were not at all comfortable, and the blankets didn't help keep out the cold night air, resulting in very little sleep for my parents. The conditions didn't bother me much, for I slept soundly swaddled in my warm blanket, cradled in my mother's arms.

The next morning, the boat docked in Brindisi, and an Italian MP roared into a megaphone, "Men board buses to Taranto! Women and children board buses to Bari!"

Frightened, Mom asked, "Why are they taking us to different places?"

"It's probably more efficient that way," Dad said. "We have to be examined. They want to make sure we don't bring diseases to Italy."

"How long will you be in Taranto?" she stammered.

"It shouldn't be very long. They'll process us then take us to Bari."

Dad's bus headed southwest to Taranto, and Mom's north to Bari. When the women arrived in Bari, they were led to a detention center. Mom stood against the wall and looked around the large room. There were over a hundred women standing and waiting for what was to come next. The ten infants and toddlers cried in unison as the mothers failed to calm them. Nurses walked around the room and took the crying children from their mothers.

"We have to take your child," a nurse told Mom. "She has to be bathed and examined by the doctor."

"Can I go with her? She cries and she—"

"No, you also have to bathe and be examined. When you finish, you can have her."

My mother reluctantly handed me over, and I joined the chorus of wailing children in a separate room, the cries echoing off the tiled floor. The women were ordered to undress and toss their clothing and shoes into large bags that were thrown into a monstrous machine to be disinfected. As the women lathered their bodies with soap, the water gushed from the showerheads in the ceiling, hosing them off like cattle in what had to be a dehumanizing experience. Mom didn't know then of the Nazi gas chambers. She would later see the horrors of those chambers in newsreel clips shown in movie theaters in Sicily. Had she had an inkling then, the parallels alone would have been mortifying.

The women were given towels with which to dry off. They patted themselves dry, tossed the towels into a bin, and formed a single line, where they stood totally naked, waiting to be examined by the doctors and nurses. Mom had never seen so many naked bodies. One woman's ribs and hip bones jutted out from her frame, hauntingly thin, while others jiggled as they walked. Lice were found on one woman, and the nurse shaved her head, her long blonde locks mingling with her tears as they fell to the ground.

The physical examination was uneventful for Mom, and she was declared to be in good health. When their clothes were finally returned, they were wrinkled and dingy. After the women dressed, they were reunited with their children and taken to a nearby restaurant. Mom breastfed me as she ate her sandwich and sipped orange soda.

There were Italian and American MPs and soldiers milling about the restaurant, and some of the women were chatting with the friendly soldiers. An American soldier approached Mom and offered her a Hershey's bar. Mom shook her head, refusing the candy. Offended, the soldier said something in English, pointing the candy bar in my direction. Mom didn't understand what the man said except for the word "baby." She wondered if the young soldier really believed that an eight-month-old could actually eat a chocolate bar.

The women were then led into a room lined with sleeping cots. Mom settled into the cot, with me snuggled by her side. Sometime after midnight Mom awoke to a child crying hysterically and saw that it was the toddler in the next cot. He was alone and frightened—first losing his father, and now his mother. Mom picked up the boy and tried to comfort him while looking for his mother, when an Italian guard approached.

Speaking in Italian with a smattering of Greek, he asked Mom, "Where's his mother?"

"I don't know. The boy's crying woke me up."

The guard picked up the sobbing child and walked around the room, looking for the missing mom.

When the mom returned the next morning, she was greeted by the furious guard, who screamed, "Where have you been?"

The Greek woman mumbled something Mom couldn't hear.

The guard, in a threatening voice, said, "We'll see what your husband has to say about this!"

The woman dropped her head and made her way back to her cot as the rest of the women looked on, shaking their heads.

Two days later, when the men arrived, their wives greeted them with a peck and an embrace. The shameless woman made a spectacle of herself, greeting her husband by jumping on him, wrapping her arms and legs around him, and repeatedly kissing him, while at the same time crying, "Don't ever leave me! Don't ever leave me again!"

The guard witnessing the shameless woman groused, "Yeah, don't ever leave her again!"

The women, including Mom, couldn't keep from laughing.

As they headed for the train station, Dad told Mom that they, too, had showered, had their clothes disinfected, and suffered a physical exam. He said they were also interviewed and given money for their journey.

At the station, Dad purchased tickets to Calabria and was told that the trains had no set schedule. Not knowing how long they'd have to wait in Bari, they decided to stay at a hotel nearby. In the hotel room, Mom heard voices coming from the window and looked outside. Houses encircled the courtyard, and women were sitting on their windowsills, talking across to one another.

"What language are they speaking?" Mom asked Dad.

"We're in Bari," Dad said. "They're speaking Barese."

"It doesn't sound at all like Italian."

Laughing, Dad said, "I know. I can't understand a thing they're saying."

"What do people speak in Sicily?"

"Sicilian."

"I hope Sicilian isn't like Barese."

"It isn't," Dad assured Mom.

A trip from Bari to Sicily ordinarily takes no more than fifteen hours by train and ferry. As these were not ordinary times, the journey would take twelve days, most of the time spent waiting. It would be a difficult trip, especially with a baby in tow. Disposable diapers weren't available, so Mom had to constantly wash. Mom's milk wasn't always enough, and I was often cranky. Four days passed just waiting for the train to Calabria. From there, we were to take the ferry to Messina, Sicily. Not surprisingly, ferries had no set schedule either. We waited several hours at the pier before the ferry finally arrived.

In Messina, we shared a taxi to Catania with a couple we'd met on the ferry. It was quite late when we arrived, so we stayed the night. Dad worried that with all the delays and paying for hotel rooms and meals, the money would run out. The next day, as he was heading for the railway station to check on trains to Ravanusa, he heard voices of two men calling out to him. He turned and two familiar faces beamed at him.

"Michele! Luigi!" Dad shouted.

"Totò! What on earth are you doing in Catania?" Michele asked.

"Trying to get home," Dad said. "What are you doing here?"

"We're here on business," Michele said. "We've been trying to get back home. They keep telling us tomorrow and tomorrow. We've been stuck here for two days. We're going to get a bite; why don't you join us?"

"I have to get back to the hotel. My wife and—"

"Your wife? You're married?!" Luigi asked.

"I got married in Greece. My wife's at the hotel with our baby."

"You have a baby? I thought you went off to fight!"

Smiling, Dad said, "I did some of that too."

"Your mother didn't tell us you were married."

"I don't know if she knows."

"Didn't you write to her?"

"I was busy."

"Yeah, busy hooking up and making babies!" Michele teased.

"I did write, but I don't know if she got any of my letters. I didn't get any of hers. Hey, why don't you come to the hotel and meet my wife?"

At the hotel, Dad introduced Mom to his friends. A while later, they all went to a trattoria for lunch. Dad and his friends talked animatedly while Mom sat silently, not understanding much of what was being said.

Later, Mom asked, "Was that Sicilian?"

"Yes," Dad replied.

"I couldn't understand anything. It's so different. Why don't Italians speak Italian?"

"They do. It's just that they don't want their dialects to die, and besides, the old people who didn't go to school only speak dialect."

"Does your mother speak Italian?"

"No, Sicilian only. But you'll learn it. It's not hard."

"And why do your friends call you Totò?"

"That's what they call me at home. It's a nickname for Salvatore." Dad explained.

The days were dragging. Periodically they stopped at the railway station, hoping for good news. But it was always the same: come back later!

One evening my parents went to the movies, but as I was fussing, they left before the picture ended. There wasn't much one could do without money.

After four days in Catania, Luigi came to our hotel, frantically knocking at the door.

"Totò, it's Luigi. Open up!"

It was after ten o'clock, and we were already in bed.

Dad opened the door and asked, "What's up?"

"We met a fellow who's driving to Caltanissetta tonight. He'll take us, but he wants to leave right away. He's waiting downstairs. Michele's with him."

"Caltanissetta?" Dad asked. "But we're going to Ravanusa."

"Totò, wake up! Ravanusa is half an hour from Caltanissetta. We can get a taxi or a carriage . . . or even walk!"

"He has room for us?"

"Yes, it's a good-sized car."

"We'll be down in a minute."

"Need help?"

"No, we can manage."

"OK, but hurry!"

Dad gathered our things and threw them into the suitcase.

"Ready?" he asked Mom.

"I just need to check her diaper. Why don't you go down."

"No, I'll wait."

Dad did a quick check of the room, and then we went downstairs.

The driver seemed pleased to have company, especially since the men had offered to pay for the petrol. Caltanissetta is about a three-hour drive from Catania. After that, just another hour or so, and we'd be home.

In Caltanissetta, we got out, and the kind man drove off. The men couldn't find a taxi, so they settled on a horse-drawn carriage. The carriage driver, a crusty old man, held on to the reins as everyone hopped in. The horse tottered along the bumpy unpaved road, periodically jolting the carriage, which caused me to grow more and more agitated. It was a still night, but suddenly, rustling sounds were heard coming from the bushes.

"Quiet!" Michele whispered. "Did you hear that? We'd better get down and have a look."

Dad and his friends stepped out of the carriage and, with guns drawn, walked ahead, the carriage following behind. Frightened, Mom held me close to her breast. With the war still on, Dad felt he needed to have some means of protection and had smuggled his Italian-issued revolver into our luggage. With the coast clear, the men hopped back into the carriage, and we started off again.

"Bandits roam at night looking to rob," Michele said. "If anybody was out there, the sight of three armed men must have scared them off."

As the men spoke, Mom began to understand some of what they were saying. She heard Michele tell Dad that people were afraid, especially at night, because of bandits lurking about. Mom hoped she'd misunderstood when Luigi asked Dad if Mom knew the house had no water or electricity. After all those days and nights on the road, she was looking forward to a hot bath.

We arrived in Ravanusa well after midnight. As the men stepped down and helped Mom out of the carriage, a barking dog appeared and lunged toward her, canines bared. Frightened by the ferocious creature, Mom held me up over her head. Michele grabbed the dog's collar and pulled him away.

"The dog's owner was a soldier who didn't return," the carriage driver said. "He was killed in Greece. Now the poor creature jumps on strangers."

"Probably still looking for his master," Dad said.

Mom knew why the dog had lunged at her, and it had nothing to do with his master. The beast was most likely drawn to my soiled diaper.

"Why don't we go to my house," Michele said. "It's late. I don't think it's a good idea to surprise your mother at this hour."

"We don't want to impose on your wife," Dad said.

"Don't worry, Paola bounces out of bed the moment the key hits the lock. And besides, she'll be thrilled to see you."

Just as Michele had said, when the key hit the lock, Paola was at the door.

"Paola, have I got a surprise for you!" said Michele. "Look who I found roaming the streets of Catania!"

Paola, a pleasantly plump middle-aged woman, stood at the threshold, rubbing her sleepy eyes.

"*Gesù mio!* Totò, is it really you? How good to see you!"

She embraced Dad, planting a kiss on each of his cheeks.

"It's good to be back, Paola. This is my wife, Maria, and our baby girl."

"Married and a baby! Oh my! You left a boy, and came back a man! Your mother will be thrilled. She's been so worried. You must be hungry. We can talk later. Everybody sit."

Despite the late hour, Paola pranced around the room.

"Don't bother, Paola. It's late!" Dad said.

"Speak for yourself! I'm hungry and thirsty too," Michele said.

"It's no bother," Paola said as she carried the bread and cheese to the table and went off to get the wine and glasses.

Michele cut into the loaf, placed a slice on a plate along with a chunk of cheese, and handed it to Mom.

Wine and glasses in hand, Paola asked Dad, "Does Maria speak Italian?"

"She understands more than she lets on. She's being shy right now," Dad said.

"You met in Greece?" Paola asked.

"Yes. I knew she was the one from the first moment I saw her."

"How did you speak to each other?"

"We mix Greek and Italian and use our hands when the words don't come," Dad said.

"You should hear him talking Greek!" Michele laughed. "With that name of his, it's no wonder! I always suspected he was a Greco!"

"Very funny," Dad said.

"Paola, listen to this," Michele said. "After the armistice, Maria's family hid him from the Germans."

"I don't know if I'd be alive if not for my *suoceri*," Dad said.

Crossing herself, Paola said, "God bless in-laws!"

"You know," Luigi said, "after the armistice, we thought the war would be over, and we'd go back to normal. But with the Americans and the British fighting the Germans here, the bombs fell on us from all sides!"

"And before that," Paola said, "in July the Americans came to push the Germans out. The shooting and bombing lasted more than a month. So many killed! So much destruction!"

"And that's not all!" Michele said. "What do you think those Americans and British did when they got here? They emptied the jails! Everybody out! The prisoners told them that they were political prisoners, and the idiots believed them."

"All they had to do was ask the authorities!" Luigi said. "They would have told them they were a bunch of mafiosi and crazy Communists!"

"Didn't they check the prison records?" Dad asked.

"They didn't have time to do things right," Paola lamented. "Now it's our mess."

"The mafiosi go after everybody. And the Communists! What do you think those thugs are doing?" Luigi said. "They're getting even with everybody! To them, everybody is a Fascist."

"It's late," Dad said. "Maria's tired, and we should get going."

"Luigi and I will go first to your mother. It might be too much for the old lady if you show up at this hour."

"You're probably right, although nothing scares my mother."

"I know," Michele said. "You can't put anything past her."

Michele and Luigi went off to Nonna's. They knocked on the door, and, not surprisingly, there was no answer. They knocked again and again, pleading for her to open up.

"Go away!" she called out.

"Zia Teresa, you know us! It's Michele and Luigi. Open the door!"

"I know who you are, but I don't know who's behind you! So go away!"

The men understood her reluctance. A common ploy of criminals was to use decoys. But the men didn't give up.

"We have great news! We met your son and his wife and baby girl in Catania. They are at my house right now," Michele said.

"If my son is here, why isn't he with you?" she called out from inside the house.

"Zia Teresa, just look out the window and see for yourself! There's no one here but us!"

Nonna finally looked out, and when she saw the two men were alone, she put on her shawl, opened the door, and strode ahead of the men.

When they reached Michele's house, she ran in and embraced Dad. She hadn't had any news from her son since the armistice. With the Germans occupying Greece and the Americans, British, and Germans fighting in Italy, sending and receiving mail were close to impossible. Nonna was very religious, and she'd prayed to God and all the saints for her son's safe return. She prayed especially to Saint Anthony, the saint of lost things, pleading that he find her son and bring him home. She held on to Dad for the longest time.

"I knew you would come back! I knew Saint Anthony would find you and bring you back to me!"

Tearing up, Dad said, "Mamma, this is my wife, Maria."

Nonna embraced her daughter-in-law.

"Maria! What a beautiful name for a beautiful girl."

"And this is our daughter, Teresina," Dad said proudly.

"*Che bella bambina!*" Nonna exclaimed as she took me in her arms, touched that I had been named after her.

We headed home, where Dad's stepfather greeted us. There was much excitement—so much so that no one slept except me.

That morning, Nonna served *caffè e latte* and slices of bread topped with warm ricotta and sprinkled with sugar. Afterward, she went from house to house, telling everyone she met that her son had come home, all the while exclaiming, "*Grazie a Dio!*"

Grazie a Dio! These had to be heartfelt words. I can't even begin to imagine the level of fear she must have felt in not knowing whether her son was dead or alive. She had already lost a husband and six children. How much more could she endure? Her son had to come back! He was her only surviving son, the sixth and last child fathered by her beloved husband, Giuseppe.

Our long and arduous trip to Ravanusa began on April 12. We arrived well after midnight on April 24. Four days later, on April 28, 1945, Mussolini, the deposed Italian Fascist dictator, would be dead.

10

My Father's Family

MY GRANDFATHER GIUSEPPE LA GRECA had his first taste of adventure when, in 1903, he immigrated to Tunisia with his parents. His uncles had settled there and urged the family to make the ninety-mile sea voyage to a place where the opportunities were boundless. After sailing the Strait of Sicily with their twenty-two-year-old son, my great-grandparents, Pietrina DiRosa and Calogero La Greca, settled in "Little Sicily." They were among the 105,000 Italians who had immigrated there. Their only other child, Sara, was married and remained in Sicily with her husband. With help from the DiRosa brothers, my great-grandparents opened a general store, hoping their son would join the family business. But Giuseppe had other plans, and after two years, he returned to Sicily, where his sweetheart was waiting.

In 1906, my grandmother Teresa Zagarigo married Giuseppe La Greca, the love of her life. She was eighteen, and he was twenty-five. They settled in Campobello Di Licata in Sicily in a house purchased in part with Nonna Teresa's dowry. They had a farm and a donkey, and they bred rabbits, guinea pigs, and chickens. As far as Nonna was concerned, they had all they needed to live happily ever after.

Nonno Giuseppe, however, was not content. He hated working the land. It wasn't just the drudgery; farming just wasn't lucrative. He wanted more and pined for a new start. Nonna often spoke of Nonno, saying he was a good man, a loving husband and father, but that he was also restless. She believed his restlessness stemmed from his parents insisting that he join them in Tunisia, but it wasn't Tunisia Nonno pined for. He had his sights set on America, and was stashing away every lira, longing for the day he'd set sail for the land of his dreams. But Nonno's dream would become Nonna's worst nightmare.

Nonna's mother, Angela, encouraged her son-in-law and contributed to his fare, earning her daughter's ire. We don't know whether Nonna Angela helped because she wanted to see her son-in-law realize his dream or to be rid of him. Her daughter believed it to be the latter. Nonna Angela hadn't approved of her daughter's marriage. She had disdain for Nonno's people, calling them a "band of gypsies." Nonna had to fight on two fronts: her in-laws and her own mother. My grandparents welcomed their first child, a boy, in 1907 and named him Calogero, after Nonno's father. Their elation was brief. At only two months of age, Calogero died.

By 1908, Nonno had accumulated the $30 fare and set off for America. He was joined by Nonna's two brothers, Giorlando and Antonio Zagarigo. The three traveled in steerage, where conditions were downright deplorable. Steerage rates were exorbitant when compared to the cabin rates, where a mere $20 more gave the cabin lodger clean surroundings, pure air to breathe, spotless linen to sleep on, and courteous treatment by the staff. The steerage passenger inhabited a dark hole where soap and water were luxuries.

After a grueling fourteen-day journey, the three men arrived on Ellis Island. It was there that the Zagarigo name was somehow changed to Zaro. After the weary travelers were processed, they boarded the train to Philadelphia and headed for "Little Italy," the second largest in the country, surpassed only by the one in New York. Italians were drawn to the region because of work opportunities. Nonno and his brothers-in-law soon discovered that the jobs immigrants were given were some of the dirtiest and most dangerous: ditch digging, stone cutting, and burying gas pipes. They held a sundry of backbreaking construction and factory jobs. There's a saying posted on a plaque in the Ellis Island museum that well describes the 1900 immigrant experience:

> I came to America because I heard the streets were paved with gold.
> When I got here, I found out three things:
> first, the streets weren't paved with gold;
> second, they weren't paved at all;
> and third, I was expected to pave them.

Both my grandparents were illiterate and depended on others to write and read their letters for them. Nonno's factory boss told him that with his skills, he could have held a supervisory position if only he were able to read and write. Nonno knew that the only way to get ahead in this world was to have an education. He often told Nonna, "If we have fifty children, I will see to it that one hundred go to school!"

Although travel conditions in steerage were grueling, Nonno made several trips to America. To our knowledge, he made four or five, making Nonna a "white widow" each time. His first trip back to Sicily was in 1909. He stayed only a couple of months before departing again, leaving Nonna pregnant. Later that year, their second child, a daughter, was born. She was named Pietrina, after Nonno's mother. Nonno made his second trip back to Sicily in 1911, only to depart a couple of months later, once again leaving Nonna pregnant. Nonna gave birth to their third child, a boy, in 1912. He was named Calogero, the same name given to their first boy, and was called "Caliddro." Nonno often tried to persuade Nonna to join him in America. His efforts paid off when, in 1916, Nonna; Pietrina, who was seven; and Caliddro, age four, made the voyage. They were joined by Nonna's sister-in-law, Antonia Zagarigo, and her three-year-old son, Salvatore. They arrived on Ellis Island, where they were met by their husbands.

Nonno, in anticipation of Nonna's arrival, moved from the boarding house into a two-room apartment on Chestnut Hill. That first summer, Nonna gave birth to their fourth child, a boy, and named him Salvatore, after Nonna's father. It was a summer of record-high temperatures, and the newborn was plagued with heat rash. Nights, his parents took turns carrying the crying child outdoors, where the air was slightly cooler.

Like many immigrants of the 1900s, Nonna was disillusioned. In Sicily, although by no means rich, she owned her small house and did not have to contend with anyone above or below her. The enclaves of row houses on Chestnut Hill, with less than a foot of space between them, where little light and air could enter, was not exactly a dream come true for Nonna. It was worse than she had ever imagined. The two-story houses with add-ons in the rear were nothing more than horizontal tenements separated by alleyways, with many inhabitants crammed together in close proximity. The atmosphere in their poorly lit and under-ventilated two-room apartment was suffocating, and the grimy, treeless streets with garbage piled high made it a hotbed for vermin and contagious diseases. Tenants seeking relief from their stifling dwelling headed outdoors to watch their children play ball, play hopscotch, or jump rope.

Pietrina was placed in second grade, and although her school was nearby, Nonna accompanied her each day, with four-year-old Caliddro in tow. Pietrina, a bright girl, picked up the language quickly, making Nonno proud. It's an advantage for Italians that the letters in both the Italian and English alphabets are the same, except that the Italian has five less letters: J, K, W, X, and Y. Nonno was eager to learn English and often sat with Pietrina as she did her homework. Caliddro was another matter. He'd become so unruly, his parents had a difficult time controlling him. He'd sneak out to explore the streets and picked up bad habits, even talking back. Nonna feared that he would get into trouble with the wild urchins that roamed the streets.

Nonna, who had never been afraid of anything, was afraid of everyone and everything here. How could her husband tolerate this place? How could he bear living in two cramped rooms with the only one window looking out into a dark alleyway, with walls so thin a baby's fretful wails could be heard from the next apartment? She grew more and more disillusioned with each passing day and longed for her home, her farm, her animals, her country, and her basil plants that thrived on her sunny windowsill.

If Nonna's sister-in-law Antonia had any complaints, she kept them to herself. She had been a white widow for over three years and was content just being with her husband. Unfortunately, Antonia's happiness would be short-lived. A year after she arrived, Giorlando fell ill. He was taken to the hospital, where blood tests were done, but he would succumb to his illness before the results came back. Before dying, Giorlando asked his brother, Antonio, to look after his pregnant wife and son. A year after her husband's death, Antonia, a widow with two boys, Salvatore and John, reluctantly accepted her brother-in-law's marriage proposal. Giorlando was her true love— Antonio, her savior. The couple remained in Philadelphia and went on to have four children: Sam, Steve, Joseph, and Marie.

Nonna believed her brother's death was a sign that they should return to Sicily. It was not safe here. Nonna tried to convince Nonno to give up his foolish American dream.

"How can you stand living in this squalor?" she cried. "If cholera, typhoid, smallpox, and tuberculosis don't destroy us, the trolleys surely will!"

"America is my home, and it's where I want to be! There's nothing for me in Sicily, and nothing you say will change that!"

Nonno had America in his belly. America is where he belonged, and he wouldn't be swayed by Nonna or anyone else.

In 1918, two months pregnant with their fifth child, Nonna and her three children returned to Sicily. Although relieved to be returning home, she was also sad that she was leaving without her husband. Pietrina and Caliddro were miserable. They wanted to remain in America with their father and were not looking forward to the grueling trip.

Back in Sicily, little Salvatore broke out with yet another rash. Believing he was suffering from the heat, Nonna bathed him in cool water and was relieved to see the rash disappear. Although the child seemed better, he would die just a few days later. That same year, the year that the Spanish influenza broke out, my grieving nonna gave birth to a baby girl, Angela, named after Nonna's mother. Angela became one of its fifty million victims.

In 1919 Nonno returned to Sicily, and after a few months, sailed back to America, once again leaving Nonna with child. He came back to Sicily again on March 1921, when their baby, the second Salvatore—my father—was six months old. A few months later, Nonno would make his last trip to America.

Nonno enjoyed cooking and loved experimenting with different ingredients and condiments. His creations surpassed Nonna's, whose cooking was uninspiring. He often cooked for himself and two of his boarding house friends. He loved mushrooms and was an avid forager. One Sunday evening, Nonno prepared dinner using the mushrooms he'd picked that day. His friends fell ill shortly after eating and threw up. Nonno, unfortunately, didn't have symptoms until later that night, and although he experienced severe abdominal pains, he wasn't one to call for a doctor. It wasn't until three days later that the landlady contacted Nonno's brother-in-law, who took him to the hospital. Sadly, it was too late. On August 25, 1921, when Dad was almost a year old, Nonno died. He was forty-one. Nonna, at thirty-four, was no longer a white widow, but now a *real* widow, forever to be dressed in black.

The death certificate stated that Nonno's death was due to food poisoning. It always troubled Nonna that she hadn't been with him. Things could have turned out so differently. She couldn't understand why no one at the boarding house had called for a doctor. With Nonno's money mysteriously disappearing, the only items returned to her were his clothes, her letters, and his gold wedding ring, which was passed on to my dad. At the time, widows didn't receive much in the way of government assistance. With no one to help her, Nonna, a single mother, became the sole provider for her family.

Pietrina and Caliddro had to quit school and work on the farm. Pietrina had hopes of becoming a teacher, and Caliddro, an engineer.

Sadly, their dreams died with their father. Dad also suffered, longing for the father he never knew.

But misfortune had not diminished Nonna. A single mother, she soldiered on without self-pity and bore her tragedies with dignity, raising her children with firm, unyielding principles. She taught them to hold their heads high and to defy any glimmer of scorn or pity.

Caliddro, almost ten, was now the man of the house. Nonna relied on him heavily. He cultivated the land, planted seeds, nurtured the plants, brought the harvested items to market, tended the animals, and kept the books. Unfortunately, Nonna wouldn't have his help for long. Just three years after Nonno's death, Caliddro was struck with a mysterious illness. Nonna called for the doctor, who examined Caliddro and gave him an injection. During the night, he became delirious. Nonna ran to the doctor's house, pleading for him to come see Caliddro. The doctor assured her that the boy was fine and that he would come in the morning. By the time he finally arrived, Caliddro had deteriorated. His leg had become gangrenous, and the doctor advised amputation.

Cutting off the twelve-year-old's leg didn't help. A few days after the operation, Caliddro died. Nonna never knew the nature of Caliddro's illness nor what the doctor had injected him with. Malpractice suits were unheard of in those days, and Nonna had no recourse except to excoriate the man whenever she ran into him. Caliddro's death devastated Nonna. So much sorrow and so much pain had been heaped on her. Her first child, Calogero, had died in infancy; her third, Caliddro, had been cruelly taken from her due to a misdiagnosis; and her fourth and fifth, Salvatore and Angela, had both passed in infancy.

A few months after Caliddro's death, my dad who was four years old was diagnosed with Mediterranean fever. Nonna was told that her son fortunately had a mild case that could be readily treated with a series of injections. Nonna who was still stinging from her Caliddro's death which she believed resulted from an injection, told the physicians that she'd lost one son and wasn't about to lose another.

She was only swayed when told, "You may have lost one son to an injection, but you'll surely lose this child without an injection!"

Dad went on to have the treatment, and, as far as we know, never had a recurrence of the disease.

When Pietrina was seven, she was promised in marriage to Domenico DiRosa, Nonno's first cousin. Because of the lack of work in Sicily, Domenico had immigrated to France. In 1924, when Pietrina was fifteen, Domenico returned to Sicily, and the two married. Domenico persuaded Nonna to join the couple in France. At that time, Dad was a spoiled four-year-old, and when Domenico tried disciplining his little brother-in-law, the situation became somewhat strained, resulting in mother and son returning to Sicily.

In 1925, four years after Nonno's death, Nonna contemplated marriage again. Her suitor, Tomasso Corrado, was a widower, his wife having died early on in their childless marriage. Nonna must have been drawn to Tomasso because of his love for the land. Her five-year-old son wasn't at all happy and was adamant that no man take his father's place. He tried to thwart the merger, arguing with his mother that they didn't need the lousy farmer because *he* was the man of the house, and *he* would provide for them. He fought her at every turn, making no effort to get along with the farmer. In 1926, to his dismay, his mother did marry. Now the scorned man was his stepfather. He didn't take to the man's ways and didn't like having to take orders from him. As the years passed, their relationship only worsened. Her son's failure to bend wore on Nonna. Adding to her grief were the two children she bore with her second husband, both of whom died in infancy.

When Dad turned thirteen, his stepfather told him he had to quit school and start earning his keep. He thought school was a waste of time, a way to get out of work and idle away the hours. Dad didn't agree with the man's views, and very much like his own father, he wanted nothing to do with farming. Dad loved school. He especially loved his music lessons and played trumpet in the school orchestra. He also exhibited a natural talent for drawing. He told his stepfather he would continue with school to study music and art. After, all who was he to order him around? He wasn't his father!

Nonna, too, thought school to be frivolous, believing it gave Dad foolish notions. After all, how could anyone make a living playing a trumpet or doodling? What nonsense was he being taught? As far as she was concerned, he already knew all there was to know about reading, writing, and arithmetic.

Dad's parents ultimately won the argument, and at thirteen, Dad was forced to quit school and work for his stepfather. He had no one to turn to. If he could only make his mother understand that an education would open up the world to him and that he wouldn't be limited to farming, where one toiled and shed blood, sweat, and tears, with little to no reward. Fortunately for Dad, his music teacher saw his potential, especially his powerful singing voice, and encouraged him. Continuing his lessons was a not-so-small detail he managed to keep from his mother.

Dad was much more open to talking about his evil stepfather and the tedium of farming than talking about the war. He often talked to us about his most dreaded chore, plaiting rope. He rebelled when given this chore. The many hours of twisting hay and plaiting rope caused his hands to blister and callous, impeding his trumpet playing.

Nonna, fearing that stepfather and stepson would come to blows, lent Dad out to other farms. Dad resented this even more and couldn't wait for the day when he would be on his own. He would set sail for America just as his father had done, or perhaps join his cousins in Tunisia. His opportunity to flee farm life finally arrived in 1939. However, it wouldn't be America or Tunisia beckoning, but the Italian army.

Nonno Giuseppe

Nonna Teresa

*Caliddro, Dad, Nonna,
and Pietrina*

*Antonio and Antonia Zaro
and children*

Dad and Nonna

Caliddro and Nonno

11

LIFE IN SICILY

MOM CLUNG ON TO ME AS she climbed up the ladder to the second floor. At the landing, Nonna extended her arms for Mom to hand me over. Nonna kissed me and placed me in the wooden crib that had been Dad's. She then took Mom by the hand and led her around the spacious room, pointing to the bed, dresser, two chairs, and small table that held the kerosene lamp. Mom, exhausted from the long journey and lack of sleep, sat on the bed. Nonna smiled and went back downstairs. Mom opened the shutters and peered out the window to the houses encircling the courtyard. The sunshine sparkled in the specks of dust dancing in the air, and rays of light bounced off the bins containing fava beans, legumes, chestnuts, almonds, and prickly pears.

When Dad was courting Mom, he'd boasted of his Italian villa, taking pleasure in describing in minute detail the lavish bathroom with its double-sink vanity and marble bathtub so big you could lie down in it. The best feature, he'd said, were the automatic garage doors that opened with the push of a button. Mom knew he was prone to exaggeration and that the pictures he'd painted for her were probably from some American film he'd seen, but she'd never expected this! No electricity or indoor plumbing! And she never dreamed she'd be sharing a room with the harvest. Dad climbed up the ladder and placed our bags on the floor beside the bed.

"You know," Mom said, "when we came in last night, I didn't see the garage doors . . ."

"Oh that. So I exaggerated a little."

"A little! And where's the bathroom—the one with the marble tub so big you can lie down in it?"

"The house isn't what—"

"I knew you had to be exaggerating, but I didn't expect this. You never prepared me for this! A house with no water and no electricity!"

"Lots of houses here don't have . . . You'll get used to—"

"I don't know if I can ever get used to this, but, please, no more fairytales!"

* * *

Nonna and Dad's stepfather owned two two-story houses. They lived in one and rented the other. Upon entering the one they lived in, one would come into a spacious room. At the far end, there was an alcove with a bed, a dresser, and a small table. There was not much in the way of furniture in the all-purpose room, just a table and four chairs, a cabinet, a large washbasin, and a built-in hearth for cooking.

In Greece, Mom had cooked on a wood-burning stove and found cooking on the hearth difficult at first. She was shocked and furious with Dad when she discovered that the large washbasin by the hearth was their bathtub. Her most difficult adjustment was hauling water. She couldn't manage to walk with the terra-cotta jug on her head, so she placed it on her hip, which may have been the reason she later developed scoliosis.

A second hearth, situated on the floor in the middle of the room, was used for heating the room on cold and damp days. Off to the side, there was another alcove with a separate entrance bearing oversized double doors, much like an attached garage. It served as a stall for the family's donkey. A trap door led to the rabbits' and guinea pigs' quarters. Mom was horrified to learn that the donkey's stall was also the bathroom.

Later that day, Mom was happy to see the friendly faces of Michele and Paola, the hospitable hostess she'd met the previous night. The forever-jovial Paola handed Mom a platter of pastries, and as Mom took the platter, the scrumptious fragrance assailed her senses.

"These are *zeppole*," Paola said. "Have one; they're delicious."

Mom took one and bit into it, the sweet, creamy ricotta filling her mouth with sweetness.

"*È buono?*" Paola asked.

"*Si, molto buono*," Mom replied, taking another bite.

"What are your plans?" Michele asked Dad.

"I'll probably work on my mother's farm."

"Well, don't rush," Paola said. "Give yourself some time. The farm can wait. How's your little girl?"

"She's upstairs sleeping," Dad said.

"Bonaventura was asking for you," Michele said. "He wants you to stop by. Said he has some ideas he wants to discuss with you."

"How's he doing?"

"He's doing pretty well, and he's quite busy too. There seems to be a big demand for pistachios and almonds."

A week after arriving in Dad's hometown, Mom and Dad visited the Bonaventuras, who lived just a few miles away—though it could have been on a different planet. Their two-story peach-colored villa with green shuttered windows had all the amenities of the day, including electricity and indoor plumbing. A spiral staircase led to the second floor, which had four bedrooms and a spacious bathroom suite with a white pedestal sink, a bathtub, and a toilet. Mom thought that, except for the automatic garage doors, this was the house that Dad had described to her, and she was happy that such homes could be found here.

In his mid-forties, Mr. Bonaventura had always been fond of Dad and wanted to take him on as a partner. Since Dad wasn't sure of his plans, he didn't want to commit and later disappoint his friend. Just like his father, Dad had America in his sights. In the meantime, Dad did have to earn a living, and, having few options, was forced to work for his mother and stepfather doing what he dreaded most: working the land.

Word of Dad's return had spread, and little by little, friends and neighbors trickled in, eager to greet Dad, whom they hadn't seen in five years, and meet his war bride. Some of the older women teased Dad about all the girls he'd left behind. Mom understood much of what was being said, but still had difficulty speaking the dialect. She sat quietly, wondering, *Will I ever be able to speak this strange language that is so different from Italian and sounds so guttural? Why didn't Sotiri teach me Sicilian? What good is Italian here?* She'd make herself as inconspicuous as possible, taking in all she heard, and she was beginning to understand more and more. She practiced speaking the dialect with Dad but was still self-conscious when speaking with others.

There was one visitor who'd frequently drop by, often arriving after Dad went out. She was dressed in black from head to toe, always had a black shawl draped over her shoulders, and wore her hair in a bun, which made her appear much older than her twenty-three years. Mom found her to be somewhat strange. What she found most peculiar about the woman, Calogera, was that whenever Mom turned around, she was right behind her. Calogera didn't say anything to her; she just followed her. She bombarded Nonna with questions, which Mom understood to be criticisms.

"Doesn't she speak Italian?" Calogera, asked.

"She's learning," Nonna replied.

"Does she ever say anything?"

"She does when she has something to say."

"Can she make bread? Can she make pasta? Can she make minestrone?"

Nonna, growing impatient, replied, "If she can't, she'll learn!" Then, in a lighter tone, said, "Listen, Calogera; Maria's my daughter-in-law now."

One time, Dad returned to find Calogera milling about and, practically shouting, said, "You're still here? Don't you have a home and a husband to take care of? Go on; go home!"

Calogera never came back. Mom felt bad for the woman, and wished Dad hadn't been so rude with her. Sometime later, Mom learned that Calogera and her brother, Pietro, were childhood friends of Dad's. From the time the youngsters were in grade school, their parents had hoped their children would one day marry, uniting their families.

As the years passed, Nonna periodically dropped not-so-subtle hints, telling Dad, "You know, that Calogera is such a nice girl. You couldn't ask for a better girl to marry."

"What?"

"I said Calogera is a nice girl. She's a good homemaker, she cooks, she sews. She'll make someone a good wife. And you're such good friends with Pietro and the family . . ."

"You can forget it!" Dad said. "There's no way I'd marry her! I don't even like her."

"What do you mean you don't like her?"

"I don't like her; that's all! Now, if Pietro were a girl, I'd marry him. He's even better looking."

"You're always fast with the jokes!"

A few days before Dad was to leave for the army, he went to visit Pietro's family. He was surprised to see that there were quite a few people there: Pietro's parents and siblings along with about six others who were sitting around the table drinking wine. As Dad sipped his wine, he noticed people leaving. Suspecting an *inchiusa*, Dad jumped to his feet and made a mad dash for the door. No way would he be trapped!

The *inchiusa* is an old Sicilian custom where an unwanted suitor locks himself in a room with the girl he hopes to marry. The girl, now compromised due to her lost virtue, is forced to marry the perpetrator. This sinister plot, at times, was employed by women. With the help of willing accomplices, a woman would hook the man she wanted by locking herself in the room with her victim, and then demanded that her virtue and family honor be restored.

When Dad was in Albania, Calogera, hoping to get a commitment from him, wrote to him that she'd received a marriage proposal and wanted to know if she was free to accept. Dad, ecstatic and relieved she had someone else in her sights, wrote back, saying he didn't know when the war would end or if he'd even make it back. He encouraged her to marry, saying he knew the fellow and thought him to be a good man. He signed off by wishing them both the very best. Calogera married the young man, but it was obvious that she had not gotten over her first love. Fortunately for everyone, she and her husband departed Sicily for Milan.

About two weeks after arriving, Dad was ordered to report at the Military Academy in Modena. Considering he'd been separated from the Italian army for almost two years, Mom couldn't understand why this was necessary. She was also concerned that she wouldn't have his help with the language. As it was, the only way she communicated with Nonna when Dad wasn't around was through hand gestures, which didn't always work. Dad must have viewed the situation as "swim or sink," which would compel Mom to learn the language. Mom, at times felt that Dad was deliberately not being helpful.

When she asked him what the Sicilian word for washbasin is, he replied, "I already told you what it's called. Think and it will come to you."

Mom, more than annoyed with him, started looking all around the room for the washbasin. Nonna went over to her and said, "Show me what you want . . . show me with your hands."

Mom mimicked washing her hands and face which prompted Nonna to hold up the washbasin and say, "Ah, you want the *vacile*?"

Mom smiled and said, "Yes, the *vacile*!"

"See, I told you you can do it," Dad said.

After a month in Modena, Dad was formally discharged from the Italian army. Mom wasn't the only one that was happy to greet him.

Nonna greeted him saying, "Thank God you're back! Maria hardly speaks! I don't know if she understands anything I tell her."

"She understands everything you say. She has trouble getting the words out," Dad said. "Give her time. Maria's smart; she'll be speaking in no time."

One day several women came to visit. Mom heard one say, "I hope the poor girl doesn't end up like Emma."

Later, when Dad returned, Mom asked him, "What had happened to Emma?"

Quite taken aback, Dad said, "Who told you about Emma?"

"Today I heard one of the women say that I might end up like her."

"That's ridiculous! I don't know why anybody would say such a thing!"

"But who's Emma, and what happened to her?"

"She was a girl from Palermo. She fell in love with a guy from our parts. She knew her parents wouldn't approve, so they eloped."

"Why wouldn't they approve?"

"Two different worlds. She was the daughter of a duke, and he was a common laborer—a peasant, in their eyes. But Emma found life here difficult. She had a life of privilege, probably had servants too. So you can imagine what it must have been like for her, living here."

"What happened to her?"

"It didn't end well. She learned that her husband's family was scorned because his mother had been a prostitute during the war. She also had several illegitimate children with different fathers."

"That must have also been hard on Emma's husband."

"I'm sure it was tough on him. He never brought Emma to his mother's house. He rented a small room nearby, which was a far cry from what she was accustomed to. The situation affected her so much that she never left that room. She even refused to eat, and some time later, she died."

"That's awful."

"Some say she died of a broken heart. I heard her family never stopped looking for her. But by the time her brother found where she lived, Emma was already dead."

It's hard to believe that one can die of a broken heart. Emma ran off with her great love and broke from her family. Estranged from her loving parents and thrust not only into an impoverished family, but also one of ill repute, she became disheartened by a reality that eclipsed the love she had for her husband. One can only wonder if Romeo and Juliet would have survived had they lived. Both died before their love could be tested by life. Imagine the couple on the eve of their wedding: Romeo hands Juliet a prenup, which a disheartened Juliet reluctantly signs, the first seeds of doubt planted. The two take their vows, promising to love, honor, and obey each other until death do them part. The honeymoon over, and everyday life begins, unraveling the marriage. Eager to save the love they valiantly fought for, they seek counseling. When counseling fails, they make a last-ditch attempt to save their marriage with a temporary separation. Finally, yielding to irreconcilable differences, the couple heads to divorce court. The greatest of love stories are tested in one way or another.

But Mom was not like Emma. She was—and still is—a true chameleon. She has often said that the years she lived in that small Sicilian town, without electricity, indoor plumbing, and all the conveniences she had in Greece were her happiest. After all, she had lived through a war. All that really mattered was that she had a roof over her head, a loving husband, a healthy child, and a caring mother-in-law. Not having conveniences was only an inconvenience.

The odds of my parents getting together were against them from the start. There was the war between their countries, the nine-year difference in their ages, my grandparents' attempts to prevent their union, and Dad's imprisonment. Yet they defied the odds and were well on their way to living "happily ever after." One would think there would be nothing but bliss ahead, but it wasn't all happiness. My parents' union, like most, would be tested time and again. I often wonder who coined the very accurate phrase, "One has to know unhappiness to truly appreciate happiness."

* * *

That first summer, Mom was afflicted with malaria. She experienced fever and chills and had no desire to eat. As a result, she lost a lot of weight and was sickly skinny. Because of the malaria, she wasn't allowed to nurse me, and the midwife had to pump Mom's breast milk, which, according to Mom, was almost as painful as childbirth. Mom grew weak, tired, and depressed. She pined for her mother's healing broths that surely would help her get through this illness. How she missed her mother's cooking, especially when confronted with Nonna's bland minestrone! The times Dad attempted to cook, Nonna complained that he was too liberal with the olive oil.

Mom told me of the time she earned Nonna's ire. It was on a visit to family friends. The delightful fragrance of fresh tomato sauce and sweet basil that greeted Mom at the door caused her to feel faint. When she was served homemade fettuccini topped with the delectable tomato sauce, Mom ate with relish, savoring every mouthful. This prompted Nonna to grumble, "At home, you don't eat, and here you eat!"

Later that summer, I too fell ill with debilitating diarrhea. The doctor prescribed a diet of boiled rice and directed that I drink the cooled liquid the rice had been cooked in. I wouldn't eat the rice nor drink the liquid. I was dehydrated and lost so much weight that my ribs jutted out. The hair on my frail limbs appeared longer and darker, which, according to Mom, made me look like a little old lady. I wailed whenever I smelled food cooking. My parents, in order to have their meals in peace, would have Nonna take me outdoors. When we went out and came to a house emitting fragrant cooking smells, I'd wail and point in that direction.

Frustrated and distraught by the sight of me, Dad said, "The poor girl is going to die. Let her die content and with a full stomach."

Mom couldn't bear the thought of losing her child.

"But the doctor said she can only have boiled rice."

"Well, she's not eating the rice, and if we continue to follow his orders, she will starve to death. So let her have what she wants!"

Mom mashed a couple of forkfuls of spaghetti with fresh tomato sauce, which I devoured. Later, my tummy became distended, and the dreaded diarrhea returned. The next day, my parents gave me more mashed pasta and watched in amazement as I ate with relish. As the days passed, the debilitating symptoms that had plagued me for more than a month subsided. A little boy who lived just a few doors away had contracted the illness at the same time I had. Although he didn't look half as bad as I did when I was at my worst, he unfortunately succumbed to the illness. All I can say about the whole affair is that I owe my life to pasta and to Dad for not following the doctor's orders. To this day, I can honestly say that pasta is my favorite food—all pasta topped with marinara or meat sauce, and shellfish or vegetables sautéed in garlic and olive oil.

* * *

Just as in Greece, Sicilians ventured out in the evening. Going out for a stroll was their relaxation and entertainment. People meandered through the piazza, listening to popular Italian songs, meeting up with friends, stopping to chat and indulge in delicious gelato or pasticcino, and drinking espresso. People didn't have televisions then, and so they often went to the cinema. My parents sometimes took me to the movies, and whenever I saw people on the screen eating, I'd reach out with both hands—especially if they were having spaghetti.

It was in early spring when my grandparents' tenants moved out, freeing up the house next door. It was the first time my parents had a place of their own. Dad was relieved that the two families no longer lived under the same roof, and that he no longer had to run into his stepfather. Although his stepfather had mellowed, Dad never forgot how he had been mistreated as a child and still resented his stepfather for making him quit school. Unlike Dad, who was tense around the man—the tension, so high at times that it sucked the air out of the room—Mom found him to be a gentle and kind man. He affectionately called her "Mari," the name of his first wife. I have no memory of the old man, and only know what my parents have told me: he loved having me around and especially liked when I helped him take off his boots.

That summer, the same month I turned two, my parents welcomed their second child, a son, and named him Giuseppe, after Nonno. I'm told I wasn't at all thrilled by his arrival. After having had the throne to myself, I wasn't eager to step down. When Mom picked him up, I'd tell her to put him down, and when she breastfed him, I'd say he'd had enough and that it was my turn.

An adult who witnessed my apparent displeasure teasingly asked, "Do you want me to take your little brother away?"

Mom was happy to hear me say, "No, you can't take him! He's mine!"

From that day on, I became a doting sister.

A couple of months after my brother was born, Dad's stepfather, Tomasso, died.

Nonna never spoke to us about her second husband. I never understood why. Nonna and Tomasso were simpatico and in concert especially when it came to their love of the land. He never left her to go off on a quest like Nonno repeatedly had. She had shared her life with him for many more years than she had with Nonno. And yet when Tomasso died, Nonna went out of her way to expunge him from her life, going as far as to cut him out of a portrait and superimpose his image with Nonno's.

With his stepfather out of the picture, Dad told Nonna, "I want to rent one of your farms and work the land for myself."

Nonna was kind and loving, but she was also set in her ways and didn't see it that way.

"Why talk about renting? After all, you're my son!"

Dad, seeing this as her way of controlling him, rebelled.

"Do I have to come to you when my wife or children need socks or a pair of shoes?"

There was also another matter that gnawed at Dad. He had expected to find a nice sum from his military pay waiting for him upon his return home, and was more than upset to learn that Nonna had given the money to his sister, Pietrina. He cared for his sister and would have helped her himself; he just didn't appreciate Nonna having doled out his money without his permission. Nonna's refusal to allow Dad to rent one of her farms prompted him to quit working for her altogether and get a job as a *carabinieri*—a military policeman. Nonna never understood how he got the job in the first place. For the most part, *carabinieri* in Sicily came from the mainland, most hailing from the north, the rationale being that local policemen were easy prey. The Mafia had tremendous influence and resorted to anything and everything to get their way; they bribed not only the police but also judges and politicians. Those they couldn't corrupt, they terrified and murdered.

When someone was arrested, his relatives descended on the policeman's family with gifts of meat, cheese, eggs, and sometimes money. Dad refused to be bribed and instructed Mom and Nonna to refuse any and all offerings.

One day a woman appeared at our doorstep. My mother didn't know the woman but nevertheless greeted her warmly. Once inside, she walked over to our table and began taking the items out of her basket, placing them on the table.

As she headed out, she said, "Tell Totò this is courtesy of *la famiglia* Vitale."

When Dad returned and saw the wheel of cheese, whole salamis, and some wrapped items, he asked, "What's all this?"

"A woman came by," Mom said. She said to tell you it's courtesy of *la famiglia* Vitale."

Dad turned to Nonna and said, "You know better than this! Take everything back to her now!"

Nonna did as he asked, knowing full well that his refusal to accept the "gifts" would one day cause him hardship.

Mom and Dad

*Me at two
and a half*

Me with Mom, Dad, and Giuseppe

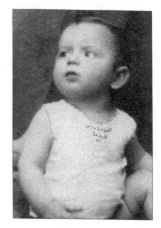

*Giuseppe at
five months*

12

COMING TO AMERICA

MOM OFTEN SAID THAT THE three and a half years she
lived in Sicily were her happiest. I find this somewhat difficult
to believe, considering she had to do without many of the amenities
she'd had in Greece. As for me, not having electricity and indoor
plumbing didn't faze me at all because I'd never had them and didn't
know anyone that did. From my perspective, I had everything and
lacked for nothing. I had a nice home, loving parents and grandmother, a comfortable bed, plenty of good food, nice clothes, a sweet
donkey, and lots of furry rabbits to play with.

When I asked my mom why we decided back then to come to
America, she replied, "I don't know why exactly. There were many
reasons. One was Nonna's fear about your father's job."

"What was she afraid of?"

"She knew there were people who could harm him."

"The Mafia?"

"The Sicilian Mafia was very powerful. It had more power than the government."

"Then why did Dad become a *carabinieri*?"

"I guess he thought he could deal with it. Besides, he didn't have many options at the time. Your nonna never understood why he was given the job since most policemen in Sicily came from the north."

"But Dad did have other options," I said. "Didn't Bonaventura offer him a partnership?"

"He did. But your father wasn't interested at the time. It was his dream to come to America. He wanted to see where his father had lived and died. In Greece, he more than once told my father that just seeing his father's grave would mean a lot to him."

"That was the first thing we did when we arrived," I recalled. "We visited Dad's uncle in Philadelphia and went to the cemetery to put flowers on Nonno's grave. I remember Dad looking sad and teary-eyed."

"I don't think he ever got over his father's senseless death."

* * *

Mom was thrilled to be going to America because she'd be reunited with her family, who would also be headed that way. Although Patras was not that far from Sicily, traveling was not easy then. Also, Greece was in the throes of a civil war that had erupted right after World War II. My grandparents didn't want to worry Mom, so they said very little about the war, although Pappou did write that the drachma had lost so much value, the paper currency was used to light fires.

"So coming to America seemed to be the answer," I said.

"It seemed to be," Mom replied, "but I worried about my parents and how my father would make a living here."

"Pappou did all right with his hot dog cart," I said.

"Yes, selling hot dogs on the street! It had to be a letdown, but I never heard him complain."

"I remember the first time Joe and I ran into him. He asked if we wanted to have a *cane caldo*. We thought he was joking, as usual."

"Your Pappou always had a sense of humor," Mom said. "He wrote to Yiayia, telling her he sold *skili zesto*. When she arrived, and first saw a hot dog, she couldn't understand why the frankfurter had been given such an unappetizing name."

"That was the first time I had one. Pappou put it in a bun and topped it with mustard and onions cooked in tomato sauce. It was delicious."

"The onions were the best part. A lot of people asked for them. It was a lot of work for Yiayia, so Eleni and I helped with peeling and slicing the onions, which made us cry."

"Onions always make me cry. I don't know how Yiayia could stand cooking so many," I said.

* * *

At this stage in my grandparents' lives—Pappou was sixty and Yiayia was forty-four—starting over in a new country had to have been a big move. It took a lot of courage, but they did it. Pappou, an American citizen, came over first, along with Taki and Eleni, arriving in New York City in 1946. Yiayia followed a year later.

They settled into a railroad apartment, one of many that lined Ninth Avenue. From the very start, Yiayia was homesick and had a difficult time adapting. She often sat by the window, dreaming of the home she'd left behind. She could see herself sitting on her veranda, gazing at the bright-red geranium pots that lined the terrace and the honeysuckle blossoms swaying in the breeze. It was evening, the best time of day to take in the spectacular views of the mountains and the blue sea. She could smell the fragrant peaches and ripe, purple figs that bloomed in her garden. She opened her eyes, hoping to find some semblance of that beauty and tranquility, only to be confronted by the four-story buildings across the avenue, their storefront windows covered with placards advertising their business: grocery store, delicatessen, restaurant, bakery, butcher shop, and fish market.

There were also fruit and vegetable stands on every street corner. This varied assortment of produce in such close proximity filled the air with a mix of odors, assaulting the senses. Sanitation trucks grunted noisily as they made their rounds at the start of each day, guaranteeing a wake-up call. The chatter and calls of pedestrians and the honking automobile horns produced an inordinate amount of noise. The flashing neon light over Rex's bar, beckoning the passersby, only added to the pandemonium.

Views from the back of the apartment building were no better, as the windows faced just more apartment buildings, separated only by a small patch of grass, which was infused with the pungent odor of cat urine. Except for the screeching of homeless cats, the noise level in the back was at least somewhat lower. But one had to draw the window shades to avoid forfeiting privacy, as so jarringly depicted in Alfred Hitchcock's suspense thriller *Rear Window*.

* * *

Pappou wrote to Mom, saying that the American Consulate advised that she and the children would travel together, but that Dad's paperwork had to be initiated by her in America. The three of us had our passports ready, but it was later decided that Mom would come alone. Pappou assured her we wouldn't be separated for long, and the United States Consulate in Italy said we'd be able to follow within six months. Six months seemed like a very long time, but Mom had little choice. Knowing Nonna would care for us made her leaving a little less stressful for her. So on December 27, 1948, Mom, pregnant with her third child, embarked on her journey.

"I have no memory of your leaving," I told her.

"It was hard leaving without you kids. I wanted to tell you I'd be gone for a little while and that we'd be together again soon, but your father thought it best if I didn't because it would upset you."

"All I remember is that you weren't there anymore and Nonna and Dad saying you were in America. I didn't know where America was or why you were there without us."

"I left with a heavy heart. Your father accompanied me on the train to Palermo. At the pier, I boarded the ship and stood on the deck waving until I couldn't see him anymore."

Pappou tried booking passage for Mom on the Vulcania and the Saturnia but was unsuccessful, so she traveled on the Marine Carp, a military ship, which was much smaller than an ocean liner and made crossing the rough Atlantic in winter even more arduous. What made the trip bearable for Mom was her traveling companion. When she was at the US Consulate in Palermo, she met a woman who was making travel arrangements for her twelve-year-old daughter, Anna, who was going to America to visit her father. Anna was a minor and required a guardian. Mom readily agreed, and as it turned out, Anna was more of Mom's keeper. Mom was seasick throughout the trip and tolerated very little food. During the entire voyage, Mom went into the dining room only a handful of times. She ate so little, her baby began kicking more and more, probably wondering why he wasn't getting nourishment. She grew weak and had difficulty standing; on most days, she stayed in her cabin.

One day, Mom asked Anna if she could bring her some bread and an orange soda.

"What's that?" she asked when Anna returned with a bottle of brown liquid.

"Pepsi-Cola, a popular soda in America."

Mom took a sip and found it sickeningly sweet. Accustomed to bread with a thick, hard crust and a soft core, Mom found the mushy slice Anna had brought her difficult to eat, as it stuck to the roof of her mouth. To this day, Mom still has distaste for colas and Wonder Bread.

Perhaps it was seeing land after all those days at sea that made Mom ravenous. She went down to the kitchen, and the obliging cook brought her a plate of spaghetti and meatballs, which she devoured. Back in her cabin, she studied herself in the mirror. How pale she looked! At almost five months pregnant, she had barely a baby bump. She pinched her cheeks, hoping to produce some color. Seeing there was little she could do to improve her appearance, she stopped trying.

Anna and Mom headed outside, and as soon as they stepped onto the deck, the frigid wind hit them. Mom, dressed in a light wool coat, woolen stockings, and flat shoes, felt the cold air travel up her legs.

"It's freezing," Anna said. "Let's go back inside."

"It's not so bad," Mom lied. "Let's walk in place. We'll warm up that way."

They took their places by the handrail, gloved hands in their pockets, and stepped from side to side, trying to keep their feet from going numb.

Looking down to the pier, Mom spotted her parents.

"I see them!" she cried. "The man with the white hair is my father. My mother is next to him."

They look much older, she thought. *And who's the tall man standing next to them? That can't possibly be my little brother, can it?*

Taki had grown and changed so much that if he weren't standing with their parents, Mom wouldn't have recognized him. When Mom left Greece, just three and half years ago, he was a twelve-year-old boy in shorts, and now he was more than a head taller than their father.

Anna then spotted her father, who was smiling and waving. With suitcases in hand, the girls proceeded to disembark. Anna's father was first to greet them, and he thanked Mom for accompanying his daughter. Mom told him she was happy to have Anna's company and that she had been a wonderful companion and friend.

Mom's parents then joined the small reunion and gave Mom a hug.

"How good it is to see you!" Mom exclaimed. "I've missed you so much! This is my friend Anna. We were roommates. And this is Anna's father."

Pappou and Anna's dad greeted each other in English and shook hands. The girls hugged and said their goodbyes.

Mom embraced her parents again and heard Taki, who was eyeing her suspiciously, whisper to their mother, "She doesn't look like Maro. She doesn't even talk like her. Maybe they sent somebody else."

"It's me, Taki," Mom reassured him. "Maybe I've changed, but not as much as you have. How big you are! I never would have recognized you!"

Taki, embarrassed at having been caught, explained, "You look different."

Yiayia, holding her daughter at arm's length, said sadly, "Child, you're so thin."

"The food on the ship wasn't very good, and I was seasick and couldn't eat much. But I feel good now that I am here with you."

"It's winter," Pappou said. "The sea is rough in winter."

"It's so cold!" Yiayia said. "Let's go home."

Taki hailed a taxi, and Mom was surprised to hear him speak English. He took her suitcase, placed it in the trunk, and sat up front with the driver as Mom huddled in the back with her parents.

"Where's Eleni?" Mom asked.

"She's at work," Pappou replied.

"She wanted to come," Yiayia said, "but she had to go to work."

"She'll be home soon," Pappou said.

"What does she do?" Mom asked.

"She adds numbers on a machine," said Taki. "It's not hard, but she complains all the time."

Within ten minutes, the taxi stopped by the curb of the four-story apartment building. Walking up the long stairway to their first-floor apartment, Mom was greeted by the familiar aroma of her mother's *avgolemono* soup. She entered the kitchen and immediately felt the warm air on her face.

Yiayia, pointing to the bathroom door, said, "Maro, why don't you go in and wash up."

Mom walked into the bathroom and hesitated a moment to gaze at the white sink. She turned on the faucet, and as the warm water caressed her hands, she thought, *No more hauling water, no more having to heat water on the hearth, and no more having to look out for the donkey!*

Mom joined her father and brother, who were already seated at the kitchen table, the steam rising from the creamy lemon-egg foam making her mouth water.

"Mamá, it smells so good! How I've missed your soup!"

Mom was deliriously happy to be sitting at the table with her family. She looked around the room, marveling at the stove, refrigerator, and—best of all—the kitchen sink with a faucet that provided hot and cold water at one's pleasure.

"What's the matter, child? Why aren't you eating?" Yiayia asked.

"Oh, I was just thinking about how good it is to be here with you."

"I'm glad. But don't let your soup get cold. Eat! I have roast lamb and potatoes."

"I love roast lamb!" Mom said. "What happened to the mama goat?"

"We left her with Chrysoula," Taki said.

"Remember crazy Tomboy?" Mom asked.

At that moment, the front door flew open, and Eleni rushed in.

"Crazy Tomboy!" Eleni exclaimed. "Don't you remember, Maro? Mamá cooked that crazy goat! Oh, Maro! It's so good to see you!"

Mom jumped up and embraced her little sister.

"It's good to see you too, Eleni!"

"You're home early," Pappou said.

"I told the boss my sister was coming today, and he said I could leave." Eleni then, sizing up her sister, asked, "Maro, did you get shorter?"

"No, I think you got taller . . . and you're wearing high heels."

"They're not so high."

Mom studied her little sister and could see no trace of the rough-and-tumble girl with bruised knees and scuffed shoes. The eighteen-year-old before her, wearing a dress that accentuated her slim figure—the top two buttons, undone, revealing a strand of pearls—was the picture of elegance. Eleni's coral lips, her rosy cheeks, the soft curls framing her face, and her shapely legs in sheer nylon stockings and three-inch pumps added to her allure. Mom, suddenly aware of her own dowdy dress, wool stockings, and unfashionable yet sensible thick-soled shoes, cringed and slid into her chair, wrapped her arms around her middle, and hid her legs under the table.

Eleni, oblivious to her sister's discomfort, went on, "We have to get you out of those old things. We'll go to Penney's; that's where I work . . . J. C. Penney. And we have to do something about your hair!"

"Clothes and hair, that's all you think about, Eleni! Sit down and eat! The first thing we have to do is put some weight on your sister."

Eleni sat at the table, beside Mom, and started on her soup.

"How was your trip?" she asked Mom. "Did you get seasick?"

"I did. The sea was rough and the ship rocked a lot. A lot of people got seasick."

"A lot of people got seasick on our ship too," Eleni said. "But I didn't, right, Babá? Taki threw up, but I didn't."

"I did not throw up!" Taki protested.

"You did too!"

"I did not!"

"All right, you two, that's enough," Pappou said. "You're tiring your sister."

"That's OK," Mom said smiling. Her siblings hadn't changed that much after all. They still liked goading each other.

"Maro, ready for some lamb and potatoes?" Yiayia asked.

"Not just yet, Mamá, maybe later."

"I don't want to force you, but you must try to eat a little more. Remember, you're eating for two now. Are you tired? Maybe you'd like to go lie down and rest a little."

"I'm not tired, Mamá. I just want to sit here with all of you. I love your house," Mom said, her eyes once again taking in the room. "It's so warm and cozy."

"It's not a house. It's an apartment. And it's *too* cozy," Eleni whined. "We need a bigger apartment and on a different street! There's so much noise here, especially in the morning. I can't wait—"

"Eleni, stop with the complaining!" Yiayia scolded.

"I'm not complaining, Mamá. It's just that . . . maybe Maro forgot what it was like in Greece. Maro, what was Sicily like? Did you like living there?"

"Sicily's nice. We lived in a small town and—" Mom caught herself. *If Eleni thinks this place awful, what might she think of the place in Sicily? Better change the subject!* "Sotiri's mother is wonderful. She loves the children and takes them everywhere. I know she's going to spoil them. Eleni, tell me about your job."

"I work in the office in Penney's, a department store. It has lots of different departments—clothes, shoes, and things for the house—and I get a discount."

"Is English hard to learn?" Mom asked.

"In the beginning it is. The alphabet is different. But when you learn the letters, it's not so hard. I went to school and got my diploma last year."

Not to be outdone, Taki said, "I get mine in two years, when I'm seventeen."

"That's great!" Mom replied. "Do you know what you want to do when you graduate?"

"Not yet. My friend says he'll work in a printing plant. I might do that."

"I'm learning a lot more English at work," Eleni added. "Everybody in the office speaks English. You won't have trouble though; you're good with languages. Maro, I just realized you sound different."

"What do you mean by 'different'?"

"I don't know . . . just different. It's your accent! Yes, you have an accent!"

"What do you mean?"

"Babá, doesn't she have an accent?"

"She talks like Sotiri," Taki quipped.

"No, I don't."

"Stop annoying your sister," Yiayia said.

"Nobody speaks Greek in Sicily," Mom explained. "Sotiri wanted me to learn Sicilian, so he stopped speaking Greek. But I haven't forgotten Greek. I understand everything and—"

"It's not so bad. In fact, you sound cute," Eleni said.

"*Cute?* She sounds like a foreigner!" Taki cackled.

"All right, all right," Pappou said. "That's enough, you two. You've had your fun."

"That's OK, Babá; they're just playing. Maybe I will go lie down now. I do feel tired."

* * *

Yiayia saw to it that Mom had plenty of nutritious food, and in no time, Mom put on all the weight she had lost and then some. She prepared dishes for Mom that brought back memories of her childhood, the good days before the war, dishes like the hearty *avgolemono* soup (chicken soup blended with eggs, fresh dill, and lemon juice—all whipped into a silky froth), *pastitsio* (long, fat noodles layered with ground meat and béchamel sauce), *dolmades* (grape or cabbage leaves stuffed with ground lamb and rice, and peppered with fragrant dill), *tiropita* and *spanakopita* (cheese and spinach pies), *koulourakia* (a crispy, orange-flavored Easter cookie), *kourabiedes* (vanilla shortbread biscuits made with minced almonds and adorned with a single spice clove), and Mom's very favorite, *diples* (thin, sheet-like dough fried in hot oil, dipped in honey, and sprinkled with minced walnuts—just like the ones that got Mom into a heap of trouble when, as a little girl, she reached for the cookie jar, dropped it, and shattered it and the *diples* too).

A month after arriving, Mom got a job as a rhinestone setter, setting rhinestones, pearls, and beads onto fabric at a factory located in the garment district, just a couple of blocks from the apartment. The owner was an Italian immigrant, as were most of the workers. There were also some Greeks and Americans. Like Mom, the Italian and Greek women spoke little English.

Eager to learn the language, Mom enrolled in night school and attended for two months—the two months, interrupted by a two-year gap. She had been compelled to quit when Yiayia was hit by a car. Although Yiayia did not suffer broken bones, her injuries were grave enough that she had to rest for a couple of months. In addition to working full time, Mom and Eleni took over the household chores.

In May, five months after arriving, Mom gave birth to a second son. He was named Antonio, after Pappou. When my grandparents visited Mom at French Hospital, they gave her the news she had been eagerly awaiting.

"All the paperwork is approved," Pappou said. "Sotiri and the children will be here soon!"

"They're finally coming! How wonderful!" Mom exclaimed.

A week later, Mom received Dad's letter, in which he wrote, "I have some bad news. Our passport is being held by the authorities." She read the line over again, hoping she was misreading it. He continued, "Some charges were filed against me, the most serious, theft of firearms from the *caserma*. Some firearms went missing, and because I had access to keys, I'm a suspect. The whole thing is ridiculous. I know I'll be cleared. There will be a trial, but I don't know when that will be."

Mom was numb. She couldn't understand any of it. She handed the letter to her father and said, "I have to go back. I have to be with my husband and children."

Pappou read the letter, folded it, and said, "No, you must not go. It will be better for you to stay here. You can help him more if you stay, as you can work and send him money. He will need money for the trial."

"But Sotiri doesn't know when the trial will be. It could be months. I don't want to be away from the children that long. My little boy was only two when I left. He may not even remember me. I can't bear the thought of that!"

"You have to be strong; things will work out. Believe me," Pappou assured her.

Adding to Mom's stress was that Antonio was constantly getting sick. The doctor said he had tonsillitis and he'd need to have his tonsils removed, but he couldn't have the operation until he was at least three. At times, Antonio's throat hurt so much, he refused to eat. Mom and Yiayia would sit with him by the window and try to distract him, pointing to the cars below and to the occasional plane in the sky while sneaking spoonfuls into his mouth.

Mom returned to her factory job that July. Work at the factory was seasonal, and during the summer when there was little to no work, she received unemployment checks. At times, the unemployment office found work for her at other factories. Once, Mom was sent to a factory and was told to bring scissors. She had no idea what scissors were until Pappou handed them to her.

When she reported for work, the floor manager asked, "Do you have experience?"

"Yes." Mom replied.

However, when the manager saw the huge pair of scissors she pulled out of her handbag, he screamed, "Get out! Get out!"

Mom couldn't understand why the man was screaming, but she was happy to be out of there. She later learned that the position required experience with dainty appliqué scissors.

Another time, she was sent to a sewing factory and was told it was for a "floor girl" position. She knew what the word *floor* meant and wondered if the job involved sweeping and mopping. She was happy to learn that neither was required. The floor girl distributed the work to the sewing machine operators, and then collected and inspected the workmanship. She liked supervising for a change, and worked at the factory for a couple of months, before she was called back to her regular job. She was asked to stay on as a floor girl, but she decided to return to her old job as a pieceworker. For Mom, it was a no-brainer. Her old crew felt like family; the job was close to home; and being a really fast worker, she made more money doing piecework. There was also another reason: her boss had cosponsored Dad's trip to America.

In the spring of 1950, Mom attended her first Greek Independence Day Parade in America. A friend pointed out to her Mr. Tofalos, that year's grand marshal of the parade. Just hearing his name caused Mom to recall the tragedy that had befallen his family. He waved somberly from the float, and Mom wondered if he, too, at that moment, was thinking of that tragic day when his brother and sister were killed by shrapnel from an exploding bomb.

When Antonio was eighteen months old, Mom returned to night school. At the start of the class, the teacher had the students read a line or two as he tried to guess their country of origin. He was doing fine until he came to Mom.

"Italian?" he asked. "No? French? Spanish?" Somewhat frustrated, he said, "You must speak more than one language!"

Mom smiled and said, "Yes. I speak Greek, Italian, and a little Sicilian."

"Three languages! No wonder I can't place you!"

Mom wanted to continue with her lessons, but between worrying about Dad's legal problems, Antonio constantly getting sick, and missing those of us who were back in Sicily, it was difficult for her to concentrate. However, with help from her father, brother, and sister, and listening to the radio, Mom continued to learn the language. She also kept up with the Italian language by listening to Italian radio stations.

Things seemed to move at a snail's pace in the Sicilian judicial system. The case dragged on with no trial date in sight. The legal fees were piling up, causing a great deal of stress and frustration for both my parents. Mom recalled the hurtful words Dad had once written her: "What am I supposed to do with this money? Buy a rope and hang myself?" Mom knew he was stressed because she, too, was stressed.

Years later, she would tell me, "Those words hurt very much. I wrote your father, saying I was doing the best I could, that I, too, had expenses and didn't want to be more of a burden to my parents than I already was."

A year passed before a trial date was set. During the trial, although only flimsy and unsubstantiated evidence had been leveled against Dad by the captain of the *caserma* and several questionable characters, he was found guilty of the most serious charge: theft of firearms.

13

LIFE WITHOUT MOM

DAD WROTE TO MOM, telling her that his lawyer had filed an appeal and that there would be another trial. She was devastated. She knew this would mean more delays, and she wanted to return to Sicily.

Nonna wrote to Mom, saying that Dad had been framed by those who wanted to harm not only him, but also his family. (Nonna couldn't read or write, so she had someone write her letters for her.) She cautioned that if he stayed in Sicily and continued in his line of work, he might be killed. She implored Mom not to give up, to be strong, and to have faith that things will work out in the end.

Of course, my brother and I were not aware of Dad's legal problems. Dad still worked at the *caserma*, and life seemed normal—except that Mom wasn't there. In the little I understood, Mom was in

America, getting our home ready. She wrote to us, saying we'd soon be together, but soon never seemed to come. I looked forward to Mom's letters, and when I learned to write, I scribbled notes at the bottom of Dad's letters, telling her I loved her and missed her and wanted to be with her. The endless waiting and pining are what I remember most.

Whenever a plane flew by, which was not very often then, Nonna would point to it and say, "Wave to your Greek Nonno, Antonio. He's going to America."

I don't think I knew then what "Greek" meant. I was happy just knowing I had another grandfather, a living grandfather who I would soon meet. With outstretched arms, my brother and I waved frantically, hoping he'd see us. It never occurred to me at that time why our Nonno was constantly going to America.

After Mom left, we moved in with Nonna. My brother and I slept in Nonna's room, and Dad slept in the upstairs room. Nonna had affectionate names for us. I was "Tre-Tre," and Giuseppe, her *picciliddro* (little one), was "Pinuccio" or "Pino." She also had a pet name for Dad, for I never heard her call him by his given name. He was "Totò" and "Pé," (a nickname for Giuseppe).

Nonna, or rather, "Mamma Teresa," as she liked to be called, was a loving grandmother. An attractive woman, she wore her long, straight dark hair in a braid rolled into a bun at the nape of her neck. Although she never wore lipstick or makeup, there were traces of vanity, as evidenced by her dainty gold earrings and the cinch around her middle, which flaunted her slender waist. She walked with a long, determined stride, which made her appear much taller than her five-foot frame.

My brother and I missed our mom, and Nonna did her best to fill the void, doting on us, entertaining us with her marvelous bedtime stories, and taking us along on trips to her farms. Those years with Nonna provided me with precious memories that still bring a smile to my face when they come to mind. When I'm watching television or riding in a car and a ray of sunlight crosses an open field, it transports me back to those dusty roads that led to Nonna's farms. I see the three of us with our donkey, Ciro, trailing behind. Some memories are vivid while others have dimmed over the years. The memories that are burned into my mind are, for the most part, imbued with warmth. Some are snippets that I try hard to hold on to, glimpses into that world of rustic country life that I would yearn for when Ninth Avenue, with all its asphalt and concrete, became my world.

Mom tells me, the farms weren't far from our house. I believe she's mistaken, because the walks seemed to take forever, and many times, we stayed overnight and slept under the stars—with Pino in the middle, shielded by Nonna and me. We'd lie on our backs and gaze at the black canvas of the night sky, sprinkled with shining stars, while listening to Nonna's stories. She'd warn us to not point at *le stelle* because if we did, we'd get warts on our fingers. She'd say that *la luna* baked all night so that we'd have fresh bread in the morning. In awe, I'd look up at the moon's smiling face, wondering how she managed all those early-morning deliveries. Although I enjoyed looking at the moon and stars and listening to Nonna's stories, sleeping out in the open at times frightened me and caused me to worry that some creature might crawl onto our blanket.

We prepared for our trips by loading Ciro with our canteens, food, and sleeping blankets, leaving early in the morning in order to avoid the midday sun. Pino was not one for walking, and Nonna often indulged him by letting him ride Ciro while we held on to the reins to prevent the spoiled brat from riding off. At times, Nonna had to coax him down in order to give the poor donkey a break. Ciro would neigh his approval as Pino reluctantly dismounted and joined us on foot. When it got too hot or we needed to rest, we took advantage of the cooled cement huts along the way. Pino and I scurried into the huts, dragging Ciro behind us and hoping Nonna would let us sit for a while. I remember wishing we'd had a carriage. We would have made better time, and would have gotten to ride, which would have prevented us from growing so tired along the journey.

On the way to the farms, we came upon a huge crater that both fascinated and terrified us. We'd stand at the outer edge, peering into the abyss, Nonna warning us to step back or we'd fall in. I often wonder why a fence hadn't been put around that crater, and imagine some poor, unsuspecting soul trudging along on a starless night and falling in!

We traveled past a farm with trees that seemed always to be chock full of incredibly delicious apples that Pino and I couldn't resist. We'd run ahead, and I'd jump up to pluck one piece of fruit for each of us. Pino couldn't reach the branches, which really infuriated him. We bit into those sweet and juicy yellow apples, savoring every bite. Ciro, too, loved munching on the chunks we gave him. Nonna reprimanded us, saying we were stealing. Her scolding didn't deter us though; the temptation was just too great.

We often came across dead snakes—their carcasses, burst open and dried out by the sun—and kicked their disgusting remains off the road. That I was able to do this back then shocks me today, because just like my yiayia, I have a morbid fear of snakes. I don't know how, why, or when my phobia began, but I believe it may have had to do with Nonna's stories, some of which were so scary, I must have blocked them from memory. All that remains is my fear of those creatures that frequently haunted my dreams, giving me nightmares that rendered me immobile and unable to scream.

Once, on the way home, we ran out of food.

"I'm sorry," Nonna said, "but there's no more food left. Let's keep walking, and we'll be home soon."

"It's too far, Nonna," I lamented, "and I'm hungry."

"Me too," Pino whined.

"Why don't we pray?" Nonna suggested.

"Will we get some food if we pray?" Pino wanted to know.

"Let's pray and ask God for some bread."

Following Nonna's lead, we knelt down, made the sign of the Cross, and recited the Lord's Prayer, giving extra emphasis to the words, *Give us this day our daily bread.* We said, "amen," crossed ourselves, and started on our way again. After taking a few steps, I was the first to spot it: sitting on a rock was a big loaf of bread.

I screamed out, "Look! There's bread on the rock!"

I ran and picked up the loaf. The warm, hard crust yielded to my touch.

I handed the loaf to Nonna and said, "Touch it, Nonna. It's warm and soft."

Nonna took the bread, gave it a gentle squeeze, and said, "Yes, it's very soft—and warm too. Don't you think we should thank God for answering our prayer?"

Nonna was very religious and encouraged us to pray, not only when we were in need, but also to give thanks.

"How did the bread get here?" I wanted to know.

"I'm hungry! Let's pray so we can eat!" Pino wailed.

"Do you think God heard us and sent the bread from Heaven?" I asked.

"There's no one around, so it had to have come from God," Nonna replied.

"No more talking! Let's pray! I want to eat!"

With that urgent order coming from the pint-sized sergeant, we once again knelt and said our prayer of thanks. Nonna cut into the loaf with her pocketknife and handed a slice to Pino and one to me. It was the best bread I'd ever tasted. But why wouldn't it have been? After all, it had come from God! While savoring the bread, I wondered if Nonna had placed the loaf there, but I quickly dismissed the thought. I wanted so much to believe that God had answered our prayer.

I don't remember seeing any of the workers on Nonna's farms, nor do I remember Dad ever going with us. It's only Nonna, Pino, and me, and the sweet and sometimes stubborn donkey that are in my memories. Nonna would point to the various fruits and vegetables, showing us the different leaves on the apple, pear, and orange trees.

"That's a pear tree," she'd say, pointing to a tree with lots of low branches. "Your father planted it when he was a little boy."

Pino and I helped Nonna collect the fruits and vegetables. She cut the stems of the tender *zarchi* (Swiss chard) with her knife and handed the bunches to us. For supper, we'd have *zarchi* sprinkled with olive oil, and a slice of bread and cheese. Afterward, we'd enjoy fruit we'd picked that day. A favorite of ours were the *fichi d'India* (prickly pears) which we called *fichidini*. *Fichi d'India* have a thick peel studded with fine, prickly spines that stick to you; they're not only a nuisance, but also painful. Pino and I waited in anticipation as Nonna cut back the peel, revealing the deep yellow, pure white, or crimson fruit. The juicy pulp emitted a citrus fragrance and had lots of tiny seeds that we had no trouble swallowing.

"Don't touch the *fichidini*," Nonna warned. "You'll get nettles on your hands!"

At times, Pino and I were impatient and dove into the basket, searching for our favorite, the prized crimson.

Our hands covered with prickly spines, we'd wail, "Take them out, Nonna! Please take them out! They hurt!"

"Didn't I tell you not to grab? See what happens when you don't listen!"

Sometimes we managed to get nettles stuck not only to our hands, arms, and legs, but also to our clothes, which kept Nonna busy in pulling them out one at a time.

Among the harvested items Nonna kept in the upstairs storage room were *carrube* (carob). *Carrube* resemble extra-wide, flat string beans, but instead of being soft and green, they're brown and hard. I tried biting into one once but couldn't sink my teeth into the wood-like texture.

One day, the Ice Man, the equivalent of Mister Softee, was making his rounds. Whenever we heard the clippety-clop of the approaching Ice Man's horse-drawn wagon, we'd run out and get in line with the other children. Nonna wasn't home that particular day, and my brother and I had no money. The Ice Man, knowing Nonna, grew *carrube*, said, "I'll give you shaved ice for *carrube*."

All excited, we climbed up the ladder to the storage room, grabbed two handfuls of *carrube* each, and ran out again.

"Are these enough?" I asked.

"Perfect," said the Ice Man, as he heaped mounds of shaved ice into cups, and topped each with *granatina*, a syrup made from pomegranates.

"That was a good deal," I said, lapping up the delicious cool treat.

"Yeah," Pino agreed. "*Carrube* taste lousy anyway."

"But maybe we shouldn't tell Nonna—"

"Shouldn't tell Nonna what?" demanded Nonna, who had appeared out of nowhere.

"The Ice Man came, and we didn't have money," I explained. "He said we could have ice for *carrube.*"

"Did he now? He's a shrewd one. I hope you didn't give him more than two for that ice!"

"Oh . . . no," I lied. "That's all he wanted, just two."

Carrube must have been a rare commodity because Nonna made us promise never to do that again.

* * *

It was Nonna who kept us occupied and entertained most days. Because of Dad's erratic work schedule, we hardly ever saw him. Whenever the *carabinieri* received a tip about a certain outlaw, they went on the chase, which at times, took them to other towns. The *carabinieri* often went to Montelepre and Partinico in search of Salvatore Giuliano, the most elusive bandit at that time. Because of his swagger, his striking good looks, his generosity to the poor, as well as a keen PR campaign, the dashing Giuliano, who led an army of six hundred loyal followers, was one of the most famous bandits in Italian history. He robbed rich landlords, gave to the poor, and then disappeared into the mountains, prompting *Time* magazine to label him the Sicilian Robin Hood. His gang killed more than a hundred police officers and forty civilians, and collected more than one million dollars from thirty kidnappings. Shielded by his loyal followers, he was able to avoid capture. In 1949, a two-thousand-man task force scoured Sicily, searching for the elusive outlaw. It was reported that in 1950, he was gunned down in a courtyard in Castelvetrano, Sicily, by the police, while resisting arrest. However, it was later revealed that the shootout was staged, and he had actually been shot by Gaspare Pisciotta, a gang member, who, four years later, would be poisoned in a Palermo prison.

When Dad returned from these chases, he made every effort to spend time with my brother and me. At times he'd take us to the *caserma*. I was in awe of the prison cells, which were never occupied when we visited. Sometimes Dad would place us in a cell and tell us that's where we'd stay if we misbehaved. I didn't like being behind bars, but Pino thought it a great adventure, one he couldn't wait to tell his friend Vito about. Dad also gave us rides on his police motorcycle. Pino and I took turns sitting on top with Dad, and in the sidecar. I loved the fast speed and the wind blowing on my face, especially on hot days. I thought it would be great to take the motorcycle to Nonna's farms. We'd not only make better time, but best of all, we wouldn't get sore feet. But there was no way we'd ever get Nonna on that motorcycle, not even in the sidecar.

Sometimes Dad took us along when he went hunting for wild rabbits and birds. I didn't like for him to shoot at the animals. It was terrible to see living creatures, minding their own business and not bothering anybody, get shot. When Dad aimed his rifle, I closed my eyes, hoping he'd miss—and sometimes he did. When he didn't, he brought home his catch and cooked it. I couldn't bring myself to eat something I'd seen hopping or flying about.

One hunt I did enjoy was the hunt for *babbaluci* (snails) that crawled on the ground and on plants. Pino and I grabbed them, placed them on the palm of our hands, admiring their spiral shells, and patiently waited for their head to come out and retreat again. Nonna sautéed the *babbaluci* in garlic and olive oil, and we had them for dinner. Pino and I giggled at the funny sucking sounds we made in trying to get the suckers out. When we couldn't remove them, Nonna would use a special pick to get the job done.

Although it's very hot in Sicily, winter mornings and nights can be quite cold and damp. On cold mornings, Nonna warmed our shoes with pieces of coal. This worked pretty well except for the time a piece got stuck inside, burning my big toe. On cold nights, Nonna cooked a special treat of ours, *frascuatula*, a polenta made of toasted, minced sweet peas, which resembles oatmeal, except that it is seasoned with salt instead of sugar. Pino and I sat around the hearth by the crackling fire, and Nonna sat between us, the large, colorful platter filled with *frascuatula* on her lap. The three of us dipped our spoons into the creamy *frascuatula*, starting at the rim, where it wasn't too hot, and working our way down. It was more of a game, and we had lots of fun with it—especially when our spoons met in the middle of the platter and clanked. When there was not a trace left, Nonna rewarded us with a story.

Nonna was a wonderful storyteller, and we were enthralled by everything she told us. At the time, I believed her stories to be true and not imaginary—that everything she said had really happened. Then it was off to bed. To take the chill from the sheets, Nonna filled the *bedouin pan* with coal and placed it between the covers. We'd then get into the warm bed—Pino, in the middle and Nonna and I, on either side of him. When we were settled in, Nonna blew out the flame in the oil lamp. I once attempted to put out the flame and burned my hand on the glass tube. My hand hurt so much, I never tried that again!

On nights Pino wet the bed, he'd climb over me and push me toward the middle. When I woke, I wondered how I got there until I felt the cold wet spot. I couldn't believe he was able to move me without waking me. But the smart aleck's scheme never worked because his underwear had the telltale signs that always did him in. However, that didn't stop him. It was an icky thing for him to do, and I wanted to give him a kick in the butt for it, but Nonna would never allow that.

There was one time of day that Pino and I absolutely hated and that was siesta time, when, after our midday meal, we had to go to bed. Being most energetic at that time of day, we found it hard to settle down. The times Nonna couldn't get us to sleep, she sent us up to Dad, who, like most adults, looked forward to siesta. Pino and I lay down on either side of Dad and tried to fall asleep but couldn't. We peeked through the shutter slats to the courtyard below to see if anything interesting was going on, but aside from birds flying around and stray cats running about, everything was still, and eventually we, too, fell asleep. The worst part for me was that after siesta, I had to go back to school for the afternoon session.

Nonna believed it was never too early to learn to be a homemaker. She taught me to sew and together we made a dress for my rag doll. She had me thread her sewing needles for as long as I can remember. She most likely needed glasses, but I don't think she ever saw a doctor. Nonna also had me help in the kitchen, placing a wooden crate for me to stand on so that I could reach the table. I loved helping Nonna make bread and pasta. Fettuccini was her specialty. My job was to dust the preparation area with flour while Nonna worked the dough, kneading it and then cutting it into long strips. A favorite of mine was orecchiette, "little ears." To make them, you cut small pieces of dough and give them a little pinch.

Nonna always managed to have two small rounds of dough left with which she made pizza for us. Sometimes she sprinkled the top with olive oil, salt, and fresh oregano and rosemary before baking, and other times, she sprinkled it with sugar. In Sicily we didn't have the fancy pizza we have in America. Pizza is said to be a Neapolitan import, but even in Naples, the pizza isn't like American pizza. Years later, when I traveled to Naples, I didn't see pizza smothered with tomato sauce and cheese, and pepperoni or sausage. For the most part, pizza was topped with olive oil and herbs, just like Nonna's.

The times I helped Nonna in the kitchen, Pino played outdoors with his best bud, Vito. A favorite game of theirs was policeman and prisoner. Pino always appointed himself *carabiniere*, and poor Vito, his prisoner, had to sit on a rock behind the eight-foot iron gate while the *carabiniere*, with a stick for a rifle, walked back and forth on the other side, guarding him. This seemed to me not only silly, but also very boring. They would do this for hours on end, never seeming to tire of it. The times I had to fetch him, Nonna told me to be gentle because, after all, he was just a *picciliddro*. But the *picciliddro* refused to come along, insisting he couldn't leave his post. It took forever trying to get ahold of him. I dodged his rapid kicks by grabbing one hand and holding his head at arm's length with the other, literally dragging him as he tried his best to land a kick on my shins, sometimes succeeding. When we finally reached home, me huffing and puffing, and he, howling and kicking, Nonna ran over to him, wanting to know if I'd hurt her little angel—while I stood there rubbing my shins, trying to make her see it was the other way around.

"But he's only a *picciliddro*," Nonna would always say.

Nonna's cuisine could be described as "peasant" style. She used oil and spices sparingly. I don't believe she cooked this way for health reasons; it had more to do with the fact that she was extremely frugal. Whatever the reason, her food choices and healthy lifestyle may account for the fact that she seldom saw a physician, didn't take prescription drugs, and went on to live a long, healthy life. It also didn't hurt that she didn't drink or smoke. Nonna's bland one-pot meals consisted of vegetables and legumes such as lentils, beans, or chickpeas that she combined with pasta. On Christmas and Easter, as well as on various saints' days, she'd splurge by cooking rabbit, chicken, or sausage. A special yummy breakfast treat Nonna made for us was warm ricotta spread on bread and sprinkled with sugar.

Nonna's cooking was definitely too bland for our dad, who had inherited his gourmet taste from both his grandmother Angela and his father. His pan-roasted meats and sausages filled the room with an intoxicating aroma that always lured Pino and me in. Nonna pooh-poohed Dad's exotic tastes, and called him a *liccuni*, an indulger of rich food. Unlike Nonna, who topped her homemade pasta with vegetables, Dad topped his store-bought pasta with tomato or meat sauce and grated cheese. My brother and I had our meals with Nonna, but always looked forward to sharing with Dad. It's a wonder we weren't obese! One day Pino and I sat at the table, watching Dad cook.

Seeing us eyeballing his every move, he asked, "Are you two hungry?"

"No, Papá. We ate already," I said. "We just want to watch."

When the spaghetti was done, Dad strained it in the *scolapasta*. (To this day, I still have trouble calling it a *colander* or *pasta strainer!*) Realizing he didn't have sauce, Dad went on to make some. Pino and I started picking at the spaghetti, our heads tilted back, spiraling into our mouths one long strand after another. When Dad returned with the tomato sauce, he stopped in his tracks at the now empty *scolapasta.*

"Where did the spaghetti go?"

"We were playing with the spaghetti and—"

"Playing with the spaghetti? Why didn't you go outside and play?" Dad grumbled as he went to cook another batch of spaghetti, but not before taking the sauce with him.

There are memories I am not sure are real or reconstructed. My earliest childhood memory was when I was about three. I'm playing in front of our house, when suddenly a horse galloped toward me, and I fell to the ground.

Years later, when I asked my mom about it, she said, "I remember that I was sitting on the stoop with your brother on my lap, watching you play by our doorstep. I heard loud thumping sounds, and when I looked up, I saw a horse running loose. Before I could reach you, the horse raced past, and you were on the ground."

"Did the horse knock me down?" I asked.

"No, you tripped trying to get out of the horse's way."

"Did I cry? I don't remember anything else."

"You were screaming. I was terrified because I didn't know how badly hurt you were. We took you to the doctor, and you had to have stitches on your forehead."

"I still have the scar."

"A couple of days later, you said your mouth hurt. Your gums were red and swollen, and pus was oozing from them. We took you back to the doctor, who recommended we take you to a dentist in Canicattì. The dentist was concerned your baby teeth might come out too early and jeopardize the new ones. Thankfully, they stayed in until it was time for them to come out."

"Did you sue the horse's owner?"

"No. I don't remember people suing then. Your father did ask her to help with the medical expenses."

"Did she do that, at least?" I asked.

"No. She said if you hadn't been playing on the street, you wouldn't have been in the horse's path."

"And she got away with that?"

"We couldn't do anything about it. She refused to help."

We made several trips to Canicattì, which is about an hour's train ride, but I only remember one. It was on that trip that my doll met her demise. Nonna and I were on our way home when my doll fell on the ground. When I picked her up, she was covered with dirt and grease. At home, Nonna filled the basin with soapy water, and I placed my doll in it. I scrubbed and scrubbed, trying to get the greasy dirt off. When I took her out of the basin, the sawdust inside her had rearranged itself and turned her into a shapeless blob. I cried at the loss of my precious rag doll.

I find it strange that while I can recall many incidents, I recall very few names and faces. My brother and I played in the courtyard and out front with the kids in the neighborhood, yet I only remember two. One was Pino's friend Vito, and the other, Tania. I remember Vito because he and Pino were inseparable, and Tania because of her bright-red curly hair, which was unusual in our area. She lived just across the street and was the girl who, according to my nonna, picked at the scab on Nonna Angela's nose, causing her to get sick and die. Tania was a few years older than I and liked teasing me, taking pleasure in telling me that her family had taken possession of Dad's dog, Giulia, when Dad was in the army. Nonna had probably found the dog a nuisance and gave her to Tania's family. Giulia was a sweet dog with a white coat and black spots. I don't know if this upset my father, but it upset me very much. Tania had what I thought to be mine, and I wanted her back.

There are two adults who still live in my memory. One is a young woman who lived down the street. She lived alone and always dressed in black, from her kerchief to her laced-up shoes. She couldn't speak and made ear-splitting sounds, especially when agitated. Because she couldn't speak, everyone, including Nonna, called her *La Muta*. Nonna and *La Muta* got along very well, and she often invited her to dine with us. Pino and I were on our best behavior when she was around because if we weren't, she'd glare at us with those black eyes of hers that cut into us like laser beams.

One day as Pino and I were playing with a stick, we accidentally poked Nonna in the eye. *La Muta* took the stick and threatened us with it, all the while fixing her laser beam eyes on us and making horrific screeching sounds.

Pino and I cried, "We didn't mean to hurt Nonna! Honest, we didn't!"

It wasn't until Nonna told her to leave us be, that she finally quieted down. At times, Nonna had me take meals to her. All there was in the stark room was a small bed, a table, and a chair. The only sources of light came from a small window and kerosene lamp, which made the room even more depressing. Even as a child, I sensed she was not only very poor, but also very lonely, and I felt sorry for her and was glad Nonna had her over often, even though she terrified me so.

The second adult I remember was an old man who appeared in a recurring nightmare that began in Sicily, followed me to America, and tormented me well into my twenties. The dream began with a man donning a black leather apron and standing over a conveyor belt while holding a hammer. His black hair partially covered his face and bounced in rhythm with each pound of the hammer on the conveyor belt. With each hammer blow, the man moved closer and closer to me until there was nothing else in the frame except his huge, frightening face. That's when I'd wake up screaming. At times, not yet asleep, I would close my eyes and star-like objects would beam light on the conveyor belt and the man. Frightened, I'd put the pillow over my head, trying to stop the man's face from coming closer. Years later, when I told my mom about my nightmare, she said there was a shoemaker, a nice man, who was not pleasant looking—Mom's way of saying he was ugly. Our shoes were custom made, so I must have gone to his shop, but I have no memory of it. The man was bent over and looked very much like Quasimodo, the sad hunchback of Notre Dame. I was about two years old the first time I saw the man, and howled at the sight of him. I had the same reaction whenever I encountered him, which must have made the poor man cringe. It had to have upset him that his appearance could frighten a child so.

Though I was in the middle of my second year in grammar school when we left Sicily, I have no memory of the classroom, my teachers, or my schoolmates; their names and faces have long since faded. I remember that we spoke Sicilian at home and standard Italian in school. This didn't seem odd, as I thought of Italian as a second language. There are more than a few differences between the Italian dialects and standard Italian. I find it amusing that words spoken in the same country can have such diametric meanings. A rather strange and funny example is the word *babbo*. In certain parts of Italy, *babbo* means *dad*, while in other parts, it means *idiot*. There's a tale of a Sicilian boy who goes off to college in Northern Italy, and when he returns, he calls his father *babbo*. His incensed father howls, "I send you off to college so you can call me an idiot? I must be an idiot!" Coming from Sicily, we'd never call our dad *babbo* unless we wanted a hard smack.

While I vividly recall the daily early-morning hair-combing ritual—during which I'd howl because my hair always managed to become tangled while I slept—I have no memory of our bathroom. One would think a person would remember a place that was used more than once a day every day. It's as though I were one of those characters you see in movies and on television who never go to the bathroom. Mom tells me we used potties, which were then emptied onto piles of hay in the barn before the hay was turned over with a pitchfork. A horse-drawn carriage made its rounds much like a sanitation truck and hauled the hay which would be used as fertilizer.

As for sanitation trucks, there wasn't any need because people didn't generate garbage. Food scraps, eggshells, and bones were turned into compost. Purchased food items were not prepackaged. Pasta was usually homemade, and if purchased, was wrapped in paper that was used to light the fire. The ricotta was supplied by the shepherd, who refilled our personal container. Having no electricity meant no refrigerators; iceboxes were used—the ice, delivered by the roving ice man.

It's said we remember a surprising amount of detail from pleasant, traumatic, and emotional events. My childhood memories in Sicily, for the most part, are quite pleasant. I remember being thrilled to be starting school, as was my proud father, who walked me to the stationer's to pick up a notebook, pencils, and an eraser. Dad said that if I ever needed anything, I could always ask the nice stationer. On the first day of school, a couple of my friends showed up without their notebooks and pencils. I told them I knew where we could get some and led them to the stationery store, where they made their selections. Sometime later, Dad received the bill.

"It looks like you bought a lot at the stationery store," Dad said.

"I didn't buy anything. My friends didn't have their notebooks or pencils, and the nice man said they could take what they wanted."

"Now the nice man wants to be paid."

"But you said—"

"I said you can get things for *yourself*, not for your friends. Their parents have to buy their supplies."

Seeing that I had misunderstood and that the stationer had taken advantage of that fact, Dad didn't reprimand me.

My first-grade report card lists good grades in all my subjects: religion; moral, civil, and physical education; Italian; arithmetic; and handwriting. I had all A's and A+ (nines and tens in Sicily) by the end of the school year. While I don't remember my teachers, I do remember the nun who taught my religion class. Nuns frightened me. It was most likely due to their black habits, which I found intimidating. The nuns I knew were also very strict and, at times, mean. One time, a nun didn't allow me to participate in an activity because I didn't have the required blue ribbon which girls wore in their hair. I imagine it had to be a blue ribbon to complement the Madonna's blue cloak. I ran home crying. Luckily, Nonna got the blue ribbon, made a bow, secured it on the top of my head, and I ran back in time to join the others.

Sometimes, just walking to and from school was an adventure. One afternoon, still groggy from the dreaded siesta, I was sauntering back to school when I spotted a woman sitting on her doorstep with a huge bowl on her lap. She was wielding a knife, repeatedly striking something in the bowl. Curious, I walked over to take a look. The sight of the disgusting slippery eel spinning around the bowl while trying to escape snapped me out of my stupor, and I ran all the way to school!

Another day, walking with a group of friends, I saw boys up ahead peering into a window of a house and laughing hysterically. My friends and I ran over, and through the window, we saw a woman sitting on the floor, slamming her head from side to side and pulling at her hair. I thought it pitiful and couldn't understand why the boys thought it funny. Years later, I saw a TV program on autism in which a little boy wearing a protective helmet slammed his head from side to side against the cabinets. It immediately reminded me of that woman in Sicily, who must also have been autistic.

While I never doubted that Nonna loved both my brother and me, and that she would never let any harm come to us, I sometimes questioned her judgment when it came to our health and well-being. When I was about five, I had a toothache. Nonna took me to the clinic, where we were greeted by a hefty nun who led us into a room. The nun picked me up and placed me on a chair so huge, three of me could've comfortably fit in it. Frightened, I gazed around the room and froze at the sight of the tray with terrifying objects. Like most children, I was afraid of doctors in general. When Mom took me for routine checkups, I'd sit on the examining table, knees pressed tightly together, with both hands clutching the hem of my dress, prompting the doctor to quip, "If only this little girl behaves like this when she grows up, you won't have any worry!"

The nun moved the torture tray closer, bent over me, and told me to say, "Ahhhh." All I could think about were the humongous pliers sitting on that tray. I didn't know what the nun was going to do with those pliers, but I didn't want to stick around to find out. I slipped down and out of the chair and bolted out of the room, running as fast as I could. The sheer terror of those pliers put wings on my feet, and I was off like a streak of lightning. I turned back to look and saw the nun and Nonna in hot pursuit, now joined by a mob of random mothers. I came to a door and dashed to freedom. I was standing outside panting when Nonna, also panting, appeared.

"Why did you run away?" she gasped.

"I was scared."

"Let's go back in, say you're sorry, the nice nun will look at your tooth, and—"

"I don't want to go back," I wailed. "I don't care that my tooth hurts!"

Nonna sighed and took my hand, and I was happy we walked away from the clinic. We came to a small building and, once inside, were greeted by a smiling young lady who led us into a room where a young man wearing a whiter-than-white jacket picked me up and sat me in a chair that was smaller than the one in the clinic. He said he had to pull my tooth out but that it wouldn't hurt very much, and when he finished, he'd give me a lollypop. He showed me the pliers and, unlike the humongous pair on the nun's torture tray, these were much smaller. When it was all over, I had a little pain, but the lollypop made me feel better. I was pleased with myself. Not only had I outrun Nonna, the nun, and all those mothers, but I also got to have my way.

However, Nonna wasn't at all pleased, and grumbled, "See how much money I had to give to the dentist! We didn't have to pay at the clinic!" As if that had any relevance to a five-year-old!

An extremely traumatic episode for me involved my brother. Whenever he had a cold or an earache, it was almost always accompanied by a fever. When Nonna thought his fever too high, she called for a nurse, surely not a medically trained one. In my opinion, the nurse was a quack. I watched as she removed Pino's shirt and had him lie face down on the bed. She then lit a flame in each of four small glasses and placed the flame-glowing glasses on his back. When a dark, round lump formed under the glass, she would remove the glass, which made a loud sucking sound. It's a wonder the glass didn't shatter. The terrifying part came next, when the quack placed a small, circular metal object over the lump, and blood squirted out. At the sight of the blood, I screamed and kicked the quack and Nonna too. They picked me up, still screaming and kicking, and threw me out so they could continue with their dastardly deed. The procedure is called *ventosa*, which our nonna called *ventusi* and is believed to rid the body of infection and lower a fever. My brother survived the barbaric treatment, but unfortunately, he was left with many tiny scars on his back. I consider myself lucky because, even to this day, I seldom have a fever.

Medical procedures weren't the only terrifying events of my childhood. The first time I went on an errand proved to be quite traumatic. Dad gave me what he said was the exact amount of money for a kilo of spaghetti. Pasta was not sold in boxes. You told the grocer how much you wanted, he weighed it, and then he wrapped it in paper. Shaky with the responsibility, I folded the lire Dad gave me, clutching the money safely in my hand, and headed out. I walked up the alleyway, onto the piazza, and into the grocery store.

The grocer seemed happy to see me on my first big mission, and said, "Hello, little girl."

"My father wants a kilo of spaghetti," I announced.

"Just a kilo?"

"That's all we want," I said.

"Very well," replied the grocer, who then proceeded to weigh and wrap the spaghetti. He handed me the package, and I handed over the money.

As I turned to leave, the grocer said, "Wait, little girl; here's your change."

Well, that threw me for a loop, but I quickly rebounded and told the grocer, "I don't want any change. My father said he gave me enough."

The grocer, looking somewhat amused, said, "When you tell your father you refused the change, he will send you back for it. If you don't take it now, I won't give it to you when you come back."

Confident that my father was always right, I defiantly told the grocer, "I won't come back!"

Having succeeded in making my first purchase, I walked home with a newfound pride. Dad greeted me with a smile and said, "Brava, Teresina, you did very well."

Thoroughly pleased with myself, I gushed, "It wasn't hard at all except when the man wanted to give me change. I told him I didn't want the change because you said you'd given me enough."

"That wasn't very smart to refuse money from the grocer, was it? He will think—"

"But you said—"

"Now go back, and tell the grocer you will take the change."

"But he said he won't give it to me."

"He will. He knows it's your first time."

I couldn't believe it. My father was making me go back! After all, he'd said he'd given me the right amount. Now I had to go back and ask for the change the grocer said he wouldn't give me. Dad must have viewed this as a teachable moment, but the experience was a painful one, as evidenced by the fact that I still remember it.

The walk back to the store took forever because I couldn't bear to face the man. When I finally arrived, instead of walking inside, I hesitated, and with my back up against the glass storefront, I slowly inched my way toward the doorway.

Seeing me standing there looking pitiful and loath to go in, the grocer said, "Oh, it's you again. I see your father sent you back. I told you he would."

I turned slowly and mumbled, "I'm sorry. You were right. Can I please have the change now?"

Appreciating that this was a tremendous ordeal for me, the grocer smiled and handed me the money. Relieved, I thanked him and ran out before he could change his mind.

After a while, going on errands became just another tedious chore. Returning from an errand one day, I stopped to watch a man who was teaching his grandson to ride a bike. I sat there hoping he would see me and offer to teach me too. After a while, they went inside. Disappointed that I didn't get to ride the bicycle, I trudged back home. A lot of time must have passed because as I approached the alleyway, I could see Dad at the other end giving me that menacing look of his, three fingers pinched together and waving his arm up and down, gesturing that I was going to get it. Seeing him looking so disagreeable, I was in no hurry to get home and walked even slower, which must have infuriated him even more. When I reached home, I was relieved that he didn't scold me. He must have realized that if a scolding were to have been waiting for him, he wouldn't have been in too much of a hurry to get home either.

While Dad never hit me, I feared him. He possessed a particularly menacing look that was more terrifying and far worse than being struck. Once, when Pino and I had been naughty and our nonna had told on us (as she always threatened to do but seldom did), Dad glared at us with that menacing look of his, his eyes open so wide, they looked as if they'd pop out. Terrified, the two of us stood there weeping.

"Why are you crying?" Nonna asked.

In unison, we said, "He hit us."

"How could he have hit you? He's at the other end of the room."

"He hit us with his eyes."

That's how intimidating his stare was.

As much as I loved my nonna, I missed my mother terribly, and was growing more and more disillusioned as the weeks, months, and years went by. Whenever I asked when we would see Mom again, I was told it would be soon. Dad helped me learn the words to the song "Mamma." He said that if I practiced, I could sing it to my mother. The first time I heard the song was in the 1941 film of the same name. The song resonated with me because it's about a son who's happy to be seeing his mother again. The Italian music is livelier and the lyrics are much more inspiring than the English lyrics I later heard Connie Francis sing. In the Italian version one is happy to be seeing their mother here on earth, while in the English version one looks forward to seeing their mother in Heaven.

Mom wrote often and at times sent photos and packages. Although I still recognized Mom, she looked different in the photos than I remembered. I liked her new hairstyle, her pretty dress and the shiny necklace and earrings she wore. She looked so pretty and modern. It seems that even as a youngster, I was aware of fashion and hairstyles. I have no memory of how I felt when I first saw the photo of Mom with a little boy. It must have been perplexing to me as a six-year-old. Added to that was the revelation that the boy was my brother. I'm sure I must have felt some level of resentment and jealousy. I must have thought: *Where did that boy come from? Why is he there with my mom? And why is she not here with us?* What I do remember is that I missed my mother terribly and couldn't wait for the day that we'd be together again.

Dad sent Mom a photo of the three of us with our names inscribed on our images and included a note saying, "I've written our names in case you've forgotten us." What Dad thought to be witty Mom thought it sarcastic and insensitive considering that the reason we were being kept apart was due to his problems.

I looked forward to the packages Mom sent because it meant that she still loved us and hadn't forgotten us. Excited, we opened our presents. There were dresses for me, shorts and shirts for my brother, and fabric to make Dad's suit. My very favorite thing in the world was a red wool coat with a matching muff and bonnet. There wasn't another like it in all of Sicily, which made me the envy of every girl. I so loved my American clothes! I'd hold fashion shows on my front stoop so that my friends would see all the wonderful things Mom had sent me. I'd tell them to sit on the stoop, and I'd run inside to put on the first dress. I don't think I had ever seen models on a runway before, but I somehow knew what to do. I walked out, did a little pirouette, and hesitated for a moment or two at each turn, giving my captivated audience just enough time to admire the front, sides, and back. Then I'd strut inside, put on the next dress, and repeat the performance.

This annoyed Nonna, who'd scold me, saying, "Stop being such a *sciusciuna*! It's not nice to make your friends jealous!" Nonna called me *sciusciuna* (shoo-shoo-nah) one of her names for me when she thought I was being haughty.

"I'm not a showoff," I protested. "My friends have their mothers at home, but my mother is far away. I want them to know that my mother sent me all these beautiful things because she loves me."

In Sicily, our clothes and shoes were custom made, which today, is considered a luxury, but back then, it was commonplace. My brother's suit—which consisted of a jacket and short pants—was made from the remnants of the fabric used to make our father's suit. Like all the boys, my brother wore shorts in both summer and winter. Our dressmaker made all my dresses, but nothing compared to the beautiful store-bought American dresses Mom sent. In the photos taken in Sicily, I'm wearing the strand of pearls that Mom left behind. Nonna scolded me whenever I wanted to finish my look with a piece of jewelry, telling me that jewelry is for big girls. I also loved wearing Mom's pin, a white enamel butterfly pin with big shiny stones for eyes and lots of small shiny stones on the wings. Nonna pinned the butterfly pin to my sweater, and when I returned from school crying, she asked, "Why are you crying?"

"My pin is gone."

"Did you lose it?"

"No, I didn't lose it!"

"Well, where is it then?"

"A lady said it was pretty, and she wanted to put it on. She took it off me and walked away."

"That's why little girls shouldn't wear jewelry!" Nonna said.

To my way of thinking, that woman, whoever she was, was a poor excuse of a human being, stealing from a child.

* * *

With the second trial hanging over Dad's head, his anxieties must have overwhelmed him at times. He knew he was innocent, but at the same time, he was not sure of what the outcome would be. Being kept in limbo and having no control over his life had to be torture for him. There were times when he must have needed to get away from it all and sought comfort, giving in to the temptations that came his way.

One day Dad took me out for what I thought was going to be a special day. We stopped at a house, and Dad knocked on the door. A woman I had never seen before let us in. She had a little boy who couldn't walk yet, and he was crawling on the floor. The woman gave her son and me some cookies and milk while she and Dad sat at a table, sipping wine. After a while, Dad and the lady stood up.

"We're going out for a little while," Dad said. "Play with the little boy. We'll be back soon."

I wanted to ask where he was going, but before I could, they left the room. I couldn't understand why he'd left me there. I didn't want to go anywhere near that boy. Not only was he dirty, with cookie crumbs all over his face, hands, and clothes, but also, he smelled. Later, when they returned, Dad made the biggest blunder he could've possibly made, one he would come to regret.

"How would you like this nice lady to be your mother?" he asked me.

206

"I have a mother!" I screamed.

After my outburst, my father said we had to go, and took my hand, leading me out the door. Outside, I pulled my hand away from his and walked in silence. I must have been five at the time, but that remark still upsets me because I couldn't understand how my father could have been so cruel and insensitive. *What was he thinking? Had he given up on my mother? Was she never coming back?* Horrible, scary thoughts were flooding my head. I needed my nonna. When we finally reached home, Dad said he was going to the piazza and headed toward the alleyway. I ran into the house and straight into Nonna's arms. The tears I had suppressed burst like a dam.

"What wrong, Tre-Tre? Why are you crying? Tell me what's wrong."

Nonna sat me on her lap and rocked me, and through my tears, I told Nonna everything. I told her about the lady, about the dirty boy, and about the worst part: Dad asking me if I wanted the woman to be my mother.

"Do you know where the woman lives?"

"Yes," I said.

"Take me there."

Nonna walked so fast, I had to run to keep up. When we reached the house, she told me to wait outside. She knocked on the door, and the woman opened it. Nonna rushed in, closing the door behind her. Even with the door closed, I could hear the woman's squeals after each slap. Nonna came out, and we headed home. I knew Nonna would set things straight. There was no way she'd ever let that woman take my mother's place! When Dad returned, Nonna told me to go out and play. She must have given him more than a piece of her mind. What was he thinking, taking his daughter as a decoy to a lover's rendezvous! Dad never said a word to me. The fact that Nonna reprimanded Dad, an adult, made me understand how powerful she was. I didn't feel any remorse for tattling on Dad. Besides, he hadn't said I couldn't tell Nonna where we'd been.

* * *

It's not surprising that, like everything else in Sicily, the wheels of justice moved ever so slowly. It would take another eighteen months before Dad's second trial would get underway. It was at this trial that the truth finally emerged: the captain of the *caserma* had taken the firearms. It appears that in addition to his day job, the captain—who hailed from Northern Italy—moonlighted for the Mafia.

This pretty much debunked the idea that Northerners couldn't or wouldn't be bribed! There was never a doubt that the captain was on the take. Mom recalls that the few times she visited the captain and his corpulent wife, their table was filled with cheese wheels, whole salamis, and other delicacies.

Dad was finally cleared of all charges, and we were free to sail to America. It was a hard-won victory that had taken three long years. The Mafia's thirst for vengeance didn't only hurt my dad; it also separated two little children from their mother and one from his father. Nonna believed it was no coincidence that the charges leveled against Dad had arisen just as we were about to leave. Mafiosi, a cruel calculating bunch, wanted to get even with Dad for not playing along and were in no rush, waiting for the right moment when they could inflict the most harm. They wielded enormous power and had their minions do their bidding, in this case, making false accusations that would hurt Dad not only financially, but also by delaying his trip and possibly preventing him from ever leaving.

Across the miles…

Mom and Antonio in New York

Dad, me, and Pino in Sicily

14

SAILING TO AMERICA

I DON'T THINK PINO UNDERSTOOD that we were not coming back. He most likely thought we were going on a boat ride, an adventure he'd share with his best friend, Vito. I did understand and was deeply torn. While thrilled I'd be seeing Mom again and meeting my brother Antonio, grandparents, and aunt and uncle for the first time, I hated having to say goodbye to my family and friends. Leaving Nonna without knowing if I'd ever see her again was hardest of all. Those three years that our mother was away, Nonna had cared for Pino and me, never looking at it as a chore, but a joy, taking us along everywhere she went. I believe she liked doing with us all the things she would have liked to have done with her own children but hadn't gotten a chance to.

At our farewell party, Pino and I received neat parting gifts. I got a miniature kitchen set with a stove, pots and pans, cups, dishes, and tiny utensils. Nonna packed it away in the big trunk we were taking to America. We also received boring gifts: knitted hats, scarves, and gloves, which came in handy when crossing the Atlantic in the dead of winter.

After having heard my early-morning wails as Nonna combed and plaited my waist-long hair that always managed to get tangled, Dad didn't want any part of it. To make this chore easier for him, it was decided that I would have my hair cut. With just two snips of the beautician's scissors, my two braids were gone. The perpetrator said she would give me pretty curls, but her words didn't ease my pain. I couldn't help think that, along with everything else, I was also parting with my braids, which had been a part of me for as long as I could remember. She then proceeded to crown my head with cylinders, dabbing them with a nasty-smelling liquid. I sat in that chair for what seemed an eternity as she unwound and rewound the cylinders, checking to see if the perm had set. When she finally removed all the cylinders, an unruly mass of curls fell over my face. She washed and towel-dried my hair and said we were almost done. Then she began rolling my hair onto rollers and placed me under a huge helmet, which was very hot and noisy. When it was finally lifted, it took a while for my head to stop humming. She removed the rollers, combed my hair, and pinned it back with two sparkly pins. Had I seen one of those Shirley Temple movies, I might have taken to the look. Nonna looked pleased, confident my new hairdo would be easier for Dad. Pino's reaction was just what I expected: he pointed at me and cackled. Considering what I'd endured to make life easier for Dad, I figured he owed me big time!

*Bon voyage! Nonna at center with Dad holding a glass to her lips;
Pino on Cousin Gina's lap; me at front right, sporting my new perm*

With our possessions packed into the humongous trunk and sent
ahead along with our luggage, we were set to go. Nonna accompanied
us to the railway station. We boarded the first car, and Pino and I
headed for the front window so that we could see the tracks ahead.
Nonna and Dad took their seats, and even though he whispered, I
could hear Dad tell Nonna that she should get off at her stop without
saying goodbye to us because we'd cry. I wanted to turn around and
give her a great big hug and tell her how much I loved her and how
much I'd miss her, but I didn't. I didn't want to make her any sadder
than she already was. When the train stopped, Nonna got off, and
I continued to stare ahead, weeping silently, knowing Nonna, too,
would be weeping.

When we reached the Palermo station, Dad hailed a taxi to take
us to the port. He pointed to the ship we'd be taking, a small dark-
gray vessel with two huge smokestacks spewing clouds of smoke.
As soon as I got on board, the foul fuel odor and incessant rocking

made me seasick. Dad rushed me into the men's room, one of many I would visit during our voyage. I was relieved when Dad said we'd be getting off that ship the next morning.

When the ship docked in Naples, I couldn't wait to have my feet on terra firma. We disembarked, and as we were walking, throngs of people swirled around us, speaking quite rapidly in a language I didn't understand.

"Papá are we in America?" I asked.

Dad chuckled and said, "No, we are still in Italy. We have a few more days to go before we reach America."

"How come people aren't speaking Italian?"

"We're in Naples," Dad said. "People in Naples speak the Neapolitan dialect."

Neapolitan didn't sound anything like Sicilian or the standard Italian we spoke in school. Dad then pointed to the SS *Constitution*, the ship that would be taking us to America. Years later, I learned that the elegant ocean liner had begun her long career of sailing the transatlantic route with her maiden voyage in June of 1951. In 1955, she was featured in an episode of *I Love Lucy* in which a hapless Lucy has to be ferried to the ship by helicopter. In April 1956, she carried Grace Kelly from New York to Europe, where she went from American movie star to Princess of Monaco. The majestic ship went on to have a featured role on the big screen in the 1957 film, *An Affair to Remember*. I wish we had traveled in summer instead of winter so that just like Cary Grant and Deborah Kerr, we would've lounged by the pool on the lido deck! However, when I think about my grandparents and their children crossing the Atlantic in steerage, I consider myself fortunate to have lived at a time when we traveled not only in comfort, but also in splendor!

Our cabin was neatly furnished, with daylight filtering in through the portholes. Pino claimed the upper bunk bed, and I was relegated to the lower one. Having always shared a bed with Pino and Nonna, I greatly enjoyed having a bed all to myself. Despite our father's scolding, Pino and I constantly flushed the toilet in our bathroom just to see the water swirling round and round. Accustomed to oil lamps, we loved turning the lights on and off by flicking the switch. There was a rather peculiar item that sat on the desk that both intrigued and stupefied Pino and me for the longest time. It was black and had a long, curly wire. Dad said it was used for speaking with others who were not in the room. I couldn't see how that was possible.

Even though the SS *Constitution* was a lot bigger than the steamboat and didn't have the nasty fuel smell, I still got seasick. Dad took me to the infirmary, where I was given seasickness pills. I had always had difficulty swallowing pills, unlike my little brother, who had no trouble at all, which really infuriated me. The time Pino and I had the same ailment, he was given pills, and I, a powder, which when dissolved in water, created a milky froth that smelled like rotten eggs. I despaired having to drink that foul concoction, the putrid-smelling bubbles making their way into my nostrils.

"Why don't you swallow the pills?" Nonna would say. "It's not hard. Your little brother does!" Couldn't she see that I wanted to but couldn't?

At times I was so seasick that I tried to swallow the pills, but to no avail.

One day Dad caught me flushing a pill down the toilet and snapped, "How are you going to get better doing that?"

Then he'd stand over me as I drank glass after glass of water, only to be disappointed at seeing the pill still sitting on my tongue. All those glasses of water eventually dissolved the immovable pill.

On days the sea was calm and my nausea didn't bother me, I joined my father and brother in the dining room. We sat at our very own table, and our friendly, Italian-speaking waiter greeted us. He recited the day's specials and told us we could make our selection from the menu. There was a lot to read and Dad helped us navigate through the *antipasti*, *primi*, *secondi*, and *dolci* sections. At first, my brother and I found it overwhelming, but we quickly got the hang of it and actually liked making our own selections, something we had never done before. Sometimes when the waiter set down our plates, Pino would have misgivings about his selection. The accommodating waiter told him he could select something else, which he happily did. When the waiter attempted to take his plate away, Pino asked him to leave it, just in case. In spite of Dad's reprimands, sometimes my little brother had three plates before him. The spunky five-year-old was not deterred.

"The nice man doesn't mind," Pino said. "And besides, we're not paying!"

Of all the diners in the dining room, I recall only one. He had a beefy face with a moustache so huge, it not only covered his upper lip, but also his lower one. I believe he dined alone, but I can't be sure because my eyes were fixed on him only. Pino and I were intrigued by the way he ate spaghetti. He loaded a huge amount onto his fork and shoved it into his mouth, leaving spaghetti strands dangling. Think of the hilarious *I Love Lucy* episode in which William Holden turns the tables on Lucy and gawks at her as she's eating spaghetti. She's at a loss as to what to do with the dangling strands until Ethel clips them with scissors she pulls out of her handbag. Our shipmate didn't need scissors. He simply chomped down and the strands fell onto his plate. Dad reprimanded us, saying we were being rude for staring at the man. I don't think we were being rude. We were simply intrigued by his technique. Anyway, I don't think our shipmate noticed because he was really into his spaghetti.

As we approached Genoa, many small boats surrounded our ship. The men in the boats sold hats, scarves, tablecloths, salami, cheese, fruit, and nuts. Thinking I'd like a better view, Dad sat me on the railing. I looked down and was terrified by the waves crashing against the ship. I wrapped my arms around his neck, not letting go until he put me down. Pino, who wasn't afraid of anything, pushed me aside so he could have his turn. Dad hoisted him up, sat him on the railing, and with both legs dangling over the side, he waved to the men below. Close to land there were lots of seagulls flying about, dipping their beaks into the water to catch fish. Eventually, the land, seagulls, and boats would desert us, leaving us to fend for ourselves in that vast ocean.

To Dad's dismay, my hair still managed to get tangled when I slept. Luckily, we met a nice lady on board who combed my hair, pinning it back with pretty pins. If only we had known, I wouldn't have had to leave my braids behind!

Pino and I, still captivated with that black thing on the desk, would periodically pick up the receiver from its cradle, but as soon as we heard the howling tone, we'd quickly put it back. One afternoon, several passengers came to visit us in our cabin. One of the ladies, seeing Pino holding an orange, took it and peeled it for him. Pino didn't want the orange peeled and began crying. Dad told him to stop his tears that he'd get him more oranges. He then walked over to the desk, picked up the handle-looking part, and held one end to his mouth and the other to his ear.

Then he spun the wheel with holes a few times and said, "We'd like some oranges, apples, and pears."

Wishful thinking, I thought as Pino kept crying.

A short time later, there was a knock at the door. Dad opened it, and a man carrying a bowl of fruit walked in. *How did the man know we wanted fruit? Did that black thing really talk to people?!* That was the day we first experienced the amazing power of the telephone!

When it wasn't too cold, we'd go out on deck to play shuffleboard or sit in deck chairs, cover ourselves with blankets, and watch the people strolling by. On days it was too cold or too windy, we would stay inside and venture into the library, which not only contained books, magazines, and newspapers, but also board games. It was on the ship that Pino and I learned to play checkers.

Sometimes Dad took us to the movie theater. The only film I recall seeing was set in the African jungle. And in the only part of the film that I remember, a man, naked except for a loincloth, is walking backward, his eyes open so wide, they look as if they'll pop out of his head. The scene then shifts to a growling lion and then fades, only to return to the lion sitting next to a pile of bones. Even though we didn't see the lion attack and eat the man, those bones told the whole story!

I was entrusted with the care of my little brother as far back as I can remember. It was my job to keep him out of trouble and see to it that no harm came to him. On the ship it was no different. My brother, much like the character Totò in *Cinema Paradiso*, always managed to get into jams, and, like Totò, he was winsome, rambunctious, and mischievous, and was never at a loss for words. Also, just like Totò, he would later transform into an exceedingly shy teenager. Once, alone in our cabin, the brat decided to climb onto the bureau to look out of the porthole. He reached for the knob and spun it round and round. With each spin, the color changed from clear to yellow, to green, to blue, to red. Worried that the window might pop open, I tried to get him down. He wouldn't budge, so I climbed up on the bureau just as Dad came in.

"What are you two doing up there?" Dad howled as he pulled us both down. "If that window opens, you'll fall into the ocean! And you . . . you're supposed to watch your little brother!"

Just like the children who followed the Pied Piper, Pino liked following the steward who rang the chimes at mealtimes. As soon as he heard the steward's chimes, he quickly set out with me following behind. We always managed to lose our way, but we were rescued by the accommodating steward, who then returned us to our cabin. The steward was so taken by my brother that on the last day of our trip, he gave him a little drum, telling him he could bang on it to announce mealtimes.

After what seemed an eternity at sea, we saw land on the horizon. As we approached the harbor, the Statue of Liberty came into view. The sight of that majestic lady as she welcomed us to her shores on that freezing February day filled me with awe. When we finally reached the pier, my eyes darted over the throngs of people, in search of my mom.

I spotted her below, tugged at my father's sleeve, and said, "Look, Papá, there's Mamma!"

Dad picked Pino up and said, "There's your Mamma; wave to her."

I don't think Pino remembered Mom because he just stood there, and for the first time, was at a loss. We stood on the deck for what seemed forever. The hat, coat, and gloves weren't enough to keep the chill out. I had never been so cold in all my life!

We finally disembarked, and Mom ran to us. We hugged and kissed, and Mom introduced us to our Pappou. I was confused because I was ready to call him Nonno. Pappou had white hair and looked very old. He kissed Pino and me and asked if we had a nice voyage. Then we all climbed into a taxi. Pappou sat in front with the driver, and Mom, Dad, Pino, and I sat in the back. As we rode, I was fascinated by all the tall buildings that looked as if they were trying to reach the sky. The taxi stopped in front of what I thought was a very tall and narrow house with lots of windows and balconies with ladders. I would soon discover that it was not a house but a building with many apartments and that the balconies with ladders were fire escapes.

We climbed up a flight of stairs to our apartment, dropped off our luggage, and headed to our grandparents' apartment just a block away. We climbed a long flight of stairs and were greeted by our yiayia, who spoke rapidly in a strange language I had never heard and didn't understand. What was more than shocking to me was that Mom and Dad also spoke that strange language. Pino and I gaped at each other and at our parents. Our mom said they were speaking Greek because Yiayia only spoke Greek.

Our brother Antonio sat at the kitchen table, quietly observing us. Mom took his hand, walked him over to us, and spoke to him in Greek and to us in Italian. It was all so strange. Pino and I looked at each other and then to Dad for guidance. As for our little brother, he just hid behind Mom's skirt.

The adults talked on and on, evidently having a lot to say, while we children quietly stared at them and at each other. Then Mom led us to our seats at the table. Sitting on our plates was a little square that looked and smelled scrumptious. The creamy béchamel sauce on top and between the alternating layers of noodles and chopped meat sauce was the best part. I later learned it was *pastitsio*, the Greek version of lasagna.

Sometime later, Aunt Eleni and Uncle Taki returned from work. They, too, spoke that strange language. I was disappointed we weren't able to speak with our new relatives and wondered how long it would be before we learned to speak Greek, and they, Italian.

PART THREE
AMERICA

15

Our New Home

T HE TWENTY LITTLE GOLD BOXES bearing the tenants' names in the foyer was an indication that twenty families lived in the four-story building. There were four apartments on each floor, with two communal bathrooms in the hall.

Our apartment was directly above the grocery store. You would enter into the eat-in kitchen, and there was a built-in hutch by the entranceway. It had two windows—one over the sink looked out to apartment buildings across the way, and the second window faced the adjoining building and was separated by a narrow tar-covered walkway. By the side of the sink there was a stove and on the other side a bathtub covered with a long white metal lid that served as a countertop. A chrome-trimmed Formica table and six chairs sat in the middle of the room. The speckled pink design on the Formica top

complemented the vinyl cushion seats. Beige vinyl flooring punctu-
ated with black flecks ran throughout the three-room apartment. The
next room had a chest of drawers and bunk beds for my brothers.
Just ahead of that was a tiny room, more of an alcove with a built-in
closet and hutch on one side and a sleeping cot for me on the other.
These two rooms had no windows. The third room faced the avenue
and served two functions: a living room by day and a bedroom for
our parents at night.

A few years ago, I walked by my old neighborhood and was
surprised to see that the two buildings were inscribed with names
of states. Our building was the *Maine,* and the adjoining one, the
Oregon. I found out that the three-room apartment that we rented
for $25 a month now rents for over $3,000 a month! For that steep
rent increase, I do hope that the bathroom is in the apartment and
not in the hall and that the bathtub with the unwieldy metal lid is
no longer in the kitchen!

On my first morning in America, I was jolted awake by a loud
clanging coming through the front window. Curious, I crept into my
parents' room to look out. On the street below, there were men lifting
metal cans and tossing the contents into a huge truck that looked
like a monstrous beast noisily chewing, spewing, and grunting as it
rumbled down the street. Everyone still asleep, I crept back into bed.

Sometime later, I heard Mom's cheery voice saying, "It's time
for all sleepyheads to wake up! We're going to Yiayia's for breakfast."

Still groggy from sleep, my brothers and I crawled out of our beds
and lined up for the hall bathroom.

Walking to our grandparents' apartment, I noticed that their
building had a bakery at the street level, while ours had a grocery
store. We climbed up to the first floor and were greeted by the aroma

of freshly brewed coffee and by our smiling pappou, who hugged and kissed us.

"Did you sleep well your first night in America?" he asked.

"Very well, Nonno," I said, quickly correcting myself: "Very well, Pappou."

"That's all right. You can call me Nonno, if you'd like."

My brothers and I took our places at the table. Mom gave us toast slathered with sweet butter and marmalade and a cup of hot milk with two spoonfuls of coffee in it. Our parents took their coffee with two spoonfuls of milk. I took a bite of the toast, savoring the sweet butter and tangy strawberry marmalade, and followed it with a sip of the creamy milk. The delightful fragrance of the butter and marmalade on warm toast and the aromatic coffee filled the apartment and lingered in the air long after breakfast. In Sicily, our breakfast consisted of either *pane e latte*, a *frittata* made with eggs and leftover pasta, a boiled vegetable and bread, or warm ricotta on bread. The Sicilian fare couldn't compare with the many American breakfast offerings we'd later enjoy, such as French toast, waffles, and pancakes doused with maple syrup; bacon and eggs; and a huge assortment of cereals.

* * *

While I'd had no preconceptions of what America was like, I may have heard stories about America having streets paved with gold. But treeless Ninth Avenue with its gray apartment buildings that formed a continuous strip was not at all what I'd expected. Even our playground was devoid of trees and grass. I also found apartment living very confining, and despaired, thinking that Ninth Avenue was my America. While our home in Sicily was by no means sumptuous, it was nonetheless warm and inviting both inside and out, with its butter-colored exterior, terra-cotta–tiled roof, and lush green trees that not only shimmered under the Sicilian sun but also provided shade and soft summer breezes.

There were a couple of things in our Manhattan apartment that fascinated Pino and me. One was the bare bulb hanging from a cord. We thrilled by being able to turn the light on and off simply by pulling on a string. Our parents later covered the bulb with a fixture, softening the glare. Another was the little box on the kitchen counter that periodically spoke and played music. When I asked Mom where the voices and music were coming from, she said they traveled through wires. Her explanation didn't make sense to me at all. I believed there had to be little people in that box, and that one day, I'd catch them coming out. A year later, when we got our television, the little people could not only be heard; they could also be seen. I had been right all along!

One thing in the apartment that should have impressed me more but didn't was the indoor plumbing. This was most likely because as a small child in Sicily, I didn't have to haul water from the well. Bathing time in Manhattan was less of an ordeal for Mom than it had been in Sicily, although she did have to remove all the items from the countertop, wrestle with the unwieldy metal lid that covered the tub and heat the water when the hot water ran out, which it usually did.

The hot water wasn't the only thing to run out in our building. On Sundays, when most tenants were cooking Sunday dinner, the gas would peter out. One time, Mom had the bright idea of precooking our Sunday dinner. While the veal was roasting, she sat on the bed, mending socks, and in the quiet of the night, she dozed off. Sometime later, she awoke to smoke and ran into the kitchen, which was engulfed in smoke. She turned off the oven and opened all the windows, relieved that she'd awakened before any real damage had occurred. However, the roast didn't fare too well, having shrunk into a small, burnt chunk!

When Dad returned from work some time later, he asked, "Was there a fire here? The hall's full of smoke."

"No, no fire, just a little smoke," Mom replied.

Needless to say, Mom never precooked Sunday dinner again.

* * *

Our parents wanted to enroll us in parochial school. However, Mother Superior at Holy Cross Catholic School, upon learning that Mom was Greek Orthodox and my three-year-old brother, Antonio, had yet to be baptized, was less than welcoming. In her view, we were not good Catholics. Our parents didn't much care for her attitude, and enrolled us in public school instead. We attended St. Raphael Catholic Church for catechism lessons, and it was there that we received our First Communion, and later, Confirmation.

Our elementary school, PS 127, was located on Thirty-Eighth Street between Tenth and Eleventh Avenues. There were two classes for each of the kindergarten–sixth grades in the quaint building. Years later when I visited my old neighborhood I was saddened to see that the building that housed my school was no longer there and in its place a skyscraper.

I was placed in second grade, and Pino, in kindergarten. I attended full day, and Pino, half day. It was in school that he was given the name *Joseph*, English for *Giuseppe*. On my first day, I cried because I didn't understand a thing my teacher said. She sat me next to an Italian-speaking girl named Anne Marie. I was relieved to hear her speak the only language I understood. A sweet and kind girl, Anne Marie was a tremendous help to me in those first days. The best part about my new school was that just down the block there were stables with real, live horses. My classmates and I frequently walked over to see them, and the friendly stable hands sometimes let us pet their shiny coats. I missed our sweet donkey, and just seeing and petting those horses reminded me of the wonderful times I'd had with Ciro.

School lunch was served in what once must have been a stately residence. Even as a seven-year-old, I thought the placement of the converted mansion incongruous to the neighborhood. What made it even more so was the prison just across the street, with its thick iron bars on all the windows.

Lunch was served in a spacious room with a high ceiling and crystal chandeliers. We made our selection from the hot and cold offerings and took a seat at one of the many round tables. The hot counter contained frankfurters sliced into thin rounds and immersed in a bowl of baked beans. There was also macaroni and cheese, and pasta swimming in tomato sauce. I preferred the cold fare, especially the peanut butter and jelly sandwich. Lunch also included a small container of milk and desserts such as Jell-O, pudding, ice cream, cookies, or fruit. I loved having lunch in that elegant room, but unfortunately, when we returned that September, our mansion was gone, and all that remained was an empty lot. From then on, only cold lunch was served in the school cafeteria, which was a far cry from our beautiful sunlit dining room.

A couple of weeks after we arrived, the city was hit by a north-easter. It was the biggest snowstorm that winter, and it was the first time Joe and I had ever seen snow. We were in awe of the big white flakes falling from the sky, which covered Ninth Avenue in a blanket of white. We each put on our boots, jacket, hat, and scarf and headed out. Navigating was a challenge, as the front steps were totally hidden, but we soon got the hang of it, kicking up the powdery snow as we made our way down. There were no cars out that morning, only children playing. Some were on the ground, making snow angels. Some were riding sleds, and others were throwing snowballs at one another. Later, the snowplow came through, spraying salt and sand, and the store owners shoveled the snow to the curb, creating huge gray mounds and rendering our winter wonderland no more.

Mom couldn't always take me to school and asked a friend if her daughter, who was in fourth grade, would take me. When the woman's daughter and her friend came to pick me up, they didn't say a word to me. They walked ahead, babbling in Greek and English, not paying any attention to me except when we came to a puddle. That's when they'd each take my hand, and on the pretext of preventing me from stepping into the puddle, lift me up high and lower me just in time to land my feet right, smack into it, getting my shoes and socks wet. These big girls most likely didn't want to have a pip-squeak—and a foreigner, to boot—tagging along, so they made the trip as miserable as possible for me.

I'd endured their cruelty for three days when I finally told my mom, "I don't want to walk with them anymore. I can walk to school by myself."

Mom protested, saying she did not want me to cross the streets on my own. However, when I told her what the girls had done, Mom relented and let me go alone. The school's crossing guard on Tenth Avenue made crossing that wide street onto Eleventh Avenue a lot easier and safer.

Unfortunately, the two mean Greek girls wouldn't be the only ones who mocked me in those early days. Children can be very cruel to those who look and sound different from them. They'd mock or play tricks on unsuspecting, naïve children. I've heard of kids who were goaded into placing their tongue on fire hydrants in winter. You had to be really stupid to lick a fire hydrant, but some kids did and got their tongue stuck to its frozen surface!

There was an incident that could have gotten me into a heap of trouble, not only with my parents, but also with the police. Since I was the new kid on the block as well as a foreigner, a couple of my so-called "friends" persuaded me to pull the handle of what I didn't know then was the fire alarm box. I don't recall what they said would happen, but they definitely didn't tell me that fire engines would come blaring down the street. As soon as I pulled the handle, the kids darted off. Frightened, I, too, ran home. A short time later, I heard sirens and ran to the window, mortified to see all those fire engines.

Mom looked out the window too, shook her head, and said, "Those terrible children set off the alarm again! If they're caught, they'll be punished, and they deserve it!"

As far as I knew, only my accomplices and I were aware that *I* was that terrible child. For the longest time, I lived in fear, thinking I would be found out!

At the end of our first school year, there was a moving-up cere-mony. Principal Cagan escorted Joe and me onto the stage and told the audience of the remarkable progress we had made. She said we had worked hard and now spoke English with barely an accent. Miss Cagan also made note of my new haircut, a short bob with bangs, saying I looked more like a little Dutch girl than an Italian one. Actually, I looked more like the famous Dutch boy on the paint can!

A week before our first Christmas in America, two girls who had to have been the original mean girls gleefully told me, "On Christmas Eve, Santa Claus comes down the chimney and puts presents under the tree."

"We don't have a chimney," I said.

"That's OK. Lots of people don't have chimneys," one of the girls replied.

"I don't have a chimney," her friend said. "Santa comes anyway."

"Who's Santa?"

"You don't know Santa Claus?"

"No."

"Santa brings presents to children who are good. Maybe he didn't come to your house because you were bad."

"I wasn't bad. My brother, maybe, but—"

"You must have been bad if Santa didn't come to your house!"

"I don't think he ever came to Sicily," I said. "Nobody ever saw him."

"You don't see him! Santa comes when you're sleeping. He comes on Christmas Eve, except . . ."

"You gonna tell her?"

"Yeah, I think we should."

"Tell me what?" I asked.

"Santa won't come anymore."

"How come?"

"Well, last year, Santa slipped off the roof, broke his neck, and died. So, no more Santa and no more presents."

With tears streaming down my face, I ran home to Mom, who listened patiently as I blurted out the sad tale.

When I finished, she wiped away my tears and said, "Those girls were just teasing. That wasn't very nice. But Santa isn't real.

He's make-believe. Parents buy the presents and put them under the Christmas tree."

I'd had Santa in my life for only a couple of minutes, and yet it was heartbreaking to learn he didn't exist. I can't imagine how the experience was for those kids who'd believed in Santa their entire lives to learn he wasn't real.

That first Christmas, Dad brought home a Christmas tree. He set it up with lights that blinked on and off and brightened up the room. Mom wrapped garland around the tree and hung sparkly ornaments on the high branches and let us hang ornaments and icicles onto the lower branches. Like most children, we loved having that tree with all the lights and ornaments but hated it when our parents said it was time to take it down.

Living in Sicily, I had never heard of the jolly, gift-giving Santa Claus. As children, we were told that Christmas was a celebration of Christ's birth, and we celebrated by going to Mass. The celebration continued with a festive meal. We received presents on January 6, Epiphany, which commemorates the visit of the Three Kings to the Christ child.

On New Year's Eve, we celebrated by going to the town square to see the fireworks display. Children flew stringed balloons and ate ice cream and cake. The main attraction was the young men who attempted to climb the slippery pole to claim the prize at the top. It was exciting to watch them trying to climb up, most failing to reach the summit. When most of the grease was wiped clean by those who'd gone before, one lucky participant made it to the top.

In Sicily we had our very own make-believe stories. Children were told that on All Souls' Day, their dearly departed relatives came down from Heaven to bring children gifts. Nonna often spoke of Nonno

Giuseppe, who had died in America when our father was a little boy. She said he loved us and always brought us gifts.

"Is Nonno really going to come?" I asked.

"Nonno always comes," Nonna replied.

"How does he come in? Do you leave the door open?"

"He knows the way in."

"Can I stay up? I want to stay up so I can see him."

"You have to go to sleep. He won't come if you're awake."

"Doesn't Nonno *want* me to see him?"

"He only comes when you're asleep."

That night I tried to stay awake, but sleep got the better of me. The next morning Joe and I began our search, and to our delight, found the marzipan fruits, chocolates, and nuts that Nonno had left for us. I was happy he'd come but terribly disappointed I didn't get to see him. Later in the day, we went to the cemetery to place flowers on the graves. I'm amazed this custom didn't frighten me as a child. The idea of a dead person, a ghost, coming to visit while one sleeps is not only frightening, but also rather morbid.

16

SIBLING RIVALRY

WHEN A FAMILY IS SEPARATED as long as ours was, it takes time for everyone to adjust. Mom worried Joe wouldn't remember her, as he was only two when she left. She also worried how Antonio, now called *Tony*, would take to his new family. It had to be harder on him because he had to contend with three strangers coming into his life. Those first days in America were difficult for us kids. Because we didn't speak the same language, it fostered an atmosphere of suspicion, mistrust, and jealousy. If only we'd had those simultaneous-translation headphones that are used in United Nations meetings, things would have run much smoother for us.

It was not easy on our parents, especially Mom, who had to be both translator and mediator. After a while, Mom grew weary of having to speak Italian to Joe and me and Greek to Tony, and decided that only English would be spoken in our home.

For Joe and me, it wasn't just our railroad apartment and the language that disappointed us. I, for one, thought our Greek relatives would be thrilled to meet us and that they'd shower us with love, attention, and toys. But that didn't happen. Our Aunt Eleni and Uncle Taki didn't spend much time with us. I imagine that between work and school, they didn't have much time to spare. When we got together, they gravitated toward Tony because he spoke their language. This made me feel unloved and homesick for my nonna, my relatives, and my friends in Sicily.

Once I heard Aunt Eleni remark that Joe and I were "dark" and not as cute as Tony. I stared into the mirror, scrutinizing myself and wondering why she'd say something like that. Our skin wasn't any darker than theirs, and why would she say we weren't cute? That remark cut deeply and troubled me for a long time. Aunt Eleni, an adult, should have been more sensitive to the difficulties we children were having.

One day when my brothers and I were fighting about something or other, we took out our anger on a family photo. I don't know who started it, but with pencil in hand, we mutilated the photo, scratching one another's eyes out. We hid the photo in a drawer, and when Mom discovered it, she wanted to know who was responsible. Ashamed and embarrassed, we all admitted our part. Mom scolded us and made us promise never to do anything like that again.

Early on, I was extremely needy for my mother's love and attention. Looking at early family photos, I appear to be clinging to both my parents, my arm draped in theirs or my hand in theirs. I resented my mom spending most of her time with Tony. After all, he'd had our mom all to himself all those years that Joe and I didn't. Now it was our turn to have our mom's undivided attention. There's a family photo that tells it all: Tony is sitting on our mom's lap and I'm sitting on the arm of the chair looking down disapprovingly at him, my knee poised to shove him off her lap!

Mom tried to make me understand that Tony needed to have his tonsils removed and that he couldn't have the operation because he was too little. She explained that she had to sit with him in order to get him to eat; otherwise, he would get sicker. I did try to understand, but I was resentful nevertheless.

I started thinking that if I, too, got sick, I'd get the attention I so craved. Outdoors, I'd unbutton my coat so I'd catch a cold, but I never succeeded. Three years later, I finally got my wish, when I, too, had to have a tonsillectomy. I was ecstatic and couldn't wait for the big day even though I had no idea what their removal entailed. When the day came, Mom took me to the clinic, which was located across the street from Central Park in a building that at one time must have been a stately residence. The original proprietor must have been an avid trophy hunter, because mounted on the walls of the large reception area were the heads of a lion, tiger, and an elk with huge antlers. It was more than unsettling to see those disembodied heads, and coming to the conclusion that those animals had met a violent end.

We were led into a room that reeked of isopropyl alcohol, the smell of which, for me, always conjured up pain.

The nurse handed Mom a hospital gown and said, "All clothes come off."

Frightened and confused, I protested, saying, "Why do I have to take my clothes off? Only my neck hurts!"

"You have to wear the gown, sweetie," the nurse replied.

I trembled as Mom undressed me and put me in the gown. Mom took my hand, and the nurse led the way down a long hallway. I stopped at the sight of a stretcher being wheeled out of a doorway, my eyes fixed on the occupant's blood-splattered face. When I realized I was being led into the same room the bloodied face had come out of, my legs gave way. Someone picked me up, and I cried and struggled to get free. I was then strapped to a stretcher, and doctors wearing masks clamped a black cone over my face, muffling my cries.

Someone said, "Count from one to ten."

With tears flowing, I had barely begun counting, when the room suddenly turned black.

I woke up with a burning pain in my throat and began to cry. Mom told me not to because it would make my throat hurt even more. After that horrifying ordeal, I never tempted fate again, and did my best to stay healthy.

As for Joe, he wasn't as needy for our mom's attention. The only mother he had known was Nonna. I don't know how much Joe remembered about our mom. But he must have retained some memories of her because I recall that about a year after Mom left, he was sobbing calling for her. It was probably after undergoing one of those harrowing *ventusi* procedures. He was lying in bed whimpering and crying, "Mamma. Mamma." I brought him the framed photo of mom and said, "Here Pino. Here's Mamma." He waved the photo away and cried out, "I don't want her! She left me!"

He would constantly find fault with Mom, asking her, "Why don't you dress like Nonna? Why don't you comb your hair like Nonna?"

Trying to mollify him, Mom replied, "Your nonna wears black because Nonno died. Does your teacher dress like Nonna?"

"No."

"That's because your teacher likes the modern styles. You'll get used to the way ladies dress and comb their hair. You'll see."

He sometimes also complained about Mom's cooking, howling, "It's too hot! I can't eat it! It's too hot!"

It would take more than a little while before Joe stopped complaining about Mom's clothes, her hairstyle, and her cooking.

Tony, too, had issues. He'd been plucked from his loving home and thrust into another with three strangers. He was uncomfortable around our father and didn't know what to make of the two older kids that had become his brother and sister. He missed Pappou, whom he loved dearly and would greet at the door when he came home from work. He missed handing him his slippers when he removed his shoes, and a towel as Pappou washed up before dinner.

*　*　*

Eleven months after arriving in America, we welcomed a new member into our family. This addition turned out to be a godsend because now, all the attention was directed toward the baby, and the sibling rivalry pretty much faded. I learned of the impending arrival quite by accident. It was on the day Mom and Aunt Eleni took me along on a shopping trip to Gimbels.

"What are you looking at baby carriages for?" I asked Mom.

Before Mom could reply, my aunt said, "We're buying a baby carriage for Tony."

"Why does he need a carriage? He's not a baby anymore."

"You know how tired Tony gets walking," my aunt said.

At times, Tony *did* fuss and asked to be carried.

"But isn't he too big for a baby carriage?" I moaned.

At that point, my aunt turned to the saleslady and said, "Isn't she a terrible girl? She's so jealous of her little brother!"

Embarrassed by her remark, which had hit a chord because there was some truth to it, I began to cry.

Mom told Eleni to stop; then, kneeling at my level, said, "The carriage is for a baby that will soon be coming to our home."

"We're getting a baby? A real baby?! Can we get a girl? Please get a girl this time! I want a sister!" I gushed.

Mom, too, must have been hoping for a girl, because when she brought him home, he was dressed in pink.

She broke the news to me gently, saying, "It's a little boy, but isn't he the *cutest* little boy?"

"Why didn't you get the girl?" I demanded.

"God gave us a little boy. Do you want me give him back?"

I looked down at him. He was so little and so cute, with such tiny fingers and toes. I hesitated, but only for an instant.

"OK we can keep him. But I still wish you *got* a girl!"

Our baby brother was named Peter, a name that turned out to be a good choice, for it honored both Mom's brother, Peter, and Dad's sister, Pietrina. By now, I was really into my catechism lessons and was thrilled that we'd added yet another important saint to our already saintly family, which included our father, Salvatore, the Savior; our mother, Maria, mother of Christ; and us children, who were named after four famous saints: Saint Teresa, Saint Joseph, Saint Anthony, and now Saint Peter, keeper of the keys to the gate of Heaven.

Unlike my three brothers, who were born in peacetime (and two of whom were born in a hospital), I came into the world at a time when Germans scoured the streets of Greece in search of young Italian children for their labor camps. I was delivered by a midwife who obviously didn't adhere to stringent sanitary rules, resulting in

Mom getting a nasty infection. At that time, parents were required to report a child's birth at City Hall, but since Mom was bedridden, and Dad, a prisoner of war, the chore fell to another. Somehow, something got lost in translation, and my birth certificate lists the wrong date of birth, resulting in my being five days younger than I am. I don't remember when I first learned about the error, but I do remember taking full advantage of it.

My Dad always asked, "Now, on which day do you want to celebrate your birthday this year?"

I'd reply, "On my real birthday of course!"

And as I took my last bite of birthday cake each year, I'd lament, "We can't just ignore my legal birthday, can we?"

It always worked. And my brothers didn't mind because five days later we got to have more cake.

I asked Mom if she and Dad had talked about names for me. She told me they'd decided to follow the custom of both their countries, naming the first boy and first girl after paternal grandparents. I was named Teresa Violetta after both of my grandmothers.

Dad had most likely hoped to have only one girl, and as it turned out, he got his wish. Being the only girl, I often felt left out. When I tried joining my brothers in playing ball, they wouldn't let me because they said I threw like a girl. As much as I love my brothers, I would have so enjoyed having a sister, an ally with whom I could share things—things brothers aren't interested in, such as makeup, hair, clothes, and talk of boyfriends. I pined for the sister I would never have.

Mom consoled me, saying, "When your brothers marry, you'll have three sisters."

243

I knew it wouldn't be the same, but I did think it would be nice to welcome into the family three sisters-in-law.

My brothers did marry, but the women they married did not want sisterhood. They didn't even want to be part of their husband's family.

"Such women," Mom sadly remarked, "should marry orphans."

On the upside, my husband's two wonderful adoring sisters welcomed me into their family with open arms.

Two months after Peter was born, our dad injured his back when he and a coworker collided while walking through the swinging doors at the restaurant where he worked. It was the first time we had seen our dad sick, and we were really scared. At the time he was hurt, Dad was working as a busboy, and the disability checks he received were not nearly enough to see us through.

Mom couldn't go back to work because she had to care for Peter and Dad. Her boss at the factory lent her a machine so that she could work from home. She placed the bulky machine near Peter's crib so she could keep an eye on him and amuse him when he got restless. I would watch as she'd place the rhinestones facedown and the nail heads onto the hopper, lining up the piece of fabric with the X mark directly under the nail head. With a push of the foot pedal, the rhinestone and nail head would meet. She worked very fast and went through those bundles in record time. I liked watching Mom putting those shiny stones and pearls on fabric. It looked like a lot of fun, and at times, Mom let me do some.

The money Mom made wasn't enough to meet our expenses. My parents didn't know enough to seek compensation from Dad's employer, who should have been held responsible for his workplace injury, and suing never crossed Dad's mind. Not wanting to be a burden to my grandparents, my parents, on the advice of friends, applied for welfare. The welfare office wasted no time in contacting our sponsors. Pappou and Mom's employer admonished my parents, saying that they should never have applied for welfare because they, as sponsors, were responsible for our welfare. The generous help we received from our sponsors kept our family afloat for the four months that our dad was on disability.

When Peter was about a year old, Mom returned to her factory job. She found a babysitter, a widow who always dressed in black. The Greek woman was short and quite rotund, and wore her graying hair in a messy bun. She had a mentally challenged adult son living with her who was often seen standing on the street near their apartment building, twirling Greek worry beads. He was perfectly harmless, but to us children, he seemed strange.

Although the babysitter had lived in America for many years, she barely spoke a word of English. There was a humorous story of her applying for US citizenship. When asked the name of the president of the United States, she replied, "My husband." She gave the same answer when asked for the names of the mayor and governor of New York. Needless to say, she wasn't granted citizenship.

Peter hated being left with anyone and cried when Mom dropped him off with the babysitter. He was ever so happy when I came to collect him after school each day. The woman, her son, and their apartment disturbed me very much, and I constantly nagged Mom to find another sitter. The situation frightened me so, it caused me to have nightmares. In one disturbing dream, I'm on my way to pick up Peter. I'm climbing up the stairs, and the apartment door is ajar. I see the old woman standing by the stove. To my horror, sticking out of the huge steaming pot are two little feet . . . and I wake up screaming. I told Mom about my nightmare and begged her not to leave Peter there anymore. Mom said it was only a bad dream and that the nice woman would never harm him.

The next day, with the nightmare still haunting me, I went to pick up Peter. I took a deep breath and knocked on the door. When the woman opened it, I was relieved to see Peter sitting on the floor, playing with his toys—and not submerged in a pot. Fortunately, a short time later, Mom found another sitter, a young Greek woman named Anna who had a little girl the same age as Peter. It was a good situation all around. Peter had a playmate, and I no longer worried. However, he still cried when Mom dropped him off, but not for very long, according to Anna.

Later, when Peter started nursery school, not only did I have to pick him up, I also had to drop him off in the morning. Unsurprisingly, Peter didn't like going to nursery school and acted up as soon as we walked out the door. He'd hold on to the stairway banister, and I had to literally peel his fingers off of it. On the street, he'd refuse to walk, and I had to drag him. When we would finally reach his school, he'd grab hold of the handrail, and I'd have to pry open his hand and drag him in. Taking off his coat was no easy feat because he would wrap his arms around his chest, making it difficult for me to get at the buttons. By the time I had removed his coat and hat and placed them in his appointed cubbyhole, I was exhausted. Considering he didn't like going to school, collecting him should have been a breeze but it wasn't. Now he didn't want to leave!

Trying to stay as cheerful as possible, I'd ask, "Did you have fun today?"

"Uh-huh."

246

"See, I told you. School is lots of fun! We have to go home now, but we'll come back tomorrow. You won't give me a hard time tomorrow, will you?"

Yet when tomorrow came, it would be more of the same. I complained to Mom that Peter was making me late for school. Her solution was that I should leave earlier. Boy, was I stuck!

There was one day that could have ended tragically. On this particular day, Peter seemed to have glued both of his hands to the banister. I couldn't budge him at all, so I tried getting him to move by poking his back with my knee, when suddenly, his arms and legs akimbo, he somersaulted down the long stairway. Horrified, I rushed down after him. At the landing, I picked him up and patted his little body as he stood immobile, as if in shock. It was a miracle he wasn't hurt. I'm sure that the many layers of clothing and the thick woolen hat he had on for that cold winter day had saved his life. From that day on, Peter no longer challenged me, and getting him to school was a lot easier. I'm sure he must have thought that his deranged sister meant business, and he'd better not do anything to provoke her!

17

OUR PARENTS

*D*AD DIDN'T KNOW HOW he'd be able to earn a living in the United States. Uncle Nick, Aunt Eleni's fiancé, helped Dad get his first job at the restaurant where he worked. Joe and I had a special affinity for Uncle Nick because he was the only member of our extended family, besides Pappou, who spoke Italian. He spoke the language because he'd lived in Greece during Italy's occupation of the Dodecanese islands from 1912 to 1947, when it was mandatory that Italian be taught in schools.

Although Dad was thankful to have a job, he wasn't thrilled about being a busboy or the meager wages. Due to the stresses new immigrants face—not only financially, but also in having to adapt to the culture—our parents sometimes quarreled. They had the additional stress of having to adapt to one another after their three-year separation and the four thousand miles between them. Years later, Mom confided that because Dad had strayed while they were apart, he suspected her of doing the same. She said that while he was never physically abusive, he was emotionally abusive.

"In those early days, your father was terribly jealous and insecure," Mom said. "When he first arrived and saw a photo of me, Eleni, Taki, and two young men at my parents' apartment, he wanted to know which of the two my suitor was. I told him the young men were family friends and were recent immigrants, like us. They didn't have family in America, and my parents often invited them for Sunday dinner. But your father was insecure, especially because of Yiayia's feelings about him, and he suspected her of trying to set me up."

"I can't believe Dad thought Yiayia would do anything like that!" I said.

"I laughed, saying I'd made a fine catch with three little children. I told him to stop imagining things, but instead of being content that we were finally together, he let his insecurities get the better of him."

I never knew my father to be insecure. To me, he always seemed strong, confident, and in control. Yet I can see why he may have been insecure under the circumstances, and especially when it came to Yiayia. He had to know my grandparents weren't thrilled about having him as a son-in-law. But at the same time, he also had to know that they'd come around. Had he forgotten that they'd risked their lives shielding him from the Germans? That they not only sponsored him to come to America, but also paid for our trip? Why would they do all that if they wanted to be rid of him? Yet he found reasons to argue and, at times, kept us from seeing our grandparents. Our mother, in order to avoid confrontation, sadly acquiesced. It saddened Yiayia that our father was so obstinate. He earned her wrath to such a degree that she put a curse on him: that his children would turn against him. It was a curse she would later rescind.

Poor Mom had to deal with a lot those early days. We children also gave her grief. Joe, at times, was so miserable, longing for his idyllic life in Sicily, that at the tender age of five, encouraged by my parents' quarrels, he began making up stories. When Dad returned from work one night, Joe woke up and told him that a man had come over after we'd gone to bed.

"Can't you see?" Mom said. "The boy makes things up because he wants to go back to Sicily. He needs time to adjust, and it doesn't help when he hears you accusing me!"

Dad ignored her and asked Joe, "What was the man wearing?"

"A dark suit."

"What was your mother wearing?"

"A pretty dress."

"Where was the man?"

"He was standing at the door."

"Where was your mother?"

"She was in the kitchen."

"Where were you?"

"In bed."

"How can you see the door from your bed?"

"Why don't you leave him alone?" Mom pleaded.

"I don't want you lying to me! Now tell me, how could you see the man from bed?"

Tangled in his web, Joe whimpered, "I don't know. I don't remember."

My father's loud voice startled me awake, and I staggered into the kitchen. Dad, seeing me approach, asked me, "Did you see the man?"

"What man?"

"The man at the door," Dad said.

Still groggy from sleep, I replied, "I don't know. No . . . I don't think so."

Mom glared at Dad, saying, "Are you satisfied now? See what you are doing to the children? They don't know what you want them to say. Leave them alone! Let them sleep!"

I stood quietly sobbing as Mom put Joe to bed, tucked him in, kissed his tearstained cheek, and told him it was OK and to go to sleep. She then walked me to my cot, tucked me in, wiped my tears, and kissed me, and I eventually fell asleep.

There were no more stories after that.

I, too, inadvertently added to our parents' woes. One day as Mom was going through photographs, I saw a photo of that bad Italian woman. The shock of seeing her in our home in America brought back that awful episode in Sicily. I blurted out the saga, not knowing it would cause my parents to quarrel. Once again, my father didn't reprimand the little tattletale. He had to know that the wounds caused by his thoughtlessness were still raw and that he once again had to suffer the consequences.

Dad, sensing that Joe and I missed our life in Sicily, decided to bring home a rabbit. Playing with that cute, little white rabbit did remind us of those fun-filled times when we'd crawl into the rabbits' hutch. We didn't know then that our playmates were being bred for consumption. Had we known, we would have set them free. Nonna rarely cooked meat, and when she did, she'd say we were having *carne*. As children, we didn't associate *carne* with rabbit.

We named the cute rabbit Bunny. Bunny hopped all over the apartment. On Easter Sunday, we couldn't find Bunny anywhere and wondered if he'd found a new hiding place. Sitting at the table, we discovered—to our horror—that Bunny was our Easter dinner. My brothers and I left the table, crying. I couldn't believe our parents were capable of doing something so horrific. The sight of three wailing children must have been enough to last a lifetime because Dad never brought home another live rabbit. Years later, I saw the film *Giant* in which three little children suffer a similar fate. The children throw morsels of food to a huge turkey they've named Pedro. On Thanksgiving Day, as the platter containing Pedro and all the trimmings is brought to the table, the children run off, crying.

When we lived in Sicily, Dad hunted rabbits and birds. He'd often say that those who don't like the idea of killing animals have to ask how the meat made it to the butcher. I have to agree. It does smack of hypocrisy that we view a neatly packaged cut of meat as just that, and not the living creature it once was. Most of us don't give a thought as to how the meat made it to the supermarket.

That first June, after one of my parents' quarrels, Dad and Joe disappeared. I wasn't allowed to go to school because Mom feared Dad might take me away too. I was terribly upset that Joe and Dad were gone and that I didn't know where they were. I was also upset about missing my last days of school. I had been looking forward to receiving the books my teacher had promised to lend me over the summer. Mom learned that Dad and Joe went to our relatives' home in Philadelphia. A whole week passed before Dad returned. Not finding us in our apartment, he went to our grandparents' place and pounded on the door, screaming for me to come out. I was frightened, sad, and confused. Pappou told Dad to leave or he'd call the police.

Dad must have come to his senses because a few days later, he returned with Joe. My parents met at Central Park. I remember, it was a warm June day and Mom had dressed Tony and me in our Sunday best. Dad wore a suit and tie, and Joe, a white shirt and slacks. At first, our parents were quiet, and so were we. Dad broke the ice by purchasing ice cream pops from the Good Humor cart. The ice cream definitely broke the ice for us kids. Mom and Dad sat together, eating their ice cream and quietly talking.

When my brothers and I finished our ice cream, we went over to the swings. A while later, Mom and Dad said it was time to go. We strolled down Fifth Avenue, at times lingering to look at the window displays. When we reached Forty-Second Street, we cut across the avenues. We loved going through Times Square, reading the movie titles on the marquees and looking at all the stills. We entered the Port Authority Bus Terminal on Eighth Avenue and exited on Ninth. By the time we got home, we were tired but happy our parents were no longer quarreling and that we were together again.

After their first separation, which lasted about two weeks, our parents patched things up, but the scars remained, and everyone seemed to be walking on eggshells. My brothers and I sensed that our parents were trying to work things out, and we didn't want to say or do anything to upset the applecart. After one of their quarrels one day, Dad told me that had I come out that day, we would have gone back to Sicily. I told him I'd never leave my mother. When I thought about it later, I realized he couldn't have been serious, and even if he had been, where would he have gotten the money for our trip?

Dad still refused to see our grandparents and also prevented us from seeing them. Our Aunt Eleni often visited us, accompanied by her fiancé. She asked Mom to be her maid of honor and for Joe and

Tony to serve as ring bearers. A couple of days before the wedding, Dad took my brothers for haircuts. When they returned, they were sporting Mohawks, red eyes, and tearstained faces. Our horrified mother took them back to the barber and had the ridiculous strip of hair shaved off, reasoning a bald head was better than a Mohawk, which was not in vogue then. On October 11, 1953, our mom attended her sister's wedding without her husband and children. Dad still harbored ill feelings toward our grandparents and avoided seeing them, even if it meant slighting our aunt and uncle-to-be on their important day.

About a year after arriving, Dad was promoted to the position of waiter and began working at high-end restaurants, where his continental accent was an advantage. He worked at the Stork Club, where ladies were given tubes of lipstick, and he often brought home tubes for Mom. He went on to work at the 21 Club, Amalfi, Marta, Gino's, Danny's Hideaway, and Asti. At Asti, the waiters entertained the patrons with popular Italian songs and arias from Italian operas. We'd come home from school and sometimes find Dad soaking his aching feet, complaining about the many trips on the long stairway at Danny's Hideaway, claiming he was not looking forward to scaling those steps for the dinner crowd. He waited on countless celebrities, including Frank Sinatra; Ed Sullivan; Lucille Ball; and Ben Cartwright and his sons, Adam, Hoss, and Little Joe of the TV hit *Bonanza*. My brothers and I asked for autographs, but Dad told us he didn't want to bother people. Dad did get Joe a signed photo of Yogi Berra, but Joe would have preferred one of Mickey Mantle, his idol. Another time he got a signed 8x10 glossy of the wrestling champ, Antonino Rocca wearing his boxing trunks. Not being wrestling fans, we were not impressed.

* * *

Holidays were a great time for tips, and Dad worked on most of them. On New Year's Eve, he wouldn't get home until the wee hours, and Mom let us stay up to wait for the festive noisemakers Dad always brought home. The times we did fall asleep, Dad woke us up with those noisemakers. We'd get up, dress, and don our New Year's hats, and Dad would snap photos of us by the Christmas tree. Mom would cook up another batch of *zeppole* and serve them with warm honey. It was the only time of the year we got to sip champagne. After our little celebration, we'd go back to bed. We'd then get up a little before noon to have more of the delicious *zeppole*.

A downside to Dad's job was that he wasn't around much. He'd usually be asleep when we left for school, and at work when we returned. He worked six days a week and had one alternating day off. It was on his day off that we'd all get to have dinner together. I often thought of Dad as our once-a-week dinner guest.

Dad was the disciplinarian in our home. For the most part, Mom had little say. There were times it seemed as if we had one parent and that Mom was one of us children. When they married, Mom was fourteen and Dad was twenty-three, which may account for Dad having taken on the dominant role. Since Mom wasn't much of disciplinarian, Dad believed that we had gotten away with murder all week long and on his day off he would grill us about school, homework, chores, and activities, which made us feel we were being interrogated for some mysterious crime.

Dad never gave us a heads-up on when he'd be off. I believe he kept us in the dark so that he could catch us in some sinister activity;

it must have been the policeman in him. Not knowing when he'd pop up did manage to keep us on our toes.

One day when I was in junior high, I was standing in the schoolyard with friends during recess when I spotted my dad across the street.

When I returned from school, I asked him, "Why didn't you come over and say hello?"

"What are you talking about?"

"Dad, you were at my school today! I saw you!" I shouted. "Were you spying on me?"

He just smiled and said, "Come help me in the kitchen."

At times Dad was so overbearing, we wished he never had a day off, which is a sad thing to admit.

When I complained that he was being too strict, he'd reply, "You don't know how lucky you are to have a father."

"But a father doesn't have to act like policeman. A father should show love and affection," I'd say.

Showing love and affection didn't come easy to our father. This was most likely because he, himself, had never had a father's love and affection.

Mom said that during the war when Dad was stationed in Albania, one of his duties was to go on patrol along the enemy line. He said he always made it a point to select an unmarried man like himself to join him on the dangerous detail. Growing up with the pain of not having a father, Dad didn't want a child to suffer the same fate if he could help it.

Whenever we children did or said something our father didn't approve of, he would glare at us and refrain from speaking to us for the longest time, his wrath expressed in chilling silence. I could never get him to tell me why he punished us in this bizarre way. Perhaps he didn't know why himself. My brothers didn't seem to mind, viewing it as a vacation from chores. Since he didn't speak to them, he couldn't very well give them things to do. For me, the silence was deafening. I hated it and would have preferred a reprimand so that it would be over and done with.

Our mom said we were to always be respectful and greet our father even if he didn't talk to us. As I got older, I tried different approaches. I'd greet him, and when he didn't respond, I'd go on chatting about different topics, such as the weather, current events, or anything else that came to mind, acting as if I were having a normal conversation. He'd pretend to be reading his newspaper, but I could see he was having a hard time suppressing the smile forming on his lips.

The only one of us kids who wasn't intimidated by Dad's glare was Peter. Reprimanding him one day Dad said, "Come here or I'll kill you!" Peter, no more than two, said, "Oh yeah? You kill me, and you go to jail!" Dad stood there, stunned and amused by Peter's pluckiness. Peter must have reminded Dad of himself as a boy. I don't think any of us would have gotten away with that. None of us ever tried, as far as I can remember.

Whenever we were late coming home from the park our dad would say, "What happened? You forgot where you live?"

We'd shove our little brother to the front and say, "It's not our fault, Dad. Peter didn't want to come home."

Our father seeing his defiant little kid staring back at him let us slide. To avoid Dad's scolding, we employed this technique whenever possible and Peter seemed happy to oblige.

It's interesting that Peter, the only one of us who stood up to our father when we were little, would be the only one of us who'd employ the silent treatment, refusing to have anything to do with the offender, acting as if the person were invisible. He could never tell us why he did this. Perhaps he, too, didn't know why. Perhaps it's a genetic flaw.

I do wish Dad had been less of a disciplinarian and more affectionate. Yet I never doubted his love for us. During those early days, I was a light sleeper and only fell asleep when Dad returned from work. Pretending to be asleep, I'd see him going over to the pullout couch where my three brothers slept and kissing them on the forehead. Then he'd walk over to my roll-up bed and plant a kiss on me. I so much wanted to sit up, give him a hug, and tell him I loved him, but I didn't dare. I was afraid I'd embarrass him and that he might never kiss us again.

At times, Dad did try to show affection. On Valentine's Day, which Dad believed was a holiday for ladies, he gave Mom and me each a box of candy. Mom got a large red heart and I, a smaller pink heart. Of course we shared the candy with my brothers.

A couple of times Dad took me to the movies, as a father-daughter date. It must have been for some special occasion, my birthday perhaps. I remember only two films that I saw with Dad. I'm not sure who decided on what to see, but one was *Psycho* which Dad thought was a ridiculous story especially when I tried to explain that it wasn't Norman Bates' mother who slashed that girl in the shower but Norman Bates, who thought he was his own mother. I remember Dad's reaction as if it were only yesterday: *"Che stupidaggine!"*

It must have been on my fifteenth birthday when Dad took me to see *A Summer Place*. This definitely was not a film a teen wants to see with her parents, let alone her father! Sandra Dee and Troy

Donahue's constant smooching and making out made me squirm in my seat. It was more than awkward especially when the characters on the screen talked about pre-marital sex and pregnancy. I couldn't wait to get out of there. Dad too must have wanted out.

Dad mostly showed affection with food. He loved to cook. Nonna was right: Dad definitely didn't go for bland. He liked spicing things up. His marinated green olives were a favorite of ours. One by one, he'd crack a whole case of olives, fill a five-gallon jar, add celery, sprigs of rosemary and thyme, oregano, bay leaves, large garlic cloves, peppercorns and red hot-pepper flakes, extra virgin olive oil, and wine vinegar, and let them marinate. We'd enjoy those meaty olives all year long. Another favorite was his *caponata*, a blend of eggplant, onion, celery, tomato, olives, capers, basil, and pine nuts that we enjoyed spreading on crusty bread. He also made jars of sauce from homegrown tomatoes.

Dad said that it was his nonna Angela who had taught him to cook. As a young boy, he loved going to her house, where she indulged him and his friends with her tasty dishes. Mom met Nonna Angela in 1945, and marveled that at age eighty-four, she didn't have a single strand of white in her long blonde hair. Tall, slim, and blonde with blue-green eyes, she looked more Scandinavian than Sicilian. When Nonna Angela died two years later, Nonna Teresa sent her brother in Philadelphia a lock of their mother's hair. He found it incredible that there still wasn't a trace of white in the golden lock.

I was two when we visited Nonna Angela at the hospital. I'm told that I refused to share my candy with her. Of course, I have no memory of that. My nonna later said that Nonna Angela's illness was a result of a tiny scab on the side of her nose. Tania, a little girl who lived across the street from us was sitting on Nonna Angela's lap and picked at the scab, causing it to bleed, never to heal. Nonna Angela most likely had melanoma. When you consider her age, she had a nice, long life that exceeded the life expectancy of women of her day. My nonna, also an attractive woman, didn't inherit her mother's tall, slender frame and fair complexion, nor did she inherit her culinary skills.

Dad also picked up tips from chefs at the restaurants where he worked. On his day off, he'd try those dishes on us—dishes like the delicate chicken francese, chicken cordon bleu with prosciutto and gruyère cheese, garlicky shrimp scampi, spaghetti with Bolognese sauce, and manicotti and lasagna that he and Mom made from scratch. One of our favorites, which we begged Dad to make time and again, was the hearty yet delicate brown sauce made with shredded beef, which he served over rigatoni. It might have been one of Dad's creations because I've never seen it in a cookbook or on any Italian restaurant menu.

He started the process by making beef broth. When the beef had cooled, he patiently pulled it apart into long shreds. He then sautéed minced onion, celery, and carrots in butter, added the shredded beef, red wine, tomato paste, and beef stock, and let it simmer for hours. The times we asked him to make it for us, he'd complain it was too much work. To our delight, he never failed to surprise us with it. A downside to Dad's cooking was that unlike Mom, who cleaned up as she cooked, Dad didn't, leaving us with a mountain of pots and pans.

Mom cooked dinner every day except on Dad's day off. She designated Wednesdays and Fridays fish days. Growing up, we didn't much care for fish and talked her into just having fish on Fridays. We didn't want to see fish heads or scales on our plate, and would only eat filet of sole or flounder—in other words, fish that didn't look like fish. Mom tried cultivating our palate by picking up the special of the day at the fishmonger's: red snapper, porgy, sea bass, shrimp, clams, squid, and the like.

Mom prided herself on her bouillabaisse, and yet, after she'd spent hours cooking, we'd come to the table holding our noses and groan, "Not that lousy fish soup again!"

Peter lamented, "Even the potatoes taste like fish!"

Dad's cooking always had an element of surprise, and at times, he went a little too far in cultivating our palate—his specialties, too exotic for our taste. Lobster fra diavolo was one dish that didn't go over too well with us kids.

Dad, more than annoyed with his ungrateful children, asked us, "Do you know how expensive lobster is?"

"Gee, Dad, think of all the money you'll save if you don't make it again," was my clever retort.

Dad tried passing off calf's brains as chicken francese. Sitting at the dinner table, I could see by my brothers' furrowed brows that something was amiss. One time, my worst fears were confirmed when my fork sank into the mushy flesh.

"This isn't chicken!" I squealed. "It's brains!"

After my outburst, my brothers dropped their forks and pushed their dishes away.

Dad glared at me and growled, "You have a big mouth!"

Tony told us of the time he saved the day. He and Dad were walking on Ninth Avenue when Tony saw the revolting mound of tripe in the butcher's window. Fearing Dad might be tempted to pick some up for dinner, he grabbed Dad's hand, pointed at something or other across the way, and steered him away from the butcher shop.

As much as he tried, Dad could never put anything over on me. I have such a keen sense of smell, which at times drove my family to the brink. One day while walking into the kitchen, I was assaulted by an odor that stopped me in my tracks.

"Phew! What's that horrible smell?"

Mom, sniffing the air, said, "What smell? I don't smell anything."

"You don't smell that?"

"You always smell something!" Joe said.

"I can't help it if you people can't smell!"

A day or two went by, and the odor had become so foul, I couldn't go anywhere near the kitchen.

"I think it smells in here," Mom said.

"You think?" I said.

Mom and Dad went on the hunt for the smelly culprit, looking under, between, and behind the counters, stove, and fridge, and finally found the offending item hiding behind the stove: a raw clam, still in its shell!

A totally unappreciated creation of Dad's was the infamous *scungilli*. I later discovered that cooking *scungilli* is quite labor intensive. It involves steaming the sea snails, removing their flesh by cracking their shells open, slicing the snails lengthwise, peeling them, rinsing them, and tenderizing them by marinating them, and finally cooking them. Presented on a plate, they didn't look very appealing.

But Dad soldiered on, saying, "You should try everything at least once."

Joe, the bravest of us, was first to sample the dish. After a couple of chews, he screwed up his face and said, "It tastes like burnt rubber."

Somewhat offended, Dad turned to me.

"Why don't you try," he suggested.

"That's OK, Dad, I don't have to. Joe said it tastes like burnt rubber, and I know I won't like eating burnt rubber."

Nothing deterred Dad. Introducing us to different and exotic foods was the way our dad showed love and affection. But children don't just need food to thrive; they need to be hugged, kissed, and told they are loved.

OUR PARENTS

Celebrating Christmas in our Manhattan apartments

18

LEARNING ENGLISH

*A*S A SOLDIER STATIONED IN GREECE, my father learned to speak Greek and was fluent enough to not only woo my mother, but also dupe the five Germans billeted in our home. However, he found the English language to be daunting.

I'd tell him, "Dad, you learned to speak Greek. English should be way easier!"

I remember his response well: *"La lingua Inglese è una lingua bastarda."* (The English language is a bastard language.)

I thought that to be rather harsh, but my father recognized long before I did that English is composed of many languages: French, German, Greek, Italian, Latin, and others, which can make the pronunciation of many words a guessing game, especially for foreigners. He found the pronunciation of vowels anything but consistent. It irked him that letters went unpronounced, and he made it his mission to voice them all. For example, he pronounced *plumber* as "ploomber." When we corrected him, he'd say, "There is a B, and I say the B!"

I had to agree. English, with all its inconsistencies and many exceptions to the rule, can be extremely difficult, especially for foreigners. One thing Dad found not only odd, but also disrespectful, is that the English language has only one version of the pronoun *you.* In Italian, there's the formal *lei,* used to address adults, strangers, and professionals, and the familiar *tu,* used to address children and friends.

Mom fared much better, but she, too, had difficulty with the pronunciation of certain words.

There was one cringeworthy moment when Mom asked the salesclerk at Macy's, "Can you tell me where the *shits* are?"

Mortified, I hissed, "Mom!"

With an awkward smile, I explained to the salesclerk, "My mother means to say *sheets.* She wants to know what floor the *sheets* are on."

"That's what I said," my indignant mother insisted. "I want to see the *shits.*"

The salesclerk, now blushing, directed us to the bedding department.

Totally exasperated, I said, "Mom, do you know what you said to that lady? You said *shits,* not *sheets!* I told you, *shit* means *merda!*"

My brothers and I tried for the longest time to correct her pronunciation, but to no avail.

Frustrated, Mom finally threw in the towel and said, "That's it! When I want to buy *shits,* I'll ask for bed linens!"

"Good idea, Mom!"

Learning English as children, we fared much better, and in less than a year, we were able to speak without an accent. It helped that our teachers were supportive and encouraged us, giving us extra attention and books to read over the summer. It wasn't always easy, and there were bumps along the way. That first summer, while reading, we came across the word *laughing*, and pronounced it *lau-ging*. That pesky word kept cropping up, confounding us. We couldn't understand why those children were constantly lau-ging. What did it mean?

When I returned to school in September, the word appeared in a passage I was reading aloud. My teacher corrected my pronunciation and told me what the word meant. I couldn't wait to tell my mom.

"Are you sure?" she asked, surprised. "But there is no F."

"The teacher said that the letters GH are pronounced like F," I explained. After mispronouncing the word all summer long, it was a joy to have the mystery solved. I later learned that the letters PH in the word *photograph* are also pronounced like an F. I thought this odd; after all, the Italian word for photograph is *fotografia* and is spelled with an F, taking out the guesswork and making it easier for anyone to read, even non-Italians.

Throughout my early school years, I came across many exceptions to the rule. Unfortunately for me, they'd always come up while I was reading aloud. When I was in the fourth grade, I mispronounced the word *vegetable*.

Instead of correcting me, my teacher, Mrs. Taub, screeched, "*Vege-table? Vege-table?* Were you raised in a barn?"

I remember her still because unlike my other teachers, who were always helpful and kind, Mrs. Taub was not. She always scowled, which made me think she didn't like children and wasn't happy being a teacher. She was quite short, and even in her platform shoes, she was shorter than her students. Years later, when I saw the witch in *The Wizard of Oz*, I immediately thought of the diminutive Mrs. Taub.

That day she mimicked me I was taken aback, and I didn't have a clue as to what a barn had to do with the word *vegetable*, but I could tell by her tone that she was not happy. I was relieved that many of my classmates, including some boys, came to my defense, telling that unkind teacher I was doing very well for someone who had come to America not very long ago. Their response and support warmed my heart.

Some years later, reading aloud again, I came upon the word *colonel*, and I pronounced it as written: *co-lo-nel*.

"I can understand why you pronounced it that way," my teacher said, "but the correct pronunciation is *kernel*."

Certain she was on the wrong line, I said, "But there is no R."

"You're right. It's one of those exceptions to the rule."

Like many immigrants learning a second language, I had difficulty with the numerous homographs and heteronyms in the English language long before I knew the meaning of those two words. I recall the time I pronounced *Arkansas* like *Are-Kansas* and was ridiculed for not knowing it was pronounced *Arkansaw*.

Frustrated, I wailed, "But there's no W!"

Of course, it was just another pesky exception!

Although I was beginning to understand more and more, I sometimes had difficulty following along when our teacher read aloud to the class.

One afternoon, as my third-grade teacher was reading, I dozed off, and still groggy from sleep, I mumbled, "Mom, can I have some water?"

"Of course you can dear," my teacher said, "but you have to get it yourself."

Hearing my teacher's voice and my classmates' giggles were enough to jolt me out of my stupor. I find it amusing that while I hated siesta in Sicily and found it difficult to fall asleep even in bed, I easily fell asleep sitting up in my chair in a classroom full of third graders!

I was extremely shy and self-conscious, and I seldom raised my hand in class. When I was in sixth grade, my teacher, Miss Taylor who bore a remarkable resemblance to Eleanor Roosevelt, especially when the bun on top of her head toppled to the side, read a newspaper clipping to the class.

She said, "Grace Kelly, an American princess, will travel to Monaco on the SS *Constitution* and will become a real-life princess when she marries Prince Rainier III of Monaco."

I had never heard of Grace Kelly, but was fascinated by the fairytale-like story. When Miss Taylor finished reading, I raised my hand.

"Yes? You have a question?" Miss Taylor asked.

"I just wanted to say that I came to America on the SS *Constitution*."

To my horror, Miss Taylor replied, "That's wonderful! Perhaps you'd like to tell us something about your trip and the beautiful *Constitution*. We'd all love to hear about it, right class? Why don't you stand so that the whole class can hear what you have to say?"

I could feel myself trembling but somehow managed to stand. My classmates fixed their eyes on me, waiting for me to speak. *How did I get myself into this?* I thought. *I just wanted to say I was on the ship. I didn't know I had to give a report!*

I swallowed hard and somehow found my voice. I started by saying that my father, brother, and I had boarded the *Constitution* in Naples in January of 1952, and as I continued speaking, my fear subsided. I can't recall much of what I said, but it must have been interesting, because my classmates listened intently, and when I finished, they asked lots of questions. They wanted to know how many days the trip took, if I got seasick, if I had seen any icebergs, and did I know how many lifeboats were on board. I imagine they had seen films about the Titanic, which had tragically sunk just forty years earlier. I'm glad I didn't know about the Titanic when I traveled. Had I known, seasickness would've been the least of my worries!

* * *

We lived in a neighborhood where there were many Italians and Greeks, a feature that must have drawn my grandparents to it. Our teachers knew that Joe and I were recent Italian immigrants, but because Mom is Greek and our last name is La Greca, some members of the school staff thought we were Greek. I was in fourth grade when I was asked to help translate for a parent who didn't speak English. The woman began speaking in a language that sounded familiar but that I didn't understand. Remembering the rule that a child should not speak when an adult is speaking, I let her go on.

The bewildered look on my face prompted the teacher to ask, "Is something wrong?"

"I don't understand what the lady is saying," I replied.

"But don't you speak Greek?"

"No, I speak Italian."

There wasn't much in the way of assistance for immigrants who didn't speak English, and they had to rely on family and friends.

Many turned to their children. As I was the eldest child, the task often fell to me.

One day I accompanied Dad to the locksmith to buy a dependable, burglar-proof lock for our front door. There had been a rash of robberies in our neighborhood, and although we didn't have very much to entice a burglar, Dad didn't want to risk bad guys breaking in on us.

In a booming voice and broken English, Dad announced to the locksmith, "I want best lock! The *poleesh* lock!"

The locksmith, scratching his head said, "I didn't know Poland made locks, let alone the best locks."

"No, no. Not Poland! *Poleesh!*"

The locksmith then turned to me.

"I don't know what your father wants."

Speaking in Italian, I said, "Dad, can you describe what the lock looks like?"

Dad went on to describe the lock, saying it had a metal bar that went from the lock on the door to the floor. Then he said the magic word: *polizia*. Upon hearing the word, even the locksmith understood: Dad wanted a police lock, not a Polish one!

There were times I didn't fare too well with my translating skills. One day I caught my index finger in the school bathroom's door latch, almost ripping the nail off. The school monitor on duty was the same mean Greek girl who had taken pleasure in landing my feet into puddles. Just seeing my bloodied hand must have stirred what little compassion she possessed. She wrapped my hand in paper towels and took me to the nurse's office. The nurse cleaned the wound, applied antiseptic, bandaged my finger, and gave me a note for my parents. That afternoon Dad took me to the doctor. After cleaning and bandaging my finger and giving me an injection, the doctor recited a list of care instructions. As he continued talking, I worried that I would not remember all he'd said.

When the doctor finally finished, Dad asked me, "What did the doctor say?"

Panic-stricken, my mind blank, all I could do was shrug.

The doctor, visibly annoyed, slowly repeated the instructions using hand gestures.

Once we got home, Dad wasted no time in telling Mom, "She doesn't understand a thing!"

"I did too understand!" I protested. "The doctor talked too much, and I couldn't remember what he'd said."

My dad especially doubted my proficiency in English when I managed to fail the school's hearing test three years in a row. The first time I took the test, I was eight. I don't remember what the test entailed, I only remember that we wore headphones. My parents received a note saying I should be seen by a hearing specialist. Dad immediately took me to the ear, nose, and throat clinic. A hearing test was administered, and we were told that my hearing was perfect. When I failed the test at school the second year, we trekked back to the clinic, where I once again passed the test with flying colors. After failing the school test the third time, my frustrated father quipped, "This time, you'd better be deaf!"

Dad kept up with world news, reading the *Il Progresso Italo-Americano* and listening to Italian radio stations, of which there were many in the 1950s. As his English improved, he went on to read the *New York Journal-American,* the *Daily Mirror,* and the *New York Daily News.* My brothers and I enjoyed the cartoons in the American newspapers, as the Italian newspaper didn't have any.

* * *

A couple of months after arriving in America, we visited our relatives in Philadelphia. I remember being in awe of their enchanting two-story house, which to me, was a world away from our Ninth Avenue railroad apartment. The large living and dining rooms were tastefully furnished, and diaphanous, cascading drapes adorned the windows. The cuckoo clock intrigued my brothers and me, and we'd wait patiently for the cuckoo bird to come out and count the hour. We lounged on the cushioned wicker chairs on the front porch, which overlooked the lawn and its evergreen bushes. On either side of the steps, rose bushes climbed up the trellises.

Uncle Antonio and Aunt Antonia had lived in America for more than forty years. They had six adult children, five of whom were born in America. They were Dad's only extended family in the States. Even though our aunt and uncle had lived in America for many years, they spoke a language that was incomprehensible. Dad asked Mom if they were speaking English, and Mom said she didn't think so. It took a lot of effort, but they somehow managed to communicate with us using a mixture of Sicilian and English and the ever-helpful hand gestures.

Our cousins took us to see the Liberty Bell and to an amusement park, where we rode on the Ferris wheel and in bumper cars. We braved the park's haunted house, which was very scary, especially at the very end when the floor fell from under us, and we slid into a canvas chute that deposited us outdoors.

Uncle Antonio had immigrated to America with our Nonno in 1908. For the most part, immigrants who came from Southern Italy and Sicily had little or no education and spoke in dialects. They communicated by combining their dialects and adding a vowel at the end of English words. For instance, the word *fence* was *fensa; bag, begga; barber, babiere*, and so on, basically creating their own unique language. It's no wonder that those immigrants who came over later had difficulty understanding those who'd come before.

Italian immigrants seemed to have a tendency to make up their own language wherever they settled. In 1970, I first met Dad's sister, Pietrina, who had been living in France for over fifty years. Dad had boasted to his sister that I was fluent in French, even bragging that I'd received my high school's three-year medal in French (this award was given to the student who received the highest grade). When we arrived, he couldn't wait for me to exhibit my proficiency in the language and encouraged my aunt and uncle to engage me.

"Why don't you say something?" Dad asked me.

"Dad, I don't understand what they're saying," I said.

"You study French for three years, get a medal, and understand nothing?"

"I don't know . . . maybe they're speaking a dialect," I said.

More than disappointed, Dad ignored me, and the three continued their conversation in Sicilian, French, and English, struggling to understand one another. Later in the day, our young cousins arrived and greeted us in French. I understood them, and they, me. We chatted for a while as Dad watched in amazement.

I was quick to tell my father, "Dad, I know what it is! Aunt Pietrina and Uncle Domenico speak French the way you speak English!"

My French aunt and uncle did pretty much what my Italian aunt and uncle did but in reverse. In an effort to sound French, they deleted not only vowels, but also consonants.

Time and again I encountered Italian-Americans who, like Uncle Antonio, spoke a mixture of dialects. When I was in my teens, Dad and I visited a couple who spoke Sicilian and some other dialect peppered with English. The couple had a daughter who was a couple of years older than I, and she spoke in what she thought was Italian, but was actually a mixture of dialects, Italian words that had been Americanized, and English words that had been Italianized. I had a vague idea of what she was saying but was appalled by the way she was butchering the Italian language.

"I'm sorry, but I don't understand what you're saying," I said in English.

In a sarcastic tone, she exclaimed, "You mean you were born there, and you don't understand Italian?"

Being American-born, she evidently took pride in mastering the Italian language.

I took delight in telling her, "I don't know what language you're speaking, but it most definitely is not Italian!"

On the way home, Dad reprimanded me: "You shouldn't be such a *superba!*"

"I'm not being haughty! And besides, I think I did her a favor!"

Early on, our parents wanted us to concentrate on learning English. That was their priority. Unlike our Greek cousins who attended after-school Greek classes and were encouraged to speak Greek at home, we weren't given instruction in either Greek or Italian. It didn't occur to our parents that children are sponges, and we could have learned all three languages, which would have been a great opportunity for us. Our parents spoke to us in Italian, and we answered in English. When they didn't understand what we said, we'd repeat it in Italian, which helped them learn English. When our parents discussed things that were not destined for our ears, they reverted to Greek. Their Greek didn't sound harsh like Yiayia's; in fact, it sounded rather melodic.

I began listening more and more, amazed that I was beginning to understand what they were saying. I'd repeat words I didn't understand to Mom, and she'd translate them for me. I thought it strange that *né* in Greek means *yes,* and *ohi* means *no.* Our mom must have been very agreeable because she said *né* an awful lot, especially when she was on the phone. My brothers and I took this opportunity to mimic her. We'd stick our thumbs in our ears, wiggle our fingers, and sway our head from side to side, all the while saying *"né."* At times Mom would get so annoyed she would threaten us with her cloth slipper, which made us laugh all the more.

One day as my parents conversed in Greek, I blurted out, "Why do we have to do that?"

More than a little surprised, Dad looked at me and then turned to Mom and speaking in Greek, said, "She understands?"

"Yes, she's beginning to understand a lot," Mom said.

I was caught. My secret was out. But Dad was thrilled. I'd picked up the language by listening, just as he had done in Greece.

In 1970, on our first trip to Greece, I made every effort to speak Greek. One relative decided to have a little fun in mimicking me.

"Why are you speaking like that?" I asked.

"Why, I'm speaking like you!"

"Please don't do that," I protested. "I want so much to learn."

I find it frustrating that while I do understand the language, I'm not comfortable speaking it. I sound like a child just learning to put words together. I don't want to sound slow or dimwitted like the person who mimicked me did. My often-repeated Greek phrase is,

"Katalavaino ellinika, all den poro na milao." ("I understand Greek, but I don't speak it.")

Of all four children, I'm the only one who has an ear for languages. My brothers either weren't interested or just didn't have the knack. One summer I thought it a good idea to hold Italian classes for my brothers. I prepared folders and did my best to make it fun. My brothers didn't find it fun at all and wanted no part of conjugating Italian verbs and after only a couple of days stormed out, leaving their folders behind.

Early on, my brothers and I were exposed to Greek and Italian language, culture, and food, and we came to love our Greco-Roman heritage. I especially enjoyed reading those wonderful tales by Homer: the *Iliad* and the *Odyssey*, and Virgil's the *Aeneid*, in which the Greek and Roman gods constantly meddle with earthly beings.

19

LIVING IN HELL'S KITCHEN

EVEN THOUGH WE LIVED THERE, we didn't know our neighborhood was called Hell's Kitchen. The first time I encountered the Jets and Sharks in New York City was on Broadway, the playhouses, not the street. Many in the neighborhood were recent immigrants, like us, where fathers worked hard to provide for their families; mothers, if they were lucky, were stay-at-home moms; and children had to do well in school and help with chores. In spite of its fiery diabolical moniker and all it conjured up, Hell's Kitchen, in its unique way, was a welcome center for recent arrivals.

It was in America where Joe and I were not only introduced to our Greek relatives, but also to many different ethnicities and races. Alongside the Greeks and Italians were the Hispanics, Irish, Polish, and Russians. America truly was (and in many ways, still is) a "melting pot" of various cultures, ethnicities, and customs.

In fact, the first black person I saw was on the ship. I remember wondering if he had spent too much time in the sun and if it had burned his skin black. I was in fourth grade when I first encountered the only two Chinese boys in my school. What fascinated me were their eyes. I asked my teacher why their eyes were so different, and he explained that China and Japan are on the continent of Asia, and that Asian eyes are shaped differently. I was both fascinated and confused. I'd had no idea up until that point that there were so many different people beyond Greek and Italian! His explanation, however, did help me to understand the little ditty kids sang in the schoolyard. With index fingers, they pulled the corners of their eyes up and down while chanting, "My mom is Chinese. My dad is Japanese. I'm a mixed up kid!" Of course, this song is now considered inappropriate, but back then in the '50s, we were just kids, singing a song in childlike innocence.

An advantage of living in the heart of Hell's Kitchen was that one was within walking distance from just about everything Manhattan had to offer, from the mom-and-pop shops to the big department stores, museums, theaters, libraries, and parks. My parents frequented the D'Amitrano-Cuomo Delicatessen, where the workers spoke Italian. It was where Mom first saw a teenaged Mario Cuomo helping behind the counter. Spina's Bakery, whose proprietor, Mr. Spina, hailed from our hometown in Sicily, was just down the block. His bakery shelves were filled with an array of delights: *millefoglie; cannoli; baba au rhum; pignoli; torroni;* rainbow cookies of red, white, and green—the colors of the Italian flag; *spumoni; gelati;* and freshly baked Italian bread. A custom Dad started early on was gifting Spina's pastries at Christmas and Easter to relatives and close friends.

A favorite haunt of mine was the New York Public Library on Forty-Second and Fifth. I would walk across the avenues from our apartment on Fortieth and Ninth through Times Square, where rows of movie theaters lined both sides of the street. My brothers and I spent many a Saturday afternoon looking at stills of coming attractions and movies currently playing. Years later, the adult movie industry took hold, changing the entire scene and attracting a depraved element that would remain until Mayor Rudy Giuliani took a broom to it. I would walk past Times Square onto Avenue of the Americas, across Bryant Park, finally reaching my destination, the library, which for me, was a welcome refuge. The two marble lions perched on either side of the entrance were the first to greet me. Years later I learned that Mayor Fiorello La Guardia named the lions Patience and Fortitude, names that embodied the qualities New Yorkers would need to survive the economic depression.

Our parents didn't allow us to hang out on the street like many of the kids did. Dad was overly protective of all his children, but more so of me. He didn't want me hanging out with the girls on our block.

He'd warn me, "I don't ever want to see you sitting on garbage cans like those girls!"

He really didn't have to worry because I certainly didn't aspire to sit on a garbage can for hours on end, chewing and smacking bubble gum, blowing huge pink bubbles until they burst all over my face.

As a result, we lived a somewhat sheltered life. I was especially naïve when it came to street slang, and lacked the street smarts kids in the neighborhood possessed, which sometimes put me at a disadvantage.

When I was about nine, I was confronted by Rico. I had seen him sitting on front stoops or garbage cans, waiting for his buddies to come along, especially his best friend, Carlos. Rico was tall, lanky, and rather cute, the last attribute contributing to his conceit. Carlos was short, hefty, and not nearly as good-looking, yet he was held in high esteem by the other boys. I imagine, if they had been part of a gang, Carlos would have been their leader. The boys were probably in their late teens. I don't think they went to school or worked, because they were permanent fixtures on the street. Rico's and Carlos' girlfriends lived in our building, and the foursome could often be found sitting on the metal garbage cans in front.

Rico, the most boisterous of the lot, always had one wisecrack or another, which he delivered with relish, especially to girls that happened by.

One day he called out to me, "Hey, you a guinea?"

"What's a guinea?" I asked.

"A wop!"

"What's a wop?"

"A dago!"

"I don't know what you're talking about!"

"A dago, a wop, a guinea! An Ital like you!" He blurted it out with such ferocity, most likely annoyed that his offensive remarks had been lost on me.

The next time I ran into the boor, he was even more offensive.

"Hey, do you have a pussy?" he jeered.

I should have kept on walking, but instead I said, "We don't have a cat."

"No, not a cat! A pussy! The pussy between your legs!"

After that, Rico didn't bother with me much. He probably didn't want to waste his talent on someone who didn't appreciate his remarkable ability to offend.

Even though my brothers and I didn't hang out on the street, we did manage to pick up a foul word here and there. One day Mom caught us saying the F-word.

Shocked by hearing us say *eff-you* this and *eff-you* that, she screamed out, "Where did you hear that?"

"The kids on the street say it," Joe said.

"It's a very bad word," Mom said icily.

"People just say it when they're mad about something," I volunteered.

"Do you know what it means?"

"No," we all said.

"It's a very bad word, and I don't ever want to hear any of you say it again. Do you understand?"

Being the inquisitive one, I asked, "What does it mean, Mom?"

"It's a bad word. That's all you need to know!"

Some years later, Rico would encounter my father's wrath. Rico was hanging out with his friends as he usually did, and when he saw me approaching with a bag full of groceries, he confronted me, "Hey, what you got there girl?"

As he tried grabbing the bag from me, I lost my balance and fell against the doorframe. I steadied myself, secured the bag, and started up the stairs. When I reached the landing I could hear my father, who must have seen what transpired, threatening Rico in his boisterous voice, "If you ever touch my daughter again, I'll kill you!"

I looked down and saw that he was gripping Rico's neck. My father then released his grip and headed up the stairs.

285

I was so angry at my father. "You didn't have to do that!" I squealed. "I'm fifteen and I can take care of myself! Now all those kids will taunt me forever."

And taunt me they did, calling me a big crybaby and daddy's little brat.

* * *

Not all kids in the neighborhood were unkind or nasty. There were those who were not only kind, but also helpful. There was Anne Marie, the daughter of Italian immigrants, who was my second-grade classmate and translator those first days in school. Also, there was Sheila, the daughter of Polish immigrants, who lived in our building. Sheila was just a year older than I and often invited me up to her apartment on the top floor. She was an only child and envied me because I had three brothers; I envied her because she had lots of dolls and toys.

When I asked for a doll, Dad said, "You don't need a doll; you have a baby brother!"

I thought that unfair. After all, playing with my baby brother meant watching him, feeding him, and changing his nappies—in other words, free babysitting. I would have preferred Betsy Wetsy. Sheila, seeing that except for my miniature kitchen set, my coloring books, and my paper doll cutouts, I didn't have much to play with, let me play with her many dolls. One day, we were outside playing, and Sheila said she'd give me Howdy Doody. She ran up and threw him down to me. Howdy came down with such a force that he cracked his skull when he landed on the pavement. Mom said that it was a lucky thing he didn't land on me, because I could have been the one with the cracked head.

After seeing TV ads for home perm kits, Sheila and I begged our mothers to get them for us. I got the Bobbi, and Sheila, the Toni. We discovered that the process wasn't as easy as it looked on TV and didn't have the same results. My thick, straight hair refused to curl, leaving me with a puffy bouffant, which was not in vogue then, and Sheila's fine, blonde hair took the curl to the extreme, giving her a wild frizz. Our mothers consoled us, saying the perm would soon wash out. Soon couldn't come soon enough!

It was Sheila who told my brothers and me about Halloween, a fun holiday when kids wore costumes and masks, went trick-or-treating, and got lots of candy. We pleaded with our mom to let us go trick-or-treating. Mom didn't like the idea, but finally relented. She took us to Woolworths, where my brothers picked the scariest Halloween masks they could find. I didn't want to look scary. I wanted to be a princess, so I selected a sparkly crown and convinced mom to let me wear her fancy dress.

"You're supposed to look *scary* when you say 'trick or treat,'" Joe snapped.

"I don't want to look scary, and anyway, Sheila's going as a princess too!"

"Bet you two won't get candy."

"Bet we will!"

"Ugh! Don't walk with us then!"

That was the first and only time I went trick-or-treating. I didn't particularly like knocking on our neighbors' doors, and besides, I didn't have any tricks up my sleeve.

Our father not only forbade us from hanging out on the street, he even limited our after-school activities, believing they were not an integral part of our education. In middle school, I played the violin and practiced at home, hoping to impress Dad with my ability to play from his sheet music. I was in my third year of music lessons when students from all over the city auditioned for a spot in the orchestra that was to perform at a concert at Hunter College. I was the only one from my school chosen to play in the orchestra, which was a great honor, not only for me, but also for my school and my music teacher. The orchestra would have to rehearse on Saturday mornings for two months. Dad didn't see it as the opportunity or the honor it truly was, and wouldn't allow me to participate. In this regard, I believe he was channeling Nonna, and I told him so. This must have stung because he finally relented.

Rehearsals were hard work but also fun, and I enjoyed them immensely. We played all five pieces of Ferde Grofé's *Grand Canyon Suite:* "Sunrise," "Painted Desert," "On the Trail," "Sunset," and "Cloudburst." My very favorite was "On the Trail." The hoofbeats of the tired donkey hoofing it up the trail brought to mind our little Sicilian donkey. Students were each given two tickets for the concert. I wanted so much for Dad to attend and was terribly disappointed he couldn't get off from work. I felt he should have made more of an effort to see his daughter performing on that stage. I would have loved to continue with the music lessons, but the high school I attended didn't have a string section. I never asked my parents for violin lessons, as I knew we couldn't afford them.

In high school, I wrote articles for the *Hughes Herald,* our school newspaper. Because meetings took place after school, I had to drop out. I wonder if Dad ever realized he was holding his children back. Mr. France, my English teacher, knew I enjoyed writing for the paper and would often assign articles to me. Once I got a plum assignment of being one of a group of students from various high schools to interview Tony Perkins. It was very exciting to see him in person! He was extremely handsome and didn't look at all like the creepy Norman Bates character he portrayed in *Psycho*.

In my junior year, my English teacher, Mrs. Edelstein, invited me to spend the summer with her family at a resort. She said I'd babysit her two young children on evenings when she and her husband went out, and I'd have the day free to partake in all the activities the resort offered: swimming, tennis, volleyball, and horseback riding. I was not only flattered, but also thrilled that I'd be spending my summer in what sounded like heaven, and not on Ninth Avenue. Mrs. Edelstein said that if I were interested, she would speak to my parents. Was I interested?! I couldn't wait! I ran home and told Mom what an honor it was that out of the whole class, Mrs. Edelstein chose me for this fantastic opportunity.

"We have to ask your father," Mom said.

Not the words I wanted to hear.

When Mom approached Dad, he flew into a rage. Glaring at both Mom and me, he bellowed, "Send my daughter away with strangers? You crazy?!"

"Mrs. Edelstein is not a stranger," I pleaded. "She's my teacher! She's a wonderful person. She must think highly of me to trust me with her children."

"I don't care she thinks highly of you! She is stranger and she has husband! You don't spend one night from this house!"

"But Dad, what do I tell Mrs. Edelstein? That you don't trust her?"

"Say you have to stay home!"

It was devastating having to tell Mrs. Edelstein that I couldn't go.

"I want to thank you for asking me," I said. "I really would love to . . . but I can't. My parents need me home."

"Would it help if I spoke to your parents?"

"No, I don't think so," I replied sadly.

The thought of Mrs. Edelstein coming face-to-face with my father was not something I wanted to contemplate. I'm sure he wouldn't have been as blunt, but I couldn't take that chance.

A few days later, my best friend, Barbara, said that her parents had readily agreed to let her go. Lucky Barbara had a wonderful summer, as she'd go on to tell me in September, while I, on the other hand, could only dream of the wonderful fun-filled days I had missed. The only consolation was that I'd been Mrs. Edelstein's first choice.

Dad definitely was clueless when it came to American ways. I was about eleven when I worked up the courage to broach the subject of an allowance, and told me father, "Dad, all my friends get an allowance."

"What is this allowance?" Dad asked.

"Allowance is money."

"Why you need money?"

"It's just a little money, like fifty cents a week."

"For what you need fifty cents?"

"No, you don't understand . . . allowance is money parents give children for washing dishes, making the bed—"

"So you want we pay you?"

"It's not *pay*. It's *allowance*. Just a little money, like ten cents for washing dishes or making the bed or throwing out the garbage . . . things like that," I explained.

"Oh, I understand. You want we pay you for what you do. OK, we pay you. But after, you have to pay your mother and me for rent, food, and—"

"No, no!" I protested. "Allowance is just a *little* money. Children don't pay for that."

"I don't like this allowance. You need something, you tell your mother and me, and we buy for you! So tell me, what is so important you need to buy?"

"Nothing! I don't need to buy *nothing*!" I said as I plodded off. What was I thinking? Dad would never understand American ways.

My brothers and I would scour the closets, concentrating on outerwear and digging into pockets, hoping to find some loose change. At times, we found pennies, nickels, and dimes, and if we were lucky, a whole quarter! A quarter bought five candy bars then. We'd scurry down to the corner candy store, and we'd each pick our favorite candy bar. Then we'd take a vote on the fifth bar, which we shared. Under my brothers' watchful eyes, I'd cut the bar into four equal parts.

A friend of Joe's said he made a lot of money selling shopping bags on Ninth Avenue. He bought the bags from a nearby store at two cents apiece and sold them for five, making a three-cent profit on each bag! Joe decided to make a go of it, and went out on Friday afternoons and Saturdays, the busiest shopping days. With the money he made, he bought baseball cards and candy. I wanted to sell bags too so that I could buy a doll and cutouts. My brother said I'd have to find my own spot because he didn't want to have to compete with me.

I started with five bags. Some people, especially men, were very generous and gave me ten cents, and sometimes even a quarter for one bag. Unfortunately, my lucrative career came to an abrupt end when I had the misfortune of running into Dad, who was out moonlighting as a detective.

Shocked at seeing his daughter peddling on the street, he hollered, "What you do here?"

"Hi, Dad . . . do you want a shopping bag?"

"Go home! Now!"

"Why?"

"I don't want my daughter on the street!"

"What about Joe? He's on the street—"

"Joe is *boy!*"

Dad definitely espoused a double standard. My brothers had far more freedom than I ever had.

Years later, my dad took the double standard to an extreme when he said, "You can marry, but you can no go out!"

I couldn't believe my ears. Was he really that clueless?

"Dad, this is America," I argued. "People go out on dates, fall in love, and then they marry! That's how it's done here. If I can't go out, how will I ever meet anyone?"

Mom, me, Tony, Joe and Peter in carriage

Me, Mom, Tony, Peter and Joe in our treeless neighborhood park

A day at the beach: Joe, Tony, Peter, Mom, and me

Joe, Tony, me, and Aunt Eleni watching television

Peter bathing in kitchen tub with unwieldy cover

Me, Peter, and Aunt Sylvia

20

GROWING UP IN 1950S AMERICA

WE ARRIVED IN AMERICA at a time when the country was enjoying peace and prosperity—the war, a distant memory. The looming threat of Communism was not on our radar then, although there was one rather telling exercise in school that should have raised a red flag: the weekly drop drill, where students were instructed to duck under their school desks and cover their heads, as if that would have shielded anyone from a nuclear attack.

We had lived in our first apartment for a little over two years when we moved two blocks away. Our new apartment, located on Fortieth Street between Ninth and Tenth Avenues, was a definite improvement. It wasn't a railroad apartment, nor was it over a grocery store, and best of all, it was off the avenue, which provided not only more pleasant views, but also less automobile and pedestrian traffic. Across the street were apartment buildings, the Church of St. Clemens Mary, a funeral home, and a corner candy store. Unlike our first building, which was four stories high and had four apartments on each landing, this building had only three stories and two apartments on each floor. Fewer families meant less noise and fewer cooking odors seeping into the hallway.

Upon entering, one would walk into the eat-in kitchen with its front-facing window that provided lots of sunlight. Just as in the first apartment, there was a stove, refrigerator, sink, and bathtub covered by a humongous white metal lid, apparently a trend of the time. Although this apartment far exceeded our first, there was one drawback: a window-like opening in the kitchen that looked into the living room. On bath nights, Mom covered the opening to prevent Joe and Tony from teasing our little brother by peeking in while he bathed. Peter would cry, saying his brothers had seen his "shame," and now he had to see theirs. Our exasperated mother told him they hadn't seen a thing, and at the same time she warned the two to get away, or they'd get a hard smack. This was an often-repeated scene that severely exhausted our mother.

The kitchen led into the living room, which faced the front and had two windows and a fire escape. Just as in our first apartment, the living room also served as a bedroom. My brothers slept on the Castro Convertible, and I, on a rollaway bed. On holidays and special occasions, the living room was transformed into a dining room in which we'd use the folding table, covering it with a festive tablecloth. Past the living room were two rooms with no windows. The larger one was our parents' bedroom, and the smaller, a storage room. The very best feature was that our bathroom was in the apartment and not out in the hall.

The landlord allowed us to have a washing machine, which we kept out in the hall, as there was no room in the kitchen. Mom would wheel it in and connect the hoses to the kitchen sink's faucet. This was a bit of a nuisance but a lot better than having to schlep to the Laundromat. Tenants dried their laundry on clotheslines. Apartments that faced the back used clotheslines that were affixed to the building across the way. Those apartments that faced the front used the clotheslines on the roof. The times I helped Mom I was careful not to get near the edge because there was no barrier, and one could easily fall off. One windy day, our sheets blew off the clothesline and flew towards the Port Authority bus route, looking like magic carpets. In the winter and on rainy days, Mom hung the clothes in the apartment on makeshift clotheslines.

There was a movie theatre on Avenue of the Americas just across the street from Bryant Park that featured foreign films. We'd often go there when an Italian film was playing. After the movie, we'd walk to the park, where my brothers and I would look out for the Good Humor cart making its rounds.

"We have ice cream home," Dad said.

"But it's not Good Humor," I said. "It's just that boring Neapolitan ice cream."

I think our parents bought Neapolitan ice cream not only because the word *Neapolitan* means "a native of Naples," but also because it had three flavors. Mom and I liked strawberry, while my brothers went for the chocolate, and Dad, the boring vanilla.

"If you no like ice cream home," our father teased, "I no buy no more."

"Oh, we like it all right, Dad," Joe said, thinking *some* ice cream was better than *no* ice cream, "but Good Humor is fun to eat."

Dad handed each of us a dime, and we joined the kids in line.

"Which one are you two getting?" I asked.

"Don't know yet," Joe said.

My eyes taking in the tempting offerings plastered on the Good Humor cart, I said, "I think I'll get the Creamsicle."

"You always get that one. I'm getting the chocolate pop with sprinkles."

"I want the ice cream sandwich," Tony said.

"And what are you kids having today?" the friendly Good Humor man asked.

We made our selections, handed over our coins, and lapped up our treats quickly so that they wouldn't drip on our clothes.

Our parents hardly ever bought packaged snacks like potato chips, cookies, or candy bars. Ice cream was the only treat in our home, and the carton of Neapolitan lasted the whole week. Our refrigerator was filled with lots of fruit. It was only on special occasions that our parents indulged us with Italian pastries and cake. Our mother made *koulourakia*, Greek cookies that we children thought boring, pining for those yummy Oreos, Chips Ahoy, and Fig Newtons we saw advertised on TV. While at the time, I felt deprived, I'm thankful I didn't get into the habit of snacking on junk food.

At times we'd venture to Central Park, which was quite a hike from our apartment. We loved exploring the park and tried to cover as much of it as we could. Once, Joe got too close to the edge of the lake and fell in. It wasn't deep, but his clothes got wet just the same, so we sat in the sun, waiting for his clothes to dry. Before heading home, Mom treated us to ice cream from the ubiquitous Good Humor man.

I became a latchkey child at the age of ten, Mom pinning the key to my dress so that I wouldn't lose it. When there was little to no work at the factory, Mom stayed home and spent most of the day baking cookies and other special treats. We'd come home from school and were greeted by the aroma of chicken and potatoes roasting. We delighted in the warmth, especially on cold winter days. On days Mom went to work, the apartment seemed cold and bare. We'd do our homework and watch TV, waiting for Mom to come home and make dinner. The factory was close by, so Mom usually got home by 5:30. We helped her by peeling potatoes, setting the table, and washing and drying the dishes.

We loved that factory work was slow in summer because we got to go to the beach on weekdays, when it wasn't too crowded. If the weather cooperated, we'd get to go two or three days a week. We discovered Sheepshead Bay in Brooklyn that first summer. My brothers and I loved splashing in the surf and never wanted to leave, pleading for just another hour. Mom always indulged us, letting us stay after most of the beachgoers had left. At times we stayed to watch the sunset lingering over the horizon, which made for a perfect end to a perfect day. We rode home on the subway, exhausted but exhilarated, our skin smelling of salty sea air. After a quick shower, Mom would make a luscious dish that Yiayia used to make for her when she was a little girl, a huge omelet filled with chopped meat sautéed with onions and a touch of tomato sauce. Mom scooped the egg onto slices of Italian bread, which we devoured.

The times our dad joined us, we ventured to Orchard Beach in the Bronx, which was quite a hike, involving not only a long subway ride, but also a trip by bus. My brothers and I didn't particularly like it when Dad came along because Dad's idea of a good time at the beach was to sit under the trees, far from the sand and sea, and grill chicken and hamburgers on the barbecue pits. We would've been happy to sit at the water's edge and just have a sandwich and a cool drink.

* * *

It was in the 1950s when most American families got their first television set. We got ours a year after arriving. Sesame Street wasn't on then, but there were lots of cartoons, which were a great help to us in learning English. A favorite of ours was Popeye the Sailor, who always ate spinach, whipped Bluto, and got his girl, Olive Oyl. We also watched Woody the Woodpecker; Mickey and Minnie Mouse; Bugs Bunny; and Tweety Bird and his nemesis, Sylvester. Later, we moved on to the Little Rascals. There was the cute but bossy Spanky; Alfalfa, with his trademark cowlick and his terrible singing voice; and Farina, which we thought a funny name for a boy. We also enjoyed the antics of the Dead End Kids, tough street-smart kids who were later called the East Side Kids, and Bowery Boys. We'd rush home from school to catch *Flash Gordon,* the science-fiction series that took place on planet Mongo, which was ruled by the evil emperor, Ming the Merciless.

In the Westerns we enjoyed, there was Gene Autry strumming his guitar, singing, "I'm Back in the Saddle Again"; Roy Rogers and Dale Evans riding their horses, Trigger and Buttermilk, and singing "Happy Trails to You"; and the Lone Ranger and Tonto galloping to the "William Tell Overture." In Westerns, the good guys wore white hats, and the bad guys wore black hats. It was incredible that no matter how long those cowboys rode on those dusty trails, they were always well groomed, without even a five-o'clock shadow. There were the inevitable saloon fights, where cowboys escaped without bruises or shedding a single drop of blood, even after being hit over the head with chairs and liquor bottles. Amazingly, the chairs just fell apart and the liquor bottles shattered when coming in contact with a person's skull!

One day as my brothers and I were watching TV, the inevitable saloon fight erupted. Peter, who was just two, must have wanted to test that principle. He picked up his milk bottle by the neck and before I could reach him, he struck Tony on the head. We were shocked and horrified to see the blood gushing from Tony's head—not the result Peter had expected. After the initial shock, I launched into big-sister mode, retrieved a clean towel, wrapped it around Tony's head, and called Mom at the factory. She then took Tony to the ER, where he got stitches.

One can only wonder if a bloodless saloon fight on TV can entice a toddler to mimic what he watched on the screen, convincing him to violently strike his older brother. Seeing Peter's reaction to play out what he had seen on TV leads me to wonder can all that gratuitous violence in movies, television, and video games spur a child to become a shooter? All through my school years I don't recall ever hearing of one single school shooting whereas today, mass shootings have sadly become an all too common occurrence. While I can't comment on other potentially contributing factors like mental illness or the misuse of opioids and other drugs, I do wonder if the constant display of violence and frequent use of abuse-themed video games add fuel the fire.

Television shows of the 1950s were, for the most part, wholesome ones that the family watched together. An all-time favorite was *The Ed Sullivan Show,* which most of America tuned into on Sunday nights. The show had something for everyone: magicians, acrobats, jugglers, high-wire acts, and circus performers; there were the comedians who didn't have to resort to foul language because they were actually funny, and a bevy of Broadway and movie stars, dancers, and singers. Best of all, one didn't have to understand English to enjoy the show!

Our very favorite show was *I Love Lucy*. We didn't always understand what was being said, but we still found it funny, mainly due to Lucy getting herself into all sorts of jams.

"What are they saying?" Dad would ask.

And we'd say, "We don't know, but it's funny."

Early on we didn't watch shows like *The George Burns and Gracie Allen Show* because there was more dialogue than slapstick, and we had difficulty following along. We loved Laurel and Hardy and called them "Fat and Skinny." Later, as our English improved, we watched *Superman, Lassie, Father Knows Best,* and *Make Room for Daddy*. One of my favorite episodes of *Make Room for Daddy* was when Danny Thomas tells his son, Rusty, "Growing up, we were so poor we didn't have toys, we played with bottle tops. We were so poor, we couldn't afford linoleum and had newspapers on the floor instead." The smart aleck replies, "Gee, Dad, aren't you glad you're living with us now?" This episode resonated with me because it reinforced the notion that parents often exaggerate and never stop telling their children how good they have it.

Watching shows like *Father Knows Best* and *Make Room for Daddy*, we'd hear kids call their mothers Mom and Mommy and their fathers Dad and Daddy, while we addressed our parents Papà and Mamma. Wanting to be more American and "hip" like those kids on TV, we decided to give it a try. Mom didn't mind but our father didn't care for it, and would make fun exaggerating the Moo sound a cow makes. Later on, we called our father Dad, to which he'd say, "Dead? I'm no dead! Why you say to me dead?"

"Papà, it's not *dead*, it's *dad!*" It would take more than a little while but eventually our father got used to our calling him dad.

* * *

Like most young girls, I couldn't wait to grow up. For as long as I could remember, I'd watched my mom apply lipstick and nail polish, dreaming of the day I'd be allowed to do the same. I'd sneak off with her nail polish, apply it to one nail, and admire it for the longest time. I watched as my mom shaped her eyebrows, plucking the stray hairs with tweezers. One day I decided to pluck mine, and not finding Mom's tweezers, I settled on a pair of scissors and proceeded to trim my thick brows. When Mom saw what I had done, she gasped so loud she woke Dad from his afternoon nap.

"What's the matter?" Dad asked.

"Look at her! Look at what she's done to herself!"

Still groggy from sleep, Dad did a double take at my missing brows and groaned, "What on earth . . ."

"I wanted to look like Mom," I explained.

"Look like Mom? Your mother has eyebrows!"

"I didn't finish."

"You didn't finish? You did plenty!"

"What are we going to do with you?" Mom said as she filled in my brows, making me the only ten-year-old wearing eyebrow pencil to school as we waited for my brows to grow back in.

When I was eleven, Dad took me shopping for a dress. It was our first and last father–daughter shopping trip. The saleswoman selected several dresses that she thought would suit me. I came out of the fitting room in a lovely chemise that featured a contrasting sash that rested on my hips.

Not to offend the saleswoman, Dad whispered in Italian, "Let's get out of here. She doesn't know what she's doing. That dress is way too big! Look where the waist is!"

"That's the way it's supposed to fit, Dad. It's a chemise. It has a drop waist." Unlike Dad, I kept up with the latest fashion trends by flipping through the pages of *Glamour* and *Seventeen* at the local candy store.

"It looks like a sack! Put your clothes on, and let's go!"

Dad wasn't the only one to call the chemise a sack. The chemise was a subject of heated debate in the American press; many commentators, particularly men, considered the figure-concealing style ugly and unnatural.

Another fashion craze of the 1950s was the poodle skirt, a wide, pastel-colored skirt with a life-size poodle appliqué. Even as a youngster, I thought the ubiquitous skirt a silly trend. To get the look just right, you had to wear lots of crinoline petticoats.

Shopping with Mom, I'd usually select a dress we couldn't possibly afford. It seems I had champagne taste on a beer budget. Mom tried finding a dress that would suit me, and more importantly, our budget.

I never demanded; I merely sighed, "That's OK, Mom. I really don't have to have a dress."

Days later, Mom would hand me the dress I had selected. I was thrilled, but at the same time, I felt a twinge of guilt, knowing that Mom went without to buy me that dress. This reminded me of how the character Mama in *I Remember Mama* always came to the rescue. While I couldn't make it up to Mom then, I knew that someday, I'd try my best to do so.

I've often told my mom that I feel lucky to have *her* as my mother rather than any of her sisters. She's the only one of her siblings to inherit Pappou's calm, reassuring nature. She's seldom rattled and reacts calmly and wisely in most situations. Throughout the years, I've found her to be not only loving and nurturing, but also very wise. This last trait was a great comfort to me, especially during my awkward preteen and teen years. Like many girls growing up, I had all sorts of body issues. One that really distressed me was my big feet. When I was twelve years old, I wore size eight, which looked humongous when compared to Mom's size five. I despaired, wanting to know why my feet had to be so big.

"You're so much taller than me," Mom said. "Why, if you had my little feet, you'd fall over."

This seemed to make sense and made me feel somewhat better.

I couldn't wait to get a part-time job. Since just about everyone said I looked older than my twelve years, I decided to use it to my advantage. I discovered, to my chagrin that employers didn't go by appearance. One was required to have working papers stating he or she was at least fourteen years old. As soon as I turned fourteen, with working papers in hand, I applied for a part-time salesclerk position at Woolworths and at Cushman's Bakery. Cushman's hired me, and I worked behind the counter at the Penn Station location. At first, I thought I'd be tempted by all those cakes and cookies, but the sweet-smelling delights that greeted me at the door nauseated me by day's end.

I liked earning money. I found it empowering. When I received my first paycheck, I spent it all on a pocketbook for my mom and a toy car for my little brother. My parents said I shouldn't spend my entire paycheck each period and encouraged me to save a portion of it, which I did. A year later, I left the bakery job and went to work at Macy's. It was a "Saturday only" position, working from 5:15 p.m. to

9:15 p.m. on Mondays and Thursdays, and 9:00 a.m. to 6:00 p.m. on Saturdays. I'd rush home from school, have a snack, do some homework, and walk to Macy's.

My job at Macy's made me quite popular with my family members. My mom and aunts had me tag along when they shopped so that they could take advantage of my employee discount. Another perk of working at Macy's was participating in the Thanksgiving Day Parade. I was all excited, thinking I'd get to wear one of those sparkly gowns and ride on a float. However, I was given a burgundy-color bodysuit with fish scales made of sequins and told I'd have to walk the entire route. I argued that fish didn't walk, but it was to no avail.

* * *

During the innocent 1950s, parents didn't seem concerned about children walking to and from school unaccompanied. Our parents told us that we were to cross the street when the light was green and only after looking both ways. Parents today wait at the bus stop with their children and wouldn't dream of sending them off on their own. They take them to and from all their activities. One can't blame them. These days, it seems a day doesn't go by that we don't hear about a pedophile priest, rabbi, or teacher of either sex preying on innocent and defenseless children. There are many news reports of children abducted, sexually abused, and killed. I don't remember hearing about pedophiles or perverts when I was growing up. But these predators did exist then and have always roamed the earth, and they have no qualms about harming their innocent young victims.

Growing up, I had two encounters with predators. The first took place when I was about ten. It was summer, and school was out. On days Mom worked, my brothers and I went to the playground so that Dad, who usually didn't get home from work until the wee hours, could sleep. It was difficult for four children to be still and not make a sound in our small apartment, especially since there were only drapes separating our parents' bedroom and the living room. On rainy days, we stayed in and watched TV without sound. If any of us made a noise, the others were quick to say "Shush!" One day the shushing got so loud that Dad sprang out of bed, walked up to each of us, and with a finger to his lips, made the shushing sound. Afterward, he screamed, "How can anybody get any sleep with all that shushing?!"

Going to the park and leaving the apartment to Dad made life easier for everyone. That way, we didn't feel as if we were in detention, and Dad was able to get his sleep. Our parents entrusted me with the care of Peter, who was one and a half. Joe and Tony knew that they had to mind me, and stand on either side of the stroller and hold on to the handlebar before crossing the street. In summer, the sprinklers at the playground were turned on, and we ran into the water to cool off. There was always some smart aleck who spoiled the fun by sitting on the sprinkler head, preventing the water from spraying out. The kids would run around him, sometimes kicking his butt until he finally got up and let the water spray out.

At noontime, my brothers and I trekked across the street to the Holy Cross School, where on weekdays, sandwiches and milk were served to all the urchins. Our favorite was the peanut butter sandwich, an item that's taboo in schools today because of the prevalence of peanut allergies. After lunch, we returned to the playground. My brothers headed for the monkey bars and I secured Peter into a chair swing, Peter asking me to make him go higher and higher. When he'd had enough, I put him in his stroller and walked over to the park bench. An elderly man came over, sat next to us and started entertaining Peter by making funny faces. He then leaned over as if trying to reach the stroller and placed his hand on my lap. Even as a ten-year-old, this didn't feel right to me, so I slid away. He then moved closer and once again put his hand on my lap. This time I pushed his hand away, got up, and called to my brothers, saying we had to leave.

The next time we went to the playground I saw the man lurking about. He smiled and tailed us as we climbed the monkey bars, slid down the slide, and swung on the swings. At noon my brothers and I headed to Holy Cross for lunch. When we returned to the playground, I was relieved the man was gone. I was sitting with Peter as Joe and Tony played ball with their friends when the man reappeared. He came over and began the same routine, fussing over Peter, only this time, he placed a quarter in Peter's hand. I gave the coin back to him and told him we were not allowed to take money from strangers. He said he wasn't a stranger and once again placed his hand on my lap. I pushed his hand away, called my brothers, and we headed home.

On the way home we'd usually stop by the photographer's studio to look at the pictures on display and make fun of the people's expressions. As we were walking by the doorway, I heard a sound, and when I looked up, I saw that ghastly man standing at the top of the stairway, exposing himself. I don't think my brothers saw him because I quickly pulled them away, saying we had to walk fast because it was late. I told them to hold on to the stroller and we took off. Peter must have enjoyed the speedy ride because he giggled all the way home, his golden Shirley Temple curls flapping in the wind.

Later when I thought about it, that pervert must have followed us at other times because he obviously knew our routine. That's why he was there waiting for us. This frightened me, and for the longest time, I found excuses to avoid going to the playground. I never once thought of telling Dad. I knew Dad was extremely protective of us, and had he known, he would have beaten or even killed the man. Having been separated from Mom all those years, I didn't want for us to be separated from Dad. I didn't even tell Mom, which looking back, was not very smart. Luckily, I never saw the man again. Hopefully, he was arrested and locked up forever.

The second incident occurred when I was thirteen and in junior high school. I was on my way home from school, and as I was going up the stairs, I heard someone coming up behind me. I was somewhat wary and waited for the person to go to wherever he was going before opening the door to our apartment. When the man reached the landing, he walked toward me wiping his brow with his handkerchief. He wore a suit and tie, and with his fedora, he looked like a businessman. He spoke rapidly and in choppy sentences, as if he were out of breath.

"Hi! I could use your help," he said. "I have some books in my car. It's not hard work. It won't take long. I'll pay you. Would you like to make some money?"

As I stood facing him, he kept coming closer. Worried he might see the key in my hand, I clenched my fist so hard that the metal ridge dug into my palm.

"No, I can't!" I blurted out. "My father is coming any minute, and I have lots of things to do."

"Hey, I have an idea. I'll help you with whatever you have to do; then you can help me, OK?"

"No, you can't help me. You should ask somebody else to help you."

Assessing me, he said, "You know, you look a lot like my little sister. I bet you even weigh the same." Then, placing his hands on my waist, he said, "Let's see."

I tried pulling away, but with my back up against the washing machine, I had nowhere to go. As he lifted me up, I heard footsteps coming up the stairs. He put me down and darted up the stairs leading to the roof. I unlocked the door, and once inside, locked it and secured the chain. I was so scared I could hardly breathe. I didn't get to see who was walking up the stairs, but I was relieved it wasn't my dad. If he had seen the state I was in, he would have chased the man up to the roof, and someone would've died that day.

By the time Dad arrived, I had managed to compose myself. And once again, I didn't tell him. However, this time, I couldn't keep from telling Mom. It was after five when she got home, Dad having already left for his second shift. As soon as Mom walked in, I fell to pieces as I recounted what happened. She told me I had done well not to open the door.

One might ask why I didn't tell my father about this episode or the one in the playground. I was afraid. Afraid because I knew how protective he was of us. I believed he might kill anyone who'd try to harm us. Where my mother was calm and steady, my father was not.

I don't think Mom ever told Dad. I believe keeping things from Dad was our way of protecting him from himself.

Years later Dad would say, "Am I always the last to know what goes on around here?"

21

ROULA, THE LAST TO ARRIVE

M Y BROTHER JOE AND I were in our second year of school and Tony was in kindergarten when our Aunt Roula arrived. I was in third grade, and Joe, in first. I learned of Roula's existence a few months earlier when my brothers and I were at Yiayia's.

I was looking out the window when Yiayia suddenly pulled me aside and, screaming in that language I didn't understand, said, "*Ohi, Ohi, Ohi, kako pedi!*"

She then removed the pin from my dress—a little pocketbook pin Aunt Eleni had given me—all the while wagging her finger and saying "Roula" over and over again. Even though I didn't understand what she'd said, I could sense she was angry.

"Aunt Eleni gave it to me," I protested. "She said it was mine."

But Yiayia didn't understand me either. She just turned away and left me crying.

Later, when my Aunt Eleni returned, I ran to her.

"Yiayia took my pin!" I said. "She thinks I stole it. She kept saying 'Ohi Roula.' What does 'Ohi Roula' mean?"

My aunt went over to Yiayia and spoke to her in Greek. Yiayia frowned, grumbled, and returned the pin to me.

When Mom came to pick us up I asked, "What does 'Ohi Roula' mean?"

"Ohi means 'no,' and Roula is my little sister's name."

"I didn't know you had another sister."

"Yes, she's my little sister, and she'll be arriving soon."

Years later Mom said that the reason Roula came to America was because she was not getting along with her adoptive parents. The problems began when Roula learned she had been adopted. What hurt her most was why, out of the four children, it was she who was given away. This knowledge deeply affected her, and she, like Yiayia, would suffer bouts of depression. Her adoptive parents were unable to deal with their fourteen-year-old daughter's mood swings and asked my grandparents to have Roula come to America. This move only intensified Roula's feelings of rejection. A tall, slender, striking girl with doleful eyes and lustrous black hair, Roula saw herself as unworthy, for she had been given up not once, but twice—the second time, by the only parents she had known. When she arrived in America, she defiantly told my mom, "The only reason I came was to let you all know how much I hate you."

Mom could see the hurt and rage on her sister's face.

"You don't really mean that, Roula."

"Yes, I do! Wouldn't you feel the same way if you were rejected, thrown away like garbage?"

"You were never rejected," Mom said.

"Why was I given away?"

"You were the youngest."

"That's no reason!"

"You're right."

"Do you know what it's like to be given away?"

"No, Roula, I don't. But try to understand. You were not given to strangers. Aunt Athena wanted you desperately and kept after our mother. The only reason our mother agreed to let her take you was because Aunt Athena convinced our mother that she would provide a substantial dowry."

"That doesn't make it any better."

"I can tell you one thing: our parents always regretted letting you go."

"But they *did* let me go!"

"When you left, the house was empty. We all missed you and wanted you back. I wanted to go to Aegion and bring you back. But it was wartime, and our parents wouldn't let me."

"Why didn't they come get me?"

"If only they had. Our mother was never the same after you left. At times she was so depressed, she didn't leave her bed. Our father had to force her up. Two years went by before Aunt Athena brought you back. You seemed so happy with them, so our parents agreed to let them adopt you. You were never rejected, Roula. Everyone loved you. Everyone wanted you."

But Roula could not be swayed, and her bitterness only grew. My grandparents had a difficult time with their daughter, which added yet another worry to Yiayia's endless list of worries.

* * *

Roula enrolled in high school, and in order to assimilate, she changed her name to an American sounding one. She thought of shortening Argyroula, her given name, to Argery but didn't like the sound of it. *Argyros* in Greek means silver, so she decided on Sylvia. At home, she was called Roula. I was happy to learn that there was only a five-year difference in our ages and considered her more of a sister than an aunt.

Sylvia spoke Greek only. She, too, had a flair for languages and learned English quickly, and learned to speak it with only a slight accent. She excelled in French, her favorite subject. Her least favorite subject was physical education; she hated all sports, including swimming. I couldn't understand that. I loved sports, especially volleyball and basketball, and thoroughly enjoyed splashing in our school's Olympic-size pool, where I learned to float and swim.

Sylvia got a part-time job at the Woolworths five-and-dime just around the corner from our apartment. Saturday evenings, my brothers and I waited anxiously for her to come over with the huge white paper bag filled to the brim with warm potato chips. Woolworths had a potato chip warmer, where one could see the chips flying up and around through the clear glass case. Sylvia would pour the chips into a huge bowl and we'd munch on them while watching *Million Dollar Movie*. The series would play the same movie every night for a week, and my brothers and I drove Mom crazy, insisting we watch the same movie night after night. By the end of the week, we had memorized many of the lines and recited them even before the characters on the screen did! We enjoyed Sylvia's company and looked forward to those Saturday visits. We thought of her as one of us kids. Sylvia liked coming over to our house because it was a place where, for a few hours, she could escape her unhappy home life. She didn't get along with her parents and often quarreled with them. One time the argument got so heated and physical that Pappou called for the police.

We didn't know at the time that in addition to suffering from depression, Sylvia also struggled with OCD, especially when it came to cleaning. At the time, we thought she was a clean freak and never gave it much thought. When washing her hands, she'd scrub and scrub, never satisfied that they were clean. Her grooming and bathing ritual took hours, which can be a problem when there's only one bathroom in the apartment.

When Sylvia was just seventeen and a senior in high school, she announced that she was to marry a man she had met only two weeks prior. We learned that our future Uncle Manoli was related to our Uncle Peter's in-laws. He was vacationing in New York and staying with relatives, where he saw a photo of Sylvia, a bridesmaid at Uncle Peter and Aunt Eugenia's wedding. Manoli was taken by the stunning beauty and asked to meet her. The two met, and it must have been love at first sight for both. However, I believe Sylvia thought marriage would be a way out of her unhappy home life.

Our Saturdays with Sylvia sadly came to an end much too soon, and things would never be the same. She would be a married woman with children and no longer one of us kids. Although I was sad about her marrying, I was thrilled that she asked me to be her bridesmaid. I got to wear a fancy gown, a tiara, and two-inch heels. I was even allowed to wear lipstick, which was a big thrill for a twelve-year-old.

A couple of months later, Sylvia invited me out for what I thought would be a day of fun. What I didn't know was that my Aunt Eleni was in the hospital having her second baby and that Sylvia had volunteered to get the baby's room ready. I was disheartened to learn that instead of a fun time, I was in for a cleaning marathon. The trip to my aunt's apartment in Washington Heights was long and complicated, requiring three subway lines, an elevator ride down to the bowels of the earth, and another elevator up to street level.

When we got to the apartment, Sylvia handed me a bucket filled with what had to be pure ammonia, because when I dipped my hands in it, I screamed, "It burns!"

"It doesn't burn," Sylvia said. "You're just not used to cleaning."

At times my mom had me help with the cleaning, but never had my hands burned like this. I soldiered on nevertheless, scrubbing the crib, which wasn't even dirty to begin with. When I finished cleaning the already-clean crib, my hands no longer burned because they were numb.

After inspecting the crib, Sylvia said, "I think it could use another going-over."

"Huh? It looks clean to me."

"Just go over it one more time."

We were in that apartment for hours, working without a break, when the phone rang.

"It's for you," Sylvia said, handing me the phone.

Great! I thought. *Someone's come to my rescue!*

I took the phone, only to hear my father holler, "What are you doing there? Come home right now. You've had enough fun!"

I decided I'd deal with the fun part later.

"Dad, please come get me. I don't know how to come home. You have to come and—"

Sylvia grabbed the phone and told my father, "Sotiri, we still have a little more to do. I'll bring Teresa home as soon as we finish."

It must have been very late when Sylvia dropped me off because Dad was fuming. As he was about to lace into me, I thrust out my swollen red hands.

Dad, looking at them in disbelief turned to Mom and said, "What's wrong with that sister of yours?"

Sylvia had been married for two years when I started high school. My homeroom teacher, Mrs. Van Kooten, had also been Sylvia's homeroom teacher. Mrs. V., as we called her, remembered Sylvia, telling me she was very fond of her.

Sylvia must have confided in Mrs. V. about her unhappy home life, because she said, "I knew Sylvia had difficulties at home, and I tried to help. Mornings she wasn't in class, I'd phone her, urging her to not miss school. She was a bright girl and one of my favorite students. I was disappointed she married so young. I wish she had stayed in school. She had so much potential."

Sylvia would regret leaving school to marry a man she barely knew, a man who had his own demons, a man who would only add to her already low self-esteem.

Passport Photos

First making the trip to America: Eleni, Pappou, and Taki in 1946

Second row, from left: Yiayia in 1947, Mom in 1949, and Sylvia in 1953

Third row: Me, Mom and Giuseppe in 1948, our first passport photo; me, Dad and Giuseppe in 1949, our second passport photo

Fourth row: Me, Dad and Giuseppe in 1952, our third passport photo

22

YIAYIA AND PAPPOU

FOR YIAYIA, STARTING A NEW LIFE in America was not easy, unlike Pappou, who simply rolled up his sleeves and dealt with the task at hand. In Greece he'd owned a business, and he would do the same in America, albeit on a smaller scale. It wasn't until 1970 when Mom and I made our first trip back to Patras since leaving in 1945 that I understood why Yiayia had a difficult time adapting to life in America. She had traded her magnificent home in her beloved Patras for a tenement on Ninth Avenue.

Patras, a port city, is the third largest city in Greece and is divided into two parts that are connected by roads and broad stairways. The upper and older part of the city, Ano Poli, is more picturesque than the lower, Kato Poli. The city is surrounded by crystal-blue waters, with mountains as a backdrop, making it an idyllic vacation spot.

Patras had been Yiayia's home from the time she was ten. Her father, Haralambos Delis, an ambitious, hardworking man, purchased the Patras property in 1913 with the proceeds from the sale of his house, farmlands, and livestock in Dervéni. The property was not developed and most likely had an attractive selling price.

We don't know how many acres there were in that parcel, but it was large enough to build thirteen houses on it, each with a generous piece of land to farm and breed cows, goats, and chickens. My great-grandfather Haralambos and his four adult sons cleared the land, and as the children wed, they were given a plot on which to build. Land closer to the city line was sold for commercial use. Clearing the land, however, was daunting and required not only cutting down many trees, weeds, and vines, but also having to deal with the dreaded *saites,* flying snakes that leaped from tree to tree, terrifying everyone, especially Yiayia, who had a morbid fear of them. It was only after her father and brothers convinced her that they had all been destroyed that she was able to venture outside.

During our visit, Mom and I walked down a long, winding road. Mom pointed to house after house belonging to aunts, uncles, and cousins. We stopped at each house and were greeted like the long lost relatives we were. Our cousins treated us to a glass of ice-cold water and to a tangy, sweet preserve, which was served on a tiny round plate. By the time we reached the last house on the strip, I was already experiencing a sugar high!

Upon first entering my grandparents' house, I had the feeling of having been there before. Mom reminded me that, after all, I did spend my first eight months there. I delighted in the summer breezes that traveled from the front balcony to the veranda in the back. I marveled at the view from the veranda, where you could see past the garden and the immense fields to the blue-domed church perched on a hill and the mountains beyond. Behind the church, not visible from the house, is the cemetery where my grandparents and their son, Constantinos, are now buried. To get an aerial view of the city, I climbed the spiral metal staircase that led to the rooftop terrace.

When Mom lived there, they walked the half mile to the beach on property belonging to the Delis family. In the early 1960s, the government acquired a portion of the land through eminent domain in order to build a highway. With the four-lane highway cutting through their property, our relatives sold the land on the other side to developers who went on to build several commercial buildings and affordable housing. And although one can still walk to the beach, crossing the four-lane highway with two-way traffic can be daunting.

The garden was still encircled by the eight-foot stone wall, but all those years of neglect had left their mark, as evidenced by the vine-strangled trees. The garden had once boasted a bevy of trees yielding fruit that Yiayia transformed into tangy, sweet preserves, figs as big as my palm, and oil-rich green and black olives. There was an array of citrus trees, which in their bloom, produced blossoms that transformed into lemons, oranges, and tangerines, emitting wondrous fragrances that greeted Mom at the gate. The citrus trees yielded a large quantity of fruit that Pappou sold to produce retailers. The income generated from the sale of produce and Yiayia's preserves provided for the family. The garden also had an assortment of vegetables, which supplied them with much-needed food during the war. Beyond the wall were the vineyards that yielded an assortment of grapes. Mom was saddened that this once-thriving garden was now overgrown with weeds.

It was on that trip that Mom and I took a bus trip to Dervéni, about seventy-three kilometers from Patras. I learned that the name *Dervéni* derives from its geographical location—squeezed between the mountains and the deep Corinthian Sea—where the houses are flanked by the old national road and the seashore. We walked along that narrow road that separates the mountains and the sea and stopped at an outdoor café. We were enjoying our lemon-flavored ice tea when a tall, middle-aged man approached us.

Speaking in English, he said, "Are you ladies by any chance Greek?"

Mom, replying in Greek said, "*Ne, imaste Ellinides.*" ("Yes, we are Greek.")

John, a friendly sort, expressed delight in Mom's fluency and continued in Greek, "Welcome to Dervéni! Are you here on vacation? Are you looking for a place to stay?"

"We're staying in Patras," Mom said. "And are here only for the day. We came hoping to find the house where my mother lived as a young girl."

"Your mother lived in Dervéni? What is her name?"

"Delis. Violetta Delis."

"Did you say *Delis?* I, too, am a Delis. John Delis. Perhaps we are related."

Mom invited John to sit at our table, and as they compared notes, they discovered, to their amazement, that they were indeed related, third cousins possibly. He told us that he knew of the house and that presently no one lived there.

We followed as John led the way, and after walking a short distance, he pointed to a small house that sat at the water's edge. We walked down a few steps, took off our shoes, and stepped into the cool water, which was as clear as glass, just as Yiayia had described it.

John said that many of the houses were not lived in and were second homes, the inhabitants having left for Patras or Athens. We were thrilled to have found that little house in that serene, idyllic town, for now we understood why my great-grandparents decided to leave all those years ago. They wanted their children to have opportunities Dervéni could never give them.

*   *   *

It can be said that Yiayia was not only class conscious, but also somewhat of a snob, especially when it came to her daughters. From the time her first daughter was born, Yiayia strived to have ample dowries. She had higher-than-high aspirations for all three of her daughters She would spend time, effort, and worry, even sacrificing her youngest daughter, a move that would plague Yiayia for her entire life.

It is both sad and ironic that all that time, effort, and worry that had consumed Yiayia would be for naught.

Her goal was that they marry highly educated, prosperous men from reputable families. She certainly didn't want a laborer or a farmer in the family, and most definitely not a man from the Greek islands, believing islanders to be poorly educated and unsophisticated.

However, all three daughters would disappoint: her eldest, my mom, when she married the enemy occupier from that foreign Sicilian island; Eleni, when she chose a common laborer from the island of Nisyros; and Roula, when she went on to marry a merchant marine who not only hailed from the inhospitable island of Kasos, but also had the temerity of being born in Egypt! The islands not only lured her daughters, they also snared her son, who chose to run off with a siren from Kasos.

Uncle Nick amused us with stories of how Yiayia tried to discourage him from calling on Aunt Eleni.

"When I was courting your aunt," he chuckled, "I had to watch for the buckets of water your yiayia poured on me from her window. The old lady managed to get me once!"

The buckets of water Uncle Nick had to dodge reminded me of Yiayia chasing Dad away with her broom. But just like Dad, Uncle Nick hung in there, his persistence paying off.

* * *

I regret I didn't really get to know my yiayia and didn't get to have the bond I had with my nonna. It didn't help that we didn't speak the same language. The Greek language sounded so harsh to me, especially when she spoke it. Her high-pitched voice made me think she was always angry and made me yearn for my nonna even more. I never felt loved by my yiayia, and at times I felt she resented me. When I shared this with Mom, she told me I was wrong.

"Yiayia always loved you," Mom said. "When you were born, and I was ill for weeks, it was Yiayia who took care of you."

While it's nice knowing that Yiayia bathed me in water suffused with rose petals and citrus leaves, I have no memory of it. I only wish she had given me some of that love and affection when I reentered her life as a seven-year-old.

Yiayia had lived through two world wars and the Greek Civil War, the latter being the most devastating, as it pit village against village, father against son, and brother against brother. She was no stranger to loss and grief. She suffered her first loss when her two-year-old son succumbed to cancer; the second, when she was pressured into giving up her three-year-old daughter; the third, when she lost her fourteen-year-old daughter to an infatuation; and now this last blow, having to leave her beloved home for a foreign land. Yiayia would sometimes fall deep into depression, keeping herself at a distance from the world, a world that had turned against her and kept her in her bed, unable to move. Unable or unwilling to adapt to her new life in America, Yiayia gave up, and in the summer of 1956, my grandparents returned to their home in Greece. It was a sad irony because my grandparents had immigrated to America to be reunited with their eldest daughter, and now they would be separated from all four children, who were now married and had made America their home. The separation added to her despair and contributed to her already poor health, and on September 2, 1960, at the age of fifty-seven, Yiayia died of a heart attack. Aunt Eleni, who happened to be vacationing in Greece with her husband and two children, was the only one of her children at her funeral.

My uncle and aunts met and wed their mates in America

Aunt Eleni and   *Uncle Peter and*   *Aunt Sylvia and*
Uncle Nick   *Aunt Eugenia*   *Uncle Manoli*

After Yiayia's death, Pappou, who was seventy-one, was inundated with many callers who came to pay their respects. Many of these callers were women—young (one was eighteen) and old, single, widowed, or divorced—hoping to charm the newly-widowed American-Greek living all alone in that big house. Both of Yiayia's sisters, Aunt Vasiliki and Aunt Zaffiroula, worried that their brother-in-law would fall prey to some unscrupulous woman and decided to take matters in their own hands. Through a matchmaker they found Evgenia (Eugenia), a sweet single woman, who at forty years old was thirty-one years his junior. Pappou and Evgenia took to each other quickly and decided to tie the knot.

All of Pappou's children, my mom included, were appalled that their father would consider marrying so soon after their mother's death. My mom wrote her father and said that she was disappointed that he would not honor the customary one-year anniversary of their mother's death. It was my father who took Pappou's side, and convinced Mom and her siblings that a man of Pappou's age should have a companion to share the rest of his life with. Pappou and Evgenia married in early 1961. Evgenia proved to be a caring and loving woman and a wonderful companion for Pappou until his death in May of 1966.

23

The American Dream

A DREAM MANY EUROPEAN IMMIGRANTS share is to own a home with land for a vegetable garden. Having lived in war-torn Europe, immigrants—like my parents and grandparents, who arrived in America in the 1950s—knew the benefits of owning a home with land. It was in 1961, nine years after arriving, that our parents finally realized that dream. They scrimped, saved, and finally had enough money for a down payment on a two-family house in Astoria. We lived on the first and second floors, and we rented the top floor, which helped pay down the mortgage. There were trees lining the street, a small patch of land in front where we planted flowers, and a strip in the back for planting vegetables. Considering that Dad hated working the land, he was a pro at cultivating our vegetable garden. His green thumb yielded tomatoes, cucumbers, zucchini, string beans, arugula, parsley, and basil.

The best thing about living in Astoria is that we were no longer living in an apartment in Hell's Kitchen. After having shared one bathroom in the hall with another family and bathing in the kitchen, having two bathrooms in our new home was the greatest of luxuries. The very best part was that the bathtub was no longer in the kitchen, but in the bathroom, where it belonged. There was a powder room on the first floor and a full bath on the second. The first time I walked into that amazing room, I closed the door behind me to take in all the room had to offer. I loved the warm peach-colored tiles from floor to ceiling, which complemented the peach-colored bathtub, vanity, and toilet. It was a world I had never known, a world where I could luxuriate in a bubble bath or an invigorating shower in complete and total privacy. I had never experienced anything like it. What luxury! What joy! I was sixteen going on seventeen, and it couldn't have happened at a better time!

Our parents purchased new furniture for all the rooms. This was the first time I was happy about being the only girl, because I got to have my very own room, whereas my three brothers had to share one. I could stay up as late as I wanted, reading and listening to the radio softly playing. I had my very own closet that I never tired of arranging and rearranging. My room faced the backyard, which was a welcome change from the Manhattan dorm room I'd shared with my brothers. I even got to select my bedroom set. Walking through the showroom, I came upon the one I wanted to call my own. The set included a bed with a headboard with sliding panels behind which I placed my books and knickknacks, a dresser with nine drawers and a large mirror at its center, and a nightstand for my lamp and clock radio. That first summer, for my seventeenth birthday, my parents gifted me with an avant-garde glass tray on which I showcased my combs and brushes and my favorite perfume, Chanel No. 5, a fragrance I have never deviated from.

Yes, one can say we had achieved the American Dream!

Our first year together in America.
My arm on Mom's shoulder, I'm
contemplating shoving Tony off her lap!

The dreaded family photo

Roula's wedding: my brothers at bottom left; I'm
in the back row third from right, and just like
Mom I look more like seventeen than twelve

Joe, Mom, Peter, me, and Tony in Astoria Park

Wishing Joe a safe tour of duty in the Navy during the Vietnam War

Dad, Tony, Peter, and Joe in Astoria Park

Mom and Dad in France

Mom and me on our first trip to Patras

Mom and Nonna in France

The vineyards, farms, and bucolic paths in Patras would give way for apartment buildings to be built. These modern edifices now tower over the landscape where my Greek grandparents' house built in 1840 once stood. I don't know what my great-grandfather, Haralambos Delis, would make of these structures erected on that rural parcel of land that he and his sons had cleared all those years ago.

24

NONNA'S VISIT

WHEN DAD, JOE, AND I left for America, Nonna grew lonely and decided to go to France and live with her daughter, Pietrina's family. I asked Dad if our donkey had gone with her. He said he had been sold along with Nonna's properties. This made me sad. Ciro was not just a working donkey, but a pet.

Now that we were living in a house with lots of rooms our parents convinced Nonna to come stay with us. After much prodding in 1961, Nonna, who was seventy-three, agreed to come. Flying over the Atlantic must have brought back memories of her previous trip to America, when she'd traveled in steerage. That arduous 1916 voyage had taken fourteen days, whereas the flight would only take seven hours!

Dad and I met Nonna at Idlewild International Airport (now JFK). Nonna must have frozen us in time because although we periodically sent family photos, she mistook me for my mom.

"This is not Maria," Dad said. "This is your granddaughter."

The tears streaming down her face, Nonna looked up at me in disbelief and said, "This is my little Tre-Tre?"

"Yes, Nonna, it's me, Tre-Tre," I said. "But I'm not so little anymore."

All the way home, Nonna stared at me, not really believing I was that little girl who'd left just nine years ago. She would have the same reaction when she saw her little *piccilidro* all grown up and towering over her. Nonna looked at Dad suspiciously. Was this really her son? Her son who had always been slim was now, at forty-one, sporting more than a middle-age spread.

Nonna only spoke Sicilian. Joe and I could easily converse with her. Tony and Peter understood some Sicilian since our father often spoke to us in Sicilian. However, speaking the language was difficult for them. The situation brought back memories of those difficult first days when the three of us kids were unable to understand one another.

Nonna was still wearing traditional Sicilian mourning attire and Dad suggested we take her shopping for some fashionable non-black dresses. At first, Nonna refused, saying she had all the dresses she needed. Nonna had always been frugal and was most definitely a true believer in "A lira saved is a lira earned." When it came to clothes, furnishings and food, she didn't indulge in extravagance. There were no gourmet dishes coming out of her kitchen. She used only the essential ingredients to sustain life. I believe her frugality stemmed from fear—fear of what calamity lay in wait.

I certainly didn't take after Nonna. The first time Nonna looked in my closet, she exclaimed, "So many clothes! When do you wear all these clothes?"

"There's not many, Nonna. We don't wear the same thing every day. We like to change."

"All you need are two dresses," Nonna said. "You wear one and when you wash it you wear the other. Two are all you need!"

I could never change Nonna's way of thinking. My yiayia, on the other hand, was the polar opposite. She enjoyed the finer things in life and delighted in surrounding herself with beauty and elegance, evident by the embroidered tablecloths that adorned her dining room table, her hand-crocheted doilies that covered her furniture and armchairs, and the porcelain vases that she filled with freshly cut flowers from her garden. She loved to cook and was lauded for her decadent desserts. Her creations were not only pleasing to the palate, but also to the eye. Even in wartime, when ingredients were scarce, Yiayia found ways to create special treats that brought joy into their lives. Yiayia, unlike Nonna, believed that a little extravagance was food for the soul, especially in difficult times.

* * *

After much cajoling, Nonna finally agreed to our shopping expedition. We started our trek from Astoria to Manhattan by subway. Nonna wasn't too thrilled to be standing on the elevated platform high above the ground and was even less so to be riding on the train, especially when it made those harrowing turns. When the train veered into the tunnel, she let out a gasp and was more than relieved when we got off at Thirty-Fourth Street and out into the open air. Nonna found the pedestrian traffic overwhelming and held on to our hands, never letting go. It was amusing to see Nonna take baby steps as we made our way into Macy's through the revolving door. Nonna stopped at every counter on the main floor, her eyes feasting on all the glitzy bottles of makeup and perfume. When we got to the escalator, Nonna backed away, not wanting any part of the moving stairs, so we headed for the elevator. The women's department had rows and rows of dresses. Nonna, of course, wanted to replace her black dress with another black one. Mom and I selected several floral-print dresses in muted blue-gray colors. It took forever to convince her that she no longer needed to wear black. Mom told her that wearing black didn't relieve grief; it only served as a constant reminder. She also told her that the color black was not good for her eyesight. The eyesight argument did the trick because she finally agreed to try on the dresses.

* * *

When we left Sicily, Nonna was trim and fit, most likely the result of walking everywhere and keeping up with two active children. Now she was heftier and not as tall as I'd remembered—a child's perspective, I'm sure—which made her look rotund. Unfortunately, she had changed in other ways too. The loving grandmother who enjoyed doting on her grandchildren had become critical and judgmental, constantly complaining to Mom that we children were ill-mannered. She kept forgetting that Tony and Peter didn't speak Sicilian and thought them to be disrespectful when they didn't respond the way she'd expected them to. Just watching television with Nonna was an ordeal. Although she didn't understand English, she insisted on filling us in on the storylines. When we attempted to explain what was really going on, she'd say we had it all wrong. When commercials came on, she would complain that we had changed the channel and that we'd made those dreaded *pupi* (Nonna's word for cartoons) appear on the screen. We'd tell her the program would resume after the commercial break, but she didn't believe us and would storm out of the room. Once she sat through a dog-food commercial and asked what the story was about.

When we said it was an advertisement for dog food, it amused her so much that she quipped, "Why if dogs in Italy find out about this, they'll be over on the next plane!"

Nonna criticized the clothes I wore, saying they were too tight or revealed too much. When she saw the scandalous one-piece bathing suits hanging on the clothesline, she asked what they were. "*Costume da bagno*," I said. "We wear it at *la spiaggia*."

She gasped, "You wear that little thing outside . . . in front of people?"

"That's what everybody wears to the beach, Nonna. The pink and orange one is mine. The blue and green one is Mamma's."

"Your mamma wears that?"

I took great pleasure replying, "Uh-huh."

Totally deflated, Nonna muttered to herself and retreated into the house.

It boggles my mind that we'd lived on an island surrounded by miles and miles of coastline—600 miles to be exact—and had never once gone to the beach. I simply can't believe that Nonna had lived in Sicily all her life and hadn't dipped her toes in the sea. One would think just getting away from the oppressive Sicilian heat and taking a dip in the ocean was not exactly an indulgence; it was a necessity. Although I'm certain that if Nonna did dip her toes in the sea, she would have donned not only her long black dress, but also her black stockings. Come to think of it, I don't think I ever saw Nonna's arms or legs. She was covered from head to toe, with only her face, neck, and hands seeing the light of day.

When I asked my mother why we'd never gone to the beach in Sicily she said, "I don't know why. I guess we didn't have time. Without modern conveniences, chores took longer."

"But you went to the beach in Patras practically every day."

"In Patras, the beach was a short walk away."

"But there were taxis, buses, and trains in Sicily," I said. "Why didn't we just go?"

"I don't know. I don't remember anybody else going."

Years later, when Mom and I toured Sicily, we stayed in a hotel in Taormina situated on a mountaintop with views of the surrounding mountains and Mount Etna. The car ride to the hotel was an adventure in itself, with hairpin curves that took your breath away. The beaches were pristine, with turquoise water and white sand. The cool, calm water was inviting, unlike the freezing water and humongous waves on Long Island and at the Jersey Shore. It saddens me that my brother Joe and I never got to enjoy those magnificent Sicilian beaches.

One way Nonna hadn't changed is that she still had a knack for storytelling. On evenings in Sicily, Joe and I sat around the hearth, the fire crackling, waiting for Nonna to recount the tale of the little shepherd boy who had failed to watch over his sheep or of the unsuspecting travelers trapped in a remote inn, unable to find their way out. She recounted these tales, which were most likely told to her as a child, and had committed them to memory. Nonna's fables, while sometimes scary, always had a happy ending and were rich in moral lessons. In one story, Nonna's father had been gored by a bull because he'd made the mistake of wearing a red kerchief on his head. The moral being that you never wear red around bulls! Nonna was thrilled that Joe and I still remembered her stories so many years later, and she went on to recite them just as she had done in Sicily.

Nonna also impressed us with the American words and phrases she learned when she lived on "Chestanotel" in Philadelphia. We had no idea where Chestanotel was until years later when we'd learn it was Chestnut Hill! She was adorably childlike when she'd utter: goo-bye, wassamatteryou, howyudu, and ezzoll (for that's all).

However, there was one story Nonna recounted that I had never heard before. She told us of the time Nonno brought home a little baby girl they named Pietrina.

Surprised at hearing this, I said, "Nonna, I didn't know Pietrina wasn't your daughter."

"Why, what do you mean? Of course, she's my daughter! Nonno picked her."

"Picked her? Picked her from where?"

"Why, he picked her where he picked all our children! From a cabbage patch!"

Mind you, I was sixteen, and I wasn't about to let her get away with that. So at the risk of being disrespectful, I took out my biology book and flipped to the page with the diagrams of the female reproductive system.

Peering at the book, she moaned, "*Che vergogna! Che scandolo!*" ("What a shame! What a scandal!")

Hearing Nonna's cries, Mom rushed into the room. When I explained to Mom what had happened, she took Nonna aside and tried without success to convince her that knowledge was a good thing.

I was seven when we'd left Sicily, and Nonna's views and beliefs weren't apparent to me then. I came to learn that she saw little value in education, even frowning upon it. She believed that school only served to corrupt the mind, especially a girl's mind. Her beliefs were in total contrast to those of Nonno, who very much wanted his children, including his daughter, Pietrina, to have a formal education. I found it hard to understand how someone who had gone through life not being able to read and write, and who had to depend on others to read and write her letters, sharing her innermost thoughts and secrets, could still maintain that education had no value. I couldn't believe that a person I loved and revered held such views.

I do have to say that although Nonna was illiterate, she did possess a certain kind of wisdom, and I came to see the subtle ways she used that wisdom.

One day, as I was plagued by interminable hiccups, she asked me, "Tre-Tre, can you help me find that pot?"

Preoccupied with my hiccups, I wanted to be left alone.

"What pot are you looking for, Nonna?"

"You know, the little one—the one I like."

I hadn't a clue as to what pot she liked, but not wanting to hear myself speak through hiccups, I got on my knees and started taking all the pots out of the kitchen cabinet.

When I reached for the last one, I said, "This is it, Nonna. There are no more pots!"

Sighing, she said, "Oh my, I wonder where that pot went. Do you think it went with your hiccups? Where did your hiccups go?"

It was only then that I realized my hiccups were gone. Having me look for that pot had distracted me from those agonizing hiccups. Her trick had worked!

* * *

After the cabbage-patch story, there was no turning back. In Sicily, Nonna had been a source of comfort to me, but in America, she had become my worst nightmare. Nonna and I slept in the same room, and on nights she had trouble sleeping—which was most nights—she woke me up wanting to talk. I pleaded that I needed to sleep because I had to get up early for school, but that didn't deter her. I'm sure it would have pleased her for me not to go to that scandalous school.

She'd then begin her nightly sermons, saying, "It's not too late. I will take you with me to France, and you'll be safe. I'll take you to a nice convent."

I couldn't believe my nonna wanted to put me in a convent. Did she believe my soul needed saving?

"If you think the convent is such a nice place, why didn't you take Pietrina there?"

"Why? What do you mean? Pietrina was a good girl."

I complained to my parents, telling them I wanted the sleeping arrangements changed. However, when I thought about it, even though Nonna had greatly disappointed me, I didn't want to offend her. So I suffered in silence. But that didn't stop me from defying her.

There was one incident I wish I could have taken back. We had seen Nonna washing dishes with barely a trickle of water dripping from the faucet, so we decided that we'd try to prevent her from washing dishes again. However, if she did wash anything, so as not to offend her, we'd wait for her to leave the kitchen before rewashing them. Nonna's technique was very disturbing. Barely using the water that trickled from the faucet, she'd wipe the dish with the same damp sponge she had wiped everything with, including drops that had spilled onto the floor. I had seen only one other person employ this method. Once, while we were visiting family friends, my parents encouraged me to offer to help with the dishes.

After seeing our hostess washing the dishes with barely a drop of water, I quietly stepped out of the kitchen and whispered to Mom, "I can't help dry because I don't want to be an accessory to a crime."

Mom looked at me questioningly.

"What do you mean?" she asked.

"She washes dishes just like Nonna."

That entire day I had the willies, thinking I may have eaten off of one of those plates. I tried to understand that the woman and Nonna had spent practically their entire lives in Sicily, having to haul water, and as a result, they used water sparingly. Still, I couldn't help but think that that was no excuse for not washing dishes properly. After all, they were in America now, where water was plentiful.

As to the hurtful incident with Nonna, I had just come home from school, and as I was apt to do, I took a couple of cookies and poured myself a glass of milk. Even before the milk had made it into my mouth I was hit by a most foul odor. The milk, unfortunately, then made it into my mouth, but went no further. I spit it out with such a force, it splattered all over the table. I knew it had to be Nonna's doing. Disgusted and angry, I had no control over the words that spilled out of my mouth with the same ferocity the milk had.

"It's no wonder your babies died," I said. "They drank from dirty glasses!"

At that point, Nonna slid down the wall onto the floor, sobbing, her hands cupping her face.

Suddenly, those terrible words that came from my lips hit me in the gut. *Did I actually just say that? Oh God, I never meant to—never in a million years. But I did say it! I hurt my nonna.*

I crouched on the floor beside Nonna, sobbing and saying I was sorry, that I didn't mean it. She took me in her arms and comforted me, telling me it was all right and to stop crying. Although she forgave me, I have never forgiven myself.

Dad, too, had unresolved issues with Nonna. On evenings when he may have had a little too much wine with dinner, he said things that would have been better left unsaid. He loved his mother, but at the same time blamed her for things that had gone wrong in his life, especially the senseless death of his father. He believed his father to be an adventurous, ambitious, courageous, and forward-thinking man who had sought a better life, and resented his mother because she hadn't shared his father's dreams, and even worse, wasn't there for him.

It was terrible to hear Dad tell Nonna, "If you had been a good wife, my father wouldn't have died the way he did! Why weren't you there with him? Your place was with your husband! But no, not you! You went off and left him to die alone!"

Hearing Dad speak those hurtful words to Nonna was heart-wrenching. It was his own pain coming to the surface after all those years—pain and hurt that he was hurling back at her.

"Dad, you shouldn't talk like that to Nonna," I said.

Ignoring me, he carried on, "And you went on to marry that tyrant who made my life miserable. You took me out of school so you could sell me to other farms."

"I sent you away because I didn't want harm to come to you," Nonna cried. "You were so stubborn, so defiant. I was afraid that you and your stepfather would kill each other!"

The most innocuous thing uttered at the dinner table would provoke an argument. One time, Dad tried to get Nonna to eat the porterhouse steak he'd placed on her plate.

343

Repelled by the sight of it, she said, "I'll eat the potatoes and vegetables. I don't want that disgusting meat."

The fireworks really kicked off when Dad heaped sautéed mushrooms onto his plate.

"*Funghi!* You eat *funghi?*" Nonna thundered. "How can you eat the food that killed your father?"

"Like my father, I love mushrooms," Dad replied, "but my father picked them in the wild, and—"

Nonna banged the table with her fist so hard it made our plates bounce.

"I don't care how he picked them!" Nonna wailed. "*Funghi* killed your father, and you sit there eating them! How could you—and in front of me!"

It went on like that for quite some time, and at some point before my high school graduation, in 1962, Nonna returned to France. It was sad that her visit ended the way it did. Drudging up unresolved issues from the past never really helps unless you're unloading to a psychiatrist. In the end, I wished Nonna had never come to America. Sometimes when a loved one comes back into your life, those memories you hold dear can be shattered, as I sadly discovered.

* * *

When I think of my nonna, I try not to be judgmental. She lived at a different time, in a different place, and was a product of her environment and circumstances. She had to endure more tragedies than one should ever have to. It isn't fair for me to judge her, unless, as the saying goes, I walk a mile in her shoes. She was born during the Victorian era and was the product of a time when girls were kept ignorant—their ignorance sometimes lasting a lifetime.

An incredible tale circulated in Sicily about a newlywed who told his clueless young bride that a baby is created body part by body part, and in order to create a complete baby, they would have to have many love-making sessions. When her husband was drafted, their baby, unfortunately, was far from complete. Distressed, the young woman sought counsel from their parish priest. When the war ended, the husband returned, and his wife happily told him that thanks to their obliging priest, they were able to have a perfectly formed child!

Nonna lived at a time when young girls did not venture out alone, and young people of the opposite sex were not permitted to go out together unless accompanied by a chaperone. She often recounted with glee the time her daughter's fiancé offered his hand in greeting.

She smacked his hand, telling him, "You can take her hand at the altar!"

One can imagine her distress when she learned that I traipsed to school on my own. I was in my junior year of high school when we moved to Astoria, and not wanting to change schools, I traveled to Manhattan. Nonna decided to accompany me part of the way on the mile-long walk to the subway. However, her zeal didn't last long because, as we walked hand in hand, in order to discourage her, I zigzagged through the streets, tiring her out completely.

Eight years after Nonna left, my parents and I went to visit our relatives in France. I was happy to see that Nonna, who was now eighty-two, had mellowed, was more accepting, and best of all, had given up talking about convents.

She handed me a pile of francs and said, "Here, take these, and buy something nice for your birthday. Make me happy." It was her way of making amends. This time, going back was good. I learned a life lesson on that trip: it is far more gratifying if we hold on to what is dear and let go of what is hurtful.

* * *

As children, we see adults, our parents, grandparents, uncles, and aunts as all-knowing beings. However, when we, ourselves, reach adulthood, we can feel the child inside us that still yearns, still wonders, and still dreams. We're not all-knowing, and if we are open to it, life teaches us every day. One of my favorite lines is from the miniseries *The Thorn Birds,* where Barbara Stanwyck's aging character says: "Let me tell you something about old age. Inside this stupid body, I am still young, I still feel, I still want, I still dream."

I do wish I could have cut Nonna some slack and hadn't been such a brat. But I was a teenager then, and my behavior could be attributed to teen angst. Now that I'm no longer a precocious teen, I find myself doing pretty much the same things I criticized my nonna for doing. After all, isn't it true that the younger generation is always disparaged by the one that came before? The older generation grumbles about the current fashion, music, films, and everything else in between. I sometimes find myself saying how sad it is that today's youth does not have the wonderful music and meaningful lyrics I listened to when I was young, songs for different moods, songs that told a story, had a beginning, middle, and an end. It's no wonder that today's performers require smoke, wind, and fire! They serve as a distraction, a way to divert the audience from the nonsensical lyrics being spewed. For the most part, these performers repeat the same line or two ad nauseam, making me want to scream out, "Hire a lyricist for Pete's sake!"

Today's youth is bombarded with rap music. I can hardly listen to these artists, and I use the term "artist" loosely, as they often perform music that celebrates violence and misogyny, polluting hearts and minds. I see many rappers as angry misfits uttering expletives and strutting around while gesturing menacingly with their hands and fists. I find that the music the youth listens to today is not moving forward, but backward to primitive times. Rap may well date back to early African tribes chanting in a rhythmic fashion to induce trance states. I wouldn't know, because I don't give it a chance to.

Another phenomenon that has surreptitiously crept into the entertainment arena is the era of reality television and performance. This nonsense that's permeating today's culture and trying to pass for entertainment disappoints me greatly. Is the television we watch truly "reality." As far as I'm concerned reality TV stars are just fatuous attention seekers! And why is it that these reality stars (and performers for that matter) today don garments that leave little to the imagination? Is it because the more revealing the outfit, the more attention they get? Don't they know it's sexier if something is left to the imagination? And why is it that males don baggy jeans that fall way below their hips, revealing their underwear? What's with all the tattered clothes that look as if they've been mauled by wildcats? And what's with those unisex hairdos in which one or both sides of the head are shaved, leaving a patch on top that looks like a poor man's toupee! And let's not get into all that facial hair and those ubiquitous piercings and tattoos. I understand that everyone strives for individualism, but these so-called individuals look as if they're all in the same sad club.

Truly gifted singers don't need gimmicks; they don't need smoke, wind, or fire. They simply walk on stage elegantly dressed and rely on their talent, inspiring music, and lyrics. It truly saddens me that today's youth is being deprived of the beauty, elegance, and civility that once was.

There I've done it! I am my Nonna! Hopefully you'll cut me some slack the way I should have to her. I guess it's just the natural progression of one generation to the next. One generation ages and holds onto the performances of their time while the new generation finds entertainment in strange, new fads, fashion, and performers.

25

Epilogue

THAT MY FATHER HAD LUCK, there is no doubt. From the very start, he had the gift of luck in spades. At the time of his birth, infant mortality in Sicily was extremely high. He and his older sister Pietrina, were the only two of eight children to survive. That same good luck saw him through the war. It made possible his meeting and falling in love with my mother, a union that would provide him refuge after the armistice. Luck also played a role in his decision to leave the barracks before the Germans took charge. It most definitely played a part when it caused the German's machine gun to jam. Luck was with him when he ran into Ioannis, who shrewdly hid him in a ditch, covering him with canes, hay, and manure, deluding the Germans and their ferocious dogs. His decision not to board that ill-fated ship bound for Italy proved to be a life-saving one. It certainly was lucky having civil Germans billeted in our home instead of the typical cruel Nazis. It was another stroke of luck for him to have left Vouchinas' farm before the Germans raided it. His good luck enabled him to survive a jump off a train—a jump that maimed many. Finally, joining the right group of partisans, who ensured his safe passage to Patras after the Germans fled Greece in October of 1944, was another stroke of good luck.

When I think of what my father endured those eight months that he was left to fend for himself, the sheer magnitude of it all makes me shudder. Imagine coming face-to-face with a band of machine-gun wielding Germans. Just the thought of it would terrorize me. But he stayed calm and pretended not to know about the armistice, telling them in the best way he could (since he didn't speak German) that he was happy to see them after having escaped from a wicked group of Greek rebels.

Yet in many World War II films, these abandoned Italian soldiers are portrayed, at best, as lovers not fighters—and, at worst, as cowards and deserters. I was in my twenties when I first saw the film *Sahara*, in which Humphrey Bogart portrays the American tank commander, and J. Carrol Naish, Giuseppe, the Italian soldier. At first, Bogart refuses to take the soldier along, and only when vultures circle overhead waiting for their prey, does he relent. Throughout the film, Giuseppe appears frightened, lost, and confused.

When Bogart discovers that the Nazi prisoner understands English, he asks Giuseppe, "You know he talked English?"

"I just found out."

"Why didn't you tell me?"

"I was afraid. I'm like a man who fights his shadow."

This didn't resonate with me. Why would Giuseppe be afraid of an unarmed German prisoner when the Allies are steps away? I believe the scene was included to reinforce the notion that Italian soldiers are cowardly, incapable of fighting or taking a stand.

At the end, Giuseppe is redeemed, when he confronts the Nazi, telling him, "Italians are not like Germans. Only the body wears the uniform, not the soul!"

Giuseppe is stabbed, and although mortally wounded, he reaches the Allies in time.

Growing up, I heard many cruel, insensitive jokes: "Want to buy an Italian rifle, never fired, just dropped once?" "Which side are the Italians on today? That depends. Who's winning?" Perhaps it was taunts like these that prevented me from asking my father about the war. I'd like to think I avoided the subject because I didn't want him to have to relive what had to be more than unpleasant memories. But I think it had more to do with shame, shame that Italy, our country, fought on the Axis side, on Hitler's side, shame that we had been the enemy of America, our new home. How naïve I was to think that a soldier, a pawn, has a say in his country's decision to go to war, when in reality, soldiers are ordered to be patriotic and to obey.

I regret never asking Dad about the war. Our conversations bordered on the mundane—discussions of unimportant things. I would have asked him, "Dad, how long were you in Albania? Is it true what they said about the White Death? What was it like being an occupier in Greece? How did you learn to speak Greek? What was it like hiding out in Mom's house with the Germans there? How were you able to jump off the train? How did you cope on that Greek terrain alone, without your buddies?" I would've loved to have heard his story. But that was not to be.

If he were here today, I'd tell him how proud of him I am, proud that he never gave up, that what he did not only took courage, it took cunning, wit, and a special kind of confidence and spirit. I'd tell him that I admire him for all he did to stay alive and find his way back to us.

ACKNOWLEDGMENTS

I FIRST WANT TO THANK MY MOTHER. This book would not have been possible without her assistance and support. I am truly fortunate that my mother possesses a remarkable memory.

I also want to thank the professors of MFA (Master of Fine Arts) at the College of New Rochelle who taught beginners' writing classes at the New Rochelle Public Library and who encouraged me to keep writing. Thanks also to Renae Williams of the MFA program for reading the manuscript, for her insights and initial edits.

Thanks to everyone on the Redwood Publishing team who helped me so much. Special thanks to Sara Stratton, the ever-patient publishing manager for her insightful comments, and Avery Auer, my amazing editor who not only did a superb job editing but for also painlessly fact-checking the manuscript, and to Michelle Manley, who created the greatest cover design I could have imagined. I am grateful for their suggestions and encouragement throughout the process and for their contributions in bringing this book to fruition.

CPSIA information can be obtained
at www.ICGtesting.com
Printed in the USA
LVHW041235151020
668887LV00002B/52

9 781952 106033